... an international fo

THE JOURNAL OF

Visualization AND Computer Animation

EDITORS

Nadia Magnenat Thalmann, *University of Geneva, Switzerland*

Daniel Thalmann, *Swiss Federal Institute of Technology, Switzerland*

ay Cat ull, *Pixar, USA*

rea University of Aizu, Japan

books ma

phenomena which may be represented on the screen of a workstation are typically time-
in order to visualize these phenomena at any given time, it is necessary to know the
the scene at this time, then computer graphics techniques can be used to build and display
ding to viewing and lighting parameters. The problems to solve are how to express time
the scene and how to make it evolve over time: this is the main challenge of computer
visualization scientists can turn mountains of numbers into animation sequences and
ements of physical variables in space and time.

nologies, animators and scientists can immerse themselves in these computer-generated
at least communicate with them using specific devices. With the existence of graphics
ble to display complex scenes and with the advent of very new 3-D interactive devices
lity, it is possible to create applications based on a full 3-D interaction metaphor in which
ions of deformations or motion are given in real-time. These new concepts provoke drastic
ethods of designing animation sequences.

mputer Animation is interdisciplinary and attracts those working in the sciences and arts
nation techniques. The range of topics covered in the journal includes all theoretical concepts,
hniques and applications in animation and visualization.

3907   **Published Quarterly**

For conditions of

Further details and subscription information from:

Dept AC, John Wiley & Sons Ltd, Baffins Lane, Chichester, West Sussex PO19 1UD, UK

Subscriptions Dept C, John Wiley & Sons Inc, 605 Third Avenue, New York, NY 10158, USA

Virtual Worlds
and Multimedia

Virtual Worlds and Multimedia

Edited by

Nadia Magnenat Thalmann
University of Geneva, Switzerland

and

Daniel Thalmann
Swiss Federal Institute of Technology, Switzerland

JOHN WILEY & SONS
Chichester · New York · Brisbane · Toronto · Singapore

Other Wiley Editorial Offices

John Wiley & Sons, Inc., 605 Third Avenue,
New York, NY 10158-0012, USA

Jacaranda Wiley Ltd, G.P.O. Box 859, Brisbane,
Queensland 4001, Australia

John Wiley & Sons (Canada) Ltd, 22 Worcester Road,
Rexdale, Ontario M9W 1L1, Canada

John Wiley & Sons (SEA) Pte Ltd, 37 Jalan Pemimpin #05-04,
Block B, Union Industrial Building, Singapore 2057

British Library Cataloguing in Publication Data

A catalogue record for this book is available from the British Library

ISBN 0 471 93972 2

Produced from camera-ready copy supplied by the editors
Printed and bound in Great Britain by Bookcraft (Bath) Ltd

Contents

6. WEBSs: An Electronic Book Shell with an Object-oriented Scripting Environment

7. Virtual Reality in Architecture

8. Virtuality Builder II: On the Topic of 3D Interaction
J.F. Balaguer, E. Gobbetti

99

9. The World of Virtual Actors
N. Magnenat Thalmann, D. Thalmann

113

10. STV—Synthetic TV: From Laboratory Prototype to Production Tool
A. Fellous

127

Preface

With 3D virtual worlds, it is now possible to simulate a situation before it happens. New buildings, clothes, trains, subways, environments or behaviors -- all these can be investigated BEFORE anything is physically expressed or built. This technology gives us the power to answer questions like "What would happen if...?" and "How would it look if...?" Moreover, we have reached the point where an operator can have real-time interaction with a virtual world simulation of a real scene. This means that the computer is able to not only provide passive virtual information, but also offer the user a satisfying interaction with virtual actors and scenes in a virtual environment.

In addition, modern networks can handle a variety of information. This information can take various forms -- images, sounds, real TV sequences, speech, text, results of calculations, graphics, etc. -- and can lead to sophisticated multimedia systems. Using virtual reality techniques, we will be able to send specific gestures, forces, positions, and attitudes through a system of networking and control equipment, to a computer anywhere in the world.

This book covers both theoretical and practical aspects of Virtual Worlds and Multimedia. It presents advanced research and surveys on key topics like: image compression, HDTV, synthetic actors, synthetic TV, 3D copying, 3D interaction, Virtual Reality, electronic books, and architectural space.

Most of the text was presented in the "Multimedia and Virtual Worlds Workshop," held in October 1993 at the University of Geneva. This workshop was sponsored by the "Troisieme Cycle Romand d'Informatique" and allowed participants to discuss the state of Swiss research in these aeras. We would like to thank Professor Yves Pigneur from HEC Lausanne for his constant encouragement and the "Troisieme Cycle Romand d'Informatique" for their generous support in offering all workshop participants a copy of this book, so nicely edited by John Wiley and Sons. Finally, we would like to thank Gaynor Redvers-Mutton for her active collaboration in the making of this book.

Nadia Magnenat Thalmann
Daniel Thalmann

List of Contributors

Jean-Francis Balaguer
Computer Graphics Laboratory
Swiss Federal Institute of Technology
CH-1015 Lausanne
Switzerland

Hanspeter Bieri
Institut für Informatik und Angewandte
  Mathematik
Universität Bern
Länggassstrasse 51
CH-3012 Bern
Switzerland

Christian Breiteneder
Centre Universitaire d'Informatique
University of Geneva
24 rue du Général-Dufour
CH-1211 Geneva 4
Switzerland

Vicki de Mey
Centre Universitaire d'Informatique
University of Geneva
24 rue du Général-Dufour
CH-1211 Geneva 4
Switzerland

Martin Dürst
Multi-Media Laboratory
Institut für Informatik der Universität Zurich
Winterthurerstrasse 190
CH-8057 Zurich
Switzerland '

Armand Fellous
Laboratoire 3D
Direction de la Recherche
Institut National de l'Audiovisuel
4 avenue de l'Europe
F-94366 Bry-sur-Marne Cedex
France

Abdelhakim Ghezal
Multi-Media Laboratory
University of Zurich-Irchel
Winterthurerstrasse 190
CH-8057 Zurich
Switzerland

Simon Gibbs
Centre Universitaire d'Informatique
University of Geneva
24 rue du Général-Dufour
CH-1211 Geneva 4
Switzerland

Enrico Gobbetti
Computer Graphics Laboratory
Swiss Federal Institute of Technology
CH-1015 Lausanne
Switzerland

Roger Hersch
Peripheral Systems Laboratory
Swiss Federal Institute of Technology
CH-1015 Lausanne
Switzerland

Prem Kalra
MIRALab
Centre Universitaire d'Informatique
University of Geneva
24 rue de Général-Dufour
CH-1211 Geneva 4
Switzerland

B. Krummenacher
Peripheral Systems Laboratory
Swiss Federal Institute of Technology
CH-1015 Lausanne
Switzerland

Murat Kunt
Signal Processing Laboratory
Swiss Federal Institute of Technology
CH-1015 Lausanne
Switzerland

Hermann Maurer
IIG – Institut für Informationsverarbeitung
Graz University of Technology
Schiessstattgasse 4A
A-8010 Graz
Austria

Denise Mayor
Institut für Informatik und Angewandte
  Mathematik
Universität Bern
Länggassstrasse 51
CH-3012 Bern
Switzerland

Laurent Moccozet
MIRALab
Centre Universitaire d'Informatique
University of Geneva
24 rue du Général-Dufour
CH-1211 Geneva 4
Switzerland

J. Monnard
Institute for Automation and Operations
  Research
University of Fribourg
Miséricorde
CH-1700 Fribourg
Switzerland

Jurg Nievergelt
Institut für Informatik
ETH Zurich
CH-8092 Zurich
Switzerland

Michael Papathomas
Centre Universitaire d'Informatique
University of Geneva
24 rue du Général-Dufour
CH-1211 Geneva 4
Switzerland

Jacques Pasquier-Boltuck
Institute for Automation and Operations
  Research
University of Fribourg
Miséricorde
CH-1700 Fribourg
Switzerland

Bernard Péroche
Departement Informatique
Ecole Nationale Supérieure des Mines de
  Saint-Etienne
158 cours Faurel
F-42023 Saint-Etienne Cedex
France

Gerhard Schmitt
ETH-Hönggerberg
Lehrstuhl für CAAD
Swiss Federal Institute of Technology
CH-8093 Zürich-Hönggerberg
Switzerland

Peter Stucki
Multi-Media Laboratory
University of Zurich-Irchel
Winterthurerstrasse 190
CH-8057 Zurich
Switzerland

Daniel Thalmann
Computer Graphics Laboratory
Swiss Federal Institute of Technology
CH-1015 Lausanne
Switzerland

Nadia Magnenat Thalmann
MIRALab
Centre Universitaire d'Informatique
University of Geneva
24 rue du Général-Dufour
CH-1211 Geneva 4
Switzerland

1

An Overview of Hypermedia and Multimedia Systems

H. Maurer
Graz University of Technology, Austria

1.1. Introduction

The terms "multimedia", "hypermedia" and "hypertext" are often used quite interchangeably in the literature. Although we concur with the by now fairly common practice to use "hypermedia" and "hypertext" synonymously (and we choose "hypermedia" throughout this chapter) we feel that it is useful to distinguish "multimedia" and "hypermedia" systems not only on the basis that "hypermedia systems are multimedia systems with link-based navigation" but also by demanding that hypermedia systems are large and networked. Also, we take the somewhat narrow view that in all such systems (be it multi- or hypermedia) all information should be stored in digital form.

We elaborate on the above points (following (Maurer 1993b)) a bit more in this section. In section 1.2 we present the main special features of Hyper-G, our largest current research and development project, and mention a few smaller projects that have materialized as "fall-outs" from our Hyper-G efforts. Section 1.3 presents the "philosophical" underpinnings of our work, i.e. the reasons why we feel that hypermedia efforts have a significant potential of impact in many areas. We conclude this chapter with a brief summary and an ample list of references.

Computer-based multimedia systems allow the integration of various types of information (misleadingly often called "media") on a computer. In addition to traditional textual and numeric data, other types of information including graphics, raster images, audio- and video-clips can be handled in such a multimedia system in digital form.

Virtual Worlds and Multimedia Edited by Nadia Magnenat Thalmann and Daniel Thalmann
© 1993 John Wiley and Sons Ltd

Two important issues should be kept in mind:

(1) We should distinguish very explicitly between graphics in the sense of pictures consisting of two- or three-dimensional geometric primitives (in the sense of GKS (Graphics Kernel System) or PHIGS (Programmer's Hierarchical Interactive Graphics Standard) (see e.g. (Bono et al. 1990) and (Van Dam 1988)) and in the sense of raster images ("pixel maps"). For the sake of this chapter let us refer to the former as computer graphics and to the latter as raster images. The main difference between the two is that in pictures based on computer graphics, objects are available in "coded form" and hence are parametrizable and can be readily manipulated, while raster images have no further "substructure": they just consist of rows of points (pixels), each with a certain colour value and can hence be manipulated only in some very trivial ways (such as moving, clipping or zooming). Observe that many computer packages (e.g. CAD software) generating technical drawings, architectural designs, or animation packages (see e.g. (Magnenat Thalmann and Thalmann 1990, 1991)) will always produce computer graphics allowing changes of views of scenes by just modifying parameters determining the attributes of some of the objects shown or the viewer's position. Raster images can be easily obtained by scanning a picture or digitizing a frame of a video-clip, i.e. without much computational effort; depending on the resolution (number of pixels and number of colours) they require a large amount of space unless sophisticated compression techniques are used: a medium-quality 640×480 raster image with 256 colours requires over 300 kByte, and a high-quality 1200×800 raster image with some 17 million colours (3 bytes colour information) - uncompressed - some 3 MByte. Also, a typical raster image may still be scaled, moved and rotated (in the plane), but changing just e.g. the view-point in a 3D scene is quite impossible. Note that most multimedia systems such as HyperCardfor the Mac, or ToolBookfor the PC, usually only support raster images with some simple compression techniques. In view of the fact that such raster images are often less flexible and more space consuming, the exclusion of computer graphics is a somewhat surprising phenomenon.

(2) In defining multimedia systems we have specifically mentioned that all data should exist in digital form. In many computer driven multimedia applications audio-clips and video-clips are often **not** stored in digitized form yet, but are obtained from an analog source, most often a video-disk player: on such a laser-disk pictures are **not** stored as raster images but just as digitized analog signals. Since it is not universally understood why this is such a drawback, let us briefly mention the two main points: (i) picture quality is restricted to TV quality; (ii) certain interactions with the picture (like zooming in at any point chosen by the user, viewing a panoramic scene in all directions at will, etc.) are not possible. The reason why video-disks are still being used is the fact that the digital storage of pictures (and audio material) is still somewhat both a storage capacity and a speed problem: while a video-disk can hold 50,000 still images of TV quality, a CD-ROM (with some 600 MByte capacity) can only hold some 2000 images of similar quality, unless sophisticated compression techniques are used. Similarly, a video-disk can hold 40 minutes of video; a large 2 GByte harddisk can hold only 5 minutes of video if no data compression is used. Further, the data transfer of

uncompressed raster images necessary to display some 20 medium-resolution pictures per second as required for a movie is only possible using very fast harddisks, and is impossible using CD-ROMs. For this reason most systems supporting "software movies" show "stamp-sized" movies only: a 2 GByte harddisk can hold - even without data compression - about 2 hours of stamp-sized movie (150 × 100 pixels with 256 colours). Above mentioned restrictions on storage and speed only apply in the absence of high-quality data compression. However, such compression techniques are by now well-known and indeed standardized for still pictures (see (Wallace 1991)) and two competing techniques (MPEG (Moving Picture coding Experts Group) vs. DVI) are available for movies (see (Le Gall 1991), (Green 1992), and (Poole 1991)). Above techniques allow the storage of tens of thousands of still pictures of reasonable quality or of 1-3 hours of TV quality movie in digitized form requiring 1 GByte. The only drawback of the compression techniques mentioned is that decompression is such a complicated process that ordinary computers require special decompression chips (JPEG (Joint Photographic Expert Group), MPEG, or DVI (Digital Video Interactive)). However, those chips (and fast CD-ROM drives that are also compatible with Kodak's photo-CD) are going to be standard components of the next generation of Mac's, PC's, and of multimedia workstations. Furthermore, new "fractal based" and "affine transformation based" high quality compression techniques requiring no special hardware for decompression are appearing on the horizon (see e.g. (CulikII and Dube 1991) and (Barnsley et al. 1988)). Thus, the integration of data in the form of text, graphics, raster images, audio and video leading to genuine digitized multimedia systems has just become possible.

The main applications of multimedia systems are in the area of information presentation, education and in the gray-zone inbetween, "edutainment" and computer games. Information presentation applications range from the presentation of companies and institutions, to public information terminals, electronic guides for exhibitions and museums (Maurer and Williams 1991), to the whole spectrum of electronic publishing (from computerized encyclopedias and dictionaries to road maps or other cartographic material). Multimedia applications can also be used for educational purposes e.g. to enhance classroom teaching, and, to a lesser degree, as partial replacement for personal instruction. Too much euphoria that multimedia applications such as cleverly designed HyperCard stacks will revolutionize the learning process is, however, unjustified: many issues more important than the display of colourful moving pictures have to be solved first (see e.g. (Makedon et al. 1987), (Huber et al. 1989)). How successful multimedia applications will be in the "edutainment" sector remains to be seen. Some of the more likeable pieces of software such as "Just Grandma and me" (Broderbond SW) still cannot rival the allure of top adventure games such as the likes of "Loom", "Space Quest" or "Larry"!

Multimedia systems clearly not only must provide a combination of various types of information, but also convenient access to that information. Various mechanisms such as simple query languages, menus, usage paradigms like "stacks of information cards", etc. are used, often combined with the notion of "links attached to clickable buttons": certain "hot-spots" (words, parts of pictures, ...) are distinguished on the screen and activating them leads "kind of associatively like we tend to think" to related information.

It is this notion of linking information together that is sometimes considered to present the step from multimedia to hypermedia (see e.g. (Jacques et al. 1993)).

We would like to suggest, however, that a multimedia system with some links does not qualify as a hypermedia system, yet. More is needed: above all, a hypermedia system must be a networked system and it must be large (i.e., capable of holding giga-quantities of chunks of information) and it must have more than a "read-only" functionality: only if (many) persons can work with, annotate and customize the information and the information paths in a multimedia system should we speak of a hypermedia system as envisaged by the pioneer Ted Nelson (1987), and as described e.g. in (Conklin 1987) (Kappe et al. 1991), or (Tomek et al. 1991).

Thus, we suggest that the term "hypermedia system" is reserved for large, networked multimedia systems that support annotation, customization, and cooperation. The linkage aspect, sometimes extolled as THE defining feature of hypermedia systems, seems to us of less importance, indeed may turn out to be as wrong an approach to structuring information as the goto has turned out to be the wrong approach to structuring programs (see (Maurer and Carlson 1992)). According to the above definitions, neither HyperCard nor ToolBook nor its variants are hypermedia systems. This does not belittle the importance of (stand-alone) multimedia systems: indeed they have been exceedingly successful in recent years. And the "Missing Organ" argument presented in section 1.3.4 applies equally well to multi- and hypermedia efforts!

However, we propose to reserve the term "hypermedia" for large networked multimedia efforts such as e.g. Nelson's Xanadu (Nelson 1987), the IRIS-systems at Brown University (Haan et al. 1992), or the Hyper-G at the Graz University of Technology (Kappe et al. 1992a). We will discuss the most important features of Hyper-G in the next section.

1.2. Hyper-G and Some of its Spin-Offs

Hyper-G is a large, networked hypermedia system (Kappe et al. 1991), (Kappe 1991) whose implementation started at the Graz University of Technology in 1990. At this point in time Hyper-G is used as a university-wide information and communication system. Its design is sufficiently modular and open that more and more modules can and will be added over the next 3 years. A first plateau will be reached in 1996 when all modules currently under development are integrated into the system. It is particularly important to understand that we are investing not only considerable efforts to obtain a system working nicely from a technical point of view but also a system containing a considerable amount of useful information. At this point in time it seems likely that Hyper-G will be adopted as major information and cooperation system by all 18 Austrian universities.

Hyper-G is a client-server based system. It resembles in many ways the IRIS-system developed at Brown University (Haan et al. 1992) and is solidly built on lessons learnt from other undertakings. There is no room in this chapter to discuss all "standard" features of Hyper-G, e.g. that it incorporates all kinds of "media" (including audio- and video-clips) and supports all kinds of navigation strategies including those based on (bidirectional) links. We rather refer for further general information concerning hypermedia to key literature such as (Conklin et al. 1987), (CACM 1988), (CACM 1991), (CGR 1991), (Champine et al. 1990), (IEEE 1991), (JMCA 1991), (Nielsen 1990), (Tomek et al. 1991), and some of the more "historic" references (Bush 1945), (Engelbart and English 1968), (Nelson 1972), and (Fedida 1975). Rather than describing all details of Hyper-G we mention some of its more outstanding features. We also want to clearly state that some of the features to be mentioned are fully functional at the time of publication of this chapter, while others are still being implemented.

Information in Hyper-G is distributed in a network consisting of a fast local area network and of connections to other networks world-wide at various speeds. Information obtained by users in Hyper-G can come from arbitrary distances, yet the basic philosophy is to keep information often accessed on servers as close as possible to the user (even if this causes information-duplication); reasons are both speed of use and reduction of the load on networks. Information "proper" and indices and linkage nformation are stored separately (and potentially on separate servers), again much decreasing response times for users. Hyper-G allows users to gateway into other systems be it Videotex, WWW (World Wide Web), Gopher, etc. with only a minimal change of the apparent user interface: many of the idiosynchrasies of different systems are taken care of by the "viewers" employed by users; and different viewers exist both for different terminal-types (dumb terminals, PCs, Mac's, X-Window-terminals, etc.) and for various user profiles.

Hyper-G is multi-lingual. The user interface (at this point) supports only German and English (... and, just for the heck, a local Styrian dialect) but can support (on principle) any number of languages. Some of the data is available in German, English, French, Spanish, Italian ... and Korean (due to the use of parts of Hyper-G at the EXPO'93 in Korea); we expect that at least Hungarian will be added (for the EXPO'96 in Budapest).

A crucial aspect of every large hypermedia system is to provide sufficiently powerful navigational facilities to allow users to find their way in the tangled web of links.

This aspect is handled in Hyper-G both conventionally (by supplying graphical browsers, guided tours, indices, etc.) and unconventionally: the latter is accomplished by imposing a semi-hierarchical structure of information databases that eliminates the need for some links and makes users aware of "where they are" in the database. The notion of "dynamic links" (links generated at run-time) is largely replaced by the notion of being able to carry out all kinds of searches within user-defined scopes of the database. Another way to state the above is to say that many links are created and maintained automatically by the system, rather than being supplied manually by "authors" or "users".

Hyper-G supports collaborative work (see (CSCW 1991) and Ziegler and Weiss 1990) for more general discussions) by providing a sophisticated annotation mechanism (allowing annotation of everything including annotations) and by providing mechanisms for viewing the annotation network. As a by-product a powerful computer conferencing facility is available.

To give an impression of the scope of Hyper-G it may be best to describe some of the facilities available when phase II (beginning of 1996) will be completed: many of the modules described are available or about to become available as stand-alone applications in museums, exhibitions or on CD-ROMs already and will be all pulled together into Hyper-G, eventually.

In addition to communicational and cooperational features briefly mentioned above, Hyper-G will include a number of transactional features typical for university life such as registration for classes or exams.

From the information point of view the system will contain a plethora of university-specific information from the University's yearbook, calendar and research report to a (multimedia) presentation of all administrative, instructional and research units, to announcements of talks, seminars, on-campus entertainment (including menus from various cafeterias); from legal information to computer-conference anonymous counselling, to agendas and minutes of meetings, to a link to the electronic catalogue of the library, to a set of hundreds of Computer-Aided Instruction (CAI) lessons, to a link to public-domain information such as telephone numbers (in all of German speaking Europe!), to train schedules, and even to (paid) advertisements from various companies, and much more. Of course, the system will also be used for anonymous lecture evaluation, as a suggestion box, etc. Hyper-G will also contain much general purpose information that comes from seven major sources:

- the "PC-library project" ("modular encyclopedia") in which we cooperate with a consortium German publisher to provide hundreds of dictionary-type books in electronic form, see (Maurer 1993a);
- the "AEIOU project" (Annotierbares Elektronisches Interaktives Oesterreich-Universallexikon) which provides an electronic encyclopedia on all aspects of Austria compiled in a substantial undertaking as part of Austria's millennium celebration in 1996;
- the "Images of Austria project" that contains some 3000 pictures with multi-lingual explanations, some cartographic material, some video- and audioclips and some "special themes" (such as Austrian inventors, or Austria's National Parks) that was prepared for EXPO'92;
- the "Electronic Worldatlas project" in which high-quality cartographic material is combined with some 2500 pictures from all over the world;
- the "City-Map project" in which electronic versions of all Austrian cities are prepared;
- the "Austria 2000 Time Capsule project" in which - with the help of the national television system - all Austrians are encouraged to submit photos and video-clips showing "Austria at the turn of the century"; and
- a number of other multimedia projects that we have carried out for various museums, exhibitions, and publishers, and where we have managed to retain the electronic rights for Hyper-G.

Altogether, Hyper-G will not only provide a modern hypermedia infrastructure, it will also incorporate an impressive body of information. Conservative aims are 500 MByte of textual information, 20000 high-quality pictures, and 2000 audio- and video-clips. It is likely that actual figures will be considerably higher. We are pursuing the implementation and data-collection for Hyper-G with much enthusiasm. And we present some of the main reasons why we "philosophically" believe in the notion of hypermedia in section 1.3.

1.3. Why Hypermedia?

In this section we present four of the main arguments why we feel the notion of hypermedia is important. Some of the arguments have been presented before to some extent, e.g. in (Maurer and Carlson 1992) and (Maurer 1992).

1.3.1. The Network Argument

A hypermedia system according to our definition in section 1.1 is a distributed database of chunks of information (if only textual information is supported some speak of hypertext systems), cross-referenced by various types of links, accessible by a large number of persons (as passive users or as authors) and supporting a variety of navigational, manipulational, communicational and cooperational activities. We can follow links, thus browsing "associatively" through some information space (much like maybe thinking processes work in our brains), we can rearrange and annotate information for later use, or we can just query the database, thus overall extending our intellect much in the sense of (Bush 1945); and we can communicate and cooperate with others over arbitrary distances: everyone of us now using high-speed computer-nets for email or cooperation via e.g. remote logins does appreciate some of those facilities already; and that a hypermedia approach to such features would enhance their usability should be clear (Maurer and Tomek 1990a). (For a survey of the state-of-the-art in computer supported cooperative work see (CSCW 1991)).

If hypermedia systems become as widespread and ubiquitous as proposed by some researchers, Nelson's vision of hypertext as the ultimate medium for electronic publishing does not seem that far-fetched anymore, hypertext as "Gutenberg 2" might indeed become reality: not just bringing some but "all" books onto everyone's desk! "All published information just a mouse-click away" (Nelson 1987).

Hypermedia systems offer a number of other potentially significant "philosophical" advantages: the fact that readers may leave notes for others may well be helpful in judging the value of a controversial report in a hypermedia newscast; many complex issues of modern society are not linear in nature, but consist of many mutually interwoven aspects: clearly such situations (a law-case, the working of a piece of machinery, ...) can be described much better using a multi-dimensional web of chunks of information than using linear text; Marshall McLuhan has pointed out that linear text has narrowed our view of the world: hypermedia is the first chance to "de-linearize" the way we communicate ideas.

There is one very important aspect, however, which cannot be overemphasized: early hypermedia pioneers have seen the main advantage of networking in pulling all kinds of information together; from today's vantage point the situation looks a bit different: the information aspect provided by such a network is surely important; but a network providing complete, up-to-date and reliable information on "everything" seems more science fiction today than colonizing the moon. Foreseeable hypermedia networks will bring access to a substantial yet clearly incomplete body of knowledge; but they will bring people and human ideas together because of the communicational facilities and their potential in providing a platform for computer moderated discussion and cooperation. It is more this cooperational aspect of hypermedia systems that makes networking important, rather than the information gathering aspect that was the original impetus for networking!

1.3.2. The Universal Argument

The hypermedia concept (linking chunks of information together within a database or even across geographically dispersed information systems) should not be seen as a monolithic concept. It is a mistake to always talk about "hypermedia systems" (as, however, we keep doing even in most of this chapter), we should talk about the "hypermedia paradigm" (Maurer and Tomek 1990a and 1990b): i.e. hypermedia principles should be applied to most computer applications: tree-like directories in today's operating systems should be replaced by annotatable, multimedia, linked webs showing the user what kind of options are available; we should have the possibility of linking pieces of email together, putting multimedia notes into them; and the same applies to textfiles, pieces of software, collections of pictures, or whatever else we are currently working on. This idea has been discussed more extensively three years ago in (Maurer and Tomek 1990) and first signs of implementations are appearing in new environments such as Apple's QuickTime!

1.3.3. The Personal Assistant Argument

Hypermedia systems have the potential to become powerful assistants in many of our computerized activities. When using a word-processing application, a hypermedia system containing dictionaries of words and rules of hyphenation, style and grammar may well go beyond "online" spell-checkers that we are starting to see today: before we have finished typing the word "airport" the computer has completed it already (as soon as we have reached "airp"), the system hyphenates for us, informs us that we have used a certain word twice in short succession (and provides a list of synonyms), it may even remark on grammatical constructions (much beyond just misspelt words!), and when further information is available the hypermedia system may indicate, while we write, that there are relevant pieces of information on the topic we are working on that we can look up with just one mouse-click.

Such computerized personal assistants who sort-of supervise users and try to guess what they want to do have probably been proposed (and implemented) first in connection with word-processing applications by Ian Witten and his team. While Witten's work continued on a more and more sophisticated experimental level, see e.g. (Witten and Maulsby 1991), some cute down-to-earth applications have been incorporated into the Ways2 package by Swiss inventor Keller, a package "supervising" (in a hopefully helpful way) our usage of arbitrary PC-based Windows applications.

There is still another facet where hypermedia systems can potentially play a more and more important role: in information verfication. We are all aware of the fact that we are flooded by information, yet often do not know how to judge the likely truth of such information. With large hypermedia archives at my fingertip and a convenient interface (whatever it may look like) we can read something in the electronic newspaper of the future and double-check facts immediately by using an appropriate archive; and indeed we may leave comments such as "this figure is blatantly wrong; see report ..." for future readers.

Thus, hypermedia systems offer us help in various ways while we compose information, and likewise when we try to ingest information: it has the potential to objectivize our information usage.

Note that such "information scrutiny" will become more and more important as the manipulation of information becomes easier and easier. In particular, there is a shift in authenticity with pictorial information: while we have been aware for a long time that a piece of text can only be trusted if we are sure of its source, pictures or movie-clips have been accepted by us as showing the "objective truth" independent of the source (since faking photos and movie-clips has not been terribly easy): thus, if we see e.g. president Clinton shake hands with Chancellor Kohl we tend to believe that such a handshake has indeed taken place; however, the manipulative possibilities of digitized information is sufficiently high that pictures and movie-clips can be faked at will, hence cannot be taken "at face value" any more, hence "second sourcing" and "information verification" (using a hypermedia system that is at our disposal wherever we are) will become more and more essential.

1.3.4. The Missing Organ Argument

We all realize that diagrams or pictures, let alone animated diagrams or movie-clips, are powerful tools for conveying information in many situations. Thus it is clear that the integration of such materials, and others (e.g. sound and speech) into information systems has been a dream for decades. This dream is now rapidly coming true.

Although everyone agrees that the wide-spread use of pictures, diagrams, animation and movies will increase the value and applicability of hypermedia systems we think that the real impact of such a media-mix is still underestimated by most people. We believe that the easy retrieval and manipulation of pictorial material in all its forms will deeply influence mankind in how knowledge is archived and communicated. The reason for this credo is based on a simple physiological observation whose significance is often overlooked: mankind is lacking one very important organ! (Maurer and Williams 1991), (Maurer and Scherbakov 1992).

To be more specific: our second most important sensory organ, the ear, has an active counterpart: the mouth, which is capable of generating utterances understood by the ear. Our most important sensory organ, the eye, has no analogous counterpart: humans have no physiological construct to display any kind of picture!

Is it not disturbing that we can produce "concrete" sounds (speech) and "abstract" sounds (music) using the vocal chords but that we are not equipped to display - in real time - high quality pictures, either "concrete" or "abstract", let alone being able to project animated pictures? Some may be tempted to answer that we can indeed produce visual information by using gestures, facial expressions, bodystance or such. Note, however, that those are what we would call "secondary" visual signals: much like the sound of hitting the table with a fist or clapping hands are crude "secondary" acoustic signals.

Let us face the fact that we can store images based on reality in our head, that we can "conjure" up images of things we have never seen; that we can "imagine"(!) things that no one has ever experienced. Yet, when it comes to externalizing these images we are markedly deficient and must resort to gestures and antics.

The only way we have had in the past to communicate mental imagery in a lasting fashion was to code it into words, and words into writing, or to draw a picture, to use sculpting techniques, or to record something as photos or movies (making it difficult to leave room for abstraction and creativity), or more recently, to use computer graphics and visualization -- and animation tools.

This is the main point to understand: humans are heavily visually based beings: about half of the human neocortex is devoted to visual information processing. We have an unconscious desire to "feed" our eyes with visual information, and this is one of the reasons for the appeal of movies and television. Yet despite all of this desire to accept visual stimuli and our excellent equipment for receiving them, we are sadly lacking a "picture generating organ".

However, this is no reason for despair. Humans are lacking many facilities of potentially great value: we have no wings to fly and no gills to swim underwater; yet we have developed airoplanes, submarines and scuba equipment as "surrogates" or "crutches" to overcome the mentioned deficiencies.

It is our contention that hypermedia systems are going to become better and better substitutes for our missing picture generating organ. As software tools and interface-mechanisms continuously improve, the externalization of mental imagery will become progressively easier. Initially, and right now, this means that the effort required to express our ideas using pictures, diagrams, animation sequences, movies, etc. is going to reduce more and more; eventually (maybe) the tools will become sophisticated enough to be used in realtime: in the same way as we are more or less capable of externalizing our thoughts in realtime by speaking (note that for a good presentation we DO need some preparation!) we might someday be able to externalize our thoughts by producing, in real time, a presentation consisting of acoustic and visual elements using a suitable technological surrogate for our missing picture generating organ.

It has to be understood that the visual component of a computer supported multi-media system is not limited to ordinary digitized photos and movies: such photos and movies of real-life situations are valuable in some cases but lack the necessary level of abstraction in others. At least as important are other techniques for visualization, among them, e.g. diagrams, maps, and abstract pictures; process visualization tools; data visualization tools; 3D modelling, animation, and abstract movies. For more information on these issues see (Maurer 1992).

1.4. Summary

In this chapter, we draw a clear distinction between computer supported multimedia systems and hypermedia systems and report on a substantial hypermedia system Hyper-G. We then present four main arguments why hypermedia systems will be more and more important, one of those arguments (the missing organ argument) also explaining the observable success of various (non-hypermedia) computer supported multimedia applications, and of all aspects of computer graphics and computer animation.

References

Barnsley MF, Deaney RL, Mandelbrot, B, Peitgan DO, Saupe D, Voss RS (1988) *The Sciences of Fractal Images*, Springer-Verlag.
Bono PR, Encarnacao JL, Herzner, W (1990) *PC Graphics with GKS* Prentice-Hall.
Bush, V (1945) *As we May Think* Atlantic Monthly, Vol.176, No.1, pp.101-108.
CACM (1988) Special Issue on Hypertext, *Comm. ACM*, Vol.31, No.7.
CACM (1990)Special Issue on Hypertext, *Comm. ACM*, Vol.33, No.3.
CACM (1991) Special Issue on Digital Multimedia Systems, *Comm. ACM*, Vol.34, No.4.
CGR (1991) Special Issue on Multimedia, *IEEE Computer Graphics and Applications*, Vol.11, No.4.
Champine GA Geer DE, Ruh, WN (1990) Project Athena as a Distributed Computer System; *IEEE Computer*, Vol.23, No.9, pp.40-51.
Conklin J (1987) Hypertext - an Introduction and Survey; *IEEE-Computer*, Vol.20, No.9, pp.17-41.
Conklin EJ, Begemann ML (1987) gIBIS: A Hypertext Tool for Team Design Deliberation; *Proc. of Hypertext'87*, TR88-013, University of North Carolina, Dept. of Computer Science, pp.247-252.
CSCW (1991) Special Issue on Collaborative Computing, *Comm. ACM*, pp.34, No.12.
CulikII K, Dube S (1991) *New Methods for Image Generation and Compression*, LNCS 555, Springer-Verlag, pp.69-90
Engelbart DC, English WK (1968) A Research Center for Augmenting Human Intellect; *AFIPS Proceedings*, Fall Joint Computer Conference, pp.395-410.
Fedida S (1975): An Interactive Information Service for the General Public, *Proc. European Conf. on Communication Networks*, pp.261-282.
Green JL (1992) The Evolution of DVI System Software, *Comm. ACM*, Vol.35, pp.53-67.
Haan BJ, Kahn P, Rilly VA, Coombs JH, Meyrowitz NK (1992) IRIS - Hypermedia Services, *Comm. ACM*, Vol.35, No.1, pp.36-51.
Huber F, Makedon F, Maurer H (1989) Hyper-COSTOC: A Comprehensive Computer-based Teaching Support System, *J.MCA*, Vol.12, pp.293-317.
IEEE (1991) Special Issue on Multimedia Information Systems, *IEEE - Computer*, Vol.24, No.10.
Jacques R, Nonnecke B, McKerlie D, Preece J (1993) Current Designs in HyperCard: What can we learn?; *J.EHM* (to appear).
JMCA (1991) Special Issue on Hypermedia Systems, *J.MCA*, Vol.14, No.2.
Kappe F, Maurer H, Tomek I (1991) Hyper-G: Specification of Requirements, *Proc. Conference on Intelligent Systems, CIS'91*, Veszprem, Hungary, pp.257-272.
Kappe F (1991) *Aspects of a Modern Multi-Media Information System*, Research Report 308, IIG Graz.
Kappe F, Maurer H, Pani G, Schnabel F (1992a) Hyper-G a Modern Hypermedia System; *Proc. Network Services Conference* Pisa, Italy, pp.35-36.

Kappe F, Maurer H, Scherbakov N (1992b) Hyper-G - A Universal Hypermedia System; *J.EHM*.

Le Gall D (1991) MPEG: A Video Compression Standard for Multimedia Applications; *Comm. ACM*, Vol.34, No.4, pp.47-58.

Magnenat-Thalmann N, Thalmann D (Eds.) (1990) *Computer Animation' 90*, Springer-Verlag.

Magnenat-Thalmann N, Thalmann D (Eds.) (1991) *Computer Animation' 91*, Springer-Verlag.

Makedon F, Maurer H, Ottmann T (1987) Presentation Type CAI in Computer Science Education at University Level, *J.MCA*, Vol.10, pp.283-295.

Maurer H, Tomek I (1990a) Broadening the Scope of Hypermedia Principles, *Hypermedia*, Vol.2, No.3, pp.201-221.

Maurer H, Tomek I (1990b) Some Aspects of Hypermedia Systems and Their Treatment in Hyper-G, *Wirtschaftinformatik*, Vol.32, pp.187-196

Maurer H, Williams MR(1991) Hypermedia Systems and Other Computer Support as Infrastructure for Museums, *J.MCA*, Vol.14, No.2, pp.117-137.

Maurer H, Carlson P (1992) Computer Visualization, a Missing Organ, and Cyber-Equivalency, *Collegiate Microcomputer*, Vol.10, No.2, pp.110-116.

Maurer H, Scherbakov N (1992) *Hypermedia Systems without Links*, IIG Report 343, IIG Graz, Austria.

Maurer H (1992) Why Hypermedia Systems are Important; *Proc. ICCAL'92*, Wolfville, LNCS 602, Springer Pub.Co., pp.1-15.

Maurer H (1993a) From Multimedia to Hypermedia; *Proc. New Zealand National Computer Conference*, Auckland.

Maurer H (1993b) *AEIOU - Annotierbares Elektronisches Interaktives Oesterreich-Universallexikon*, Internal Report Graz.

Nelson TH (1972) As We Will Think, Online 72, *Proc. Intl. Conf. on Online Interactive Computing*, Brunel University, Uxbridge, England.

Nelson TH (1987) *Literary Machines*, Edition 87.1, 702 South Michigan, South Bend, IN 46618.

Nielsen J (1990) *Hypertext and Hypermedia*; Academic Press.

Poole L (1991) QuickTime in Motion; *Mac World*, pp.154-159.

Tomek I, Khan S, Mueldner T, Nassar M, Novak G, Proszynski P (1991) Hypermedia - Introduction and Survey; *J.MCA*, Vol.14, No.2, pp.63-100.

Van Dam A (1988) Hypertext'87 Keynote Address, *Comm. ACM*, Vol.31, No.7, pp.887-895.

Wallace GK (1991) The JPEG Still Picture Compression Standard; *Comm. ACM*, Vol.34, No.4, pp.30-44.

Witten IH, Maulsby DL (1991) *Evaluation Programs Formed by Example: an Informational Heuristic*; LNCS 555, Springer-Verlag, pp.388-402.

World Wide Web - W3; *Login via telnet under info.cern.ch*

Ziegler L, Weiss G (1990) Multimedia Conferencing on Local Area Networks; *IEEE Computer*, Vol.23, No.9, pp.52-61.

2

Parallel Image Storage and Retrieval

Roger D. Hersch, B. Krummenacher
Peripheral System Laboratory, Swiss Federal Institute of Technology
Lausanne, Switzerland

2.1. Introduction

Multimedia applications require frequent access to text, graphics, sound and images stored on mass storage devices. Image manipulations required for creating appropriate multimediasequences include zooming in and out as well as panning in large size images. The best output quality can be reached if the original image data is either uncompressed or compressed by a small factor providing lossless compression. Access to images stored on disks is critical: one needs huge storage capacities for storing large image sets as well as fast access capabilities to be able to browse through such pixmap image sets. This contribution proposes a parallel multiprocessor multidisk architecture which offers at the same time high-throughput and parallel image data processing capabilities. Such an architecture, built of standard low-cost mass produced components such as processors, memory and winchester disks, provides a favorable price-performance ratio.

2.2. Image Server Architecture

Existing architectures for improving disk bandwidth and offering high reliability are based on the concept of *Redundant Arrays of Inexpensive Disks (RAID)* developed at Berkeley by Patterson et al. (1988) and Chen and Patterson (1990). Access to disk blocks is parallelized, but block and file management continues to be handled by a single CPU with

Virtual Worlds and Multimedia Edited by Nadia Magnenat Thalmann and Daniel Thalmann
© 1993 John Wiley and Sons Ltd

limited processing power and memory bandwidth. In order to access large quantities of pixmap image data at a throughput of 2 to 10 Mbytes/s, a *multiprocessor-multidisk (MPMD)* approach is proposed. Pixmap image data is partitioned into rectangular extents, each extent having a size which minimizes global access time. In order to ensure high throughput, image extents are stored on a parallel array of disk nodes. Each disk node includes one disk node processor (T800 or T9000 transputer), cache memory (6 Mbytes) and one disk (400 to 2000 Mbytes). The hardware part of this architecture is similar to the one proposed by Wilkes (1991) in the DataMesh project.

The proposed parallel image server architecture includes an array of disk nodes offering parallel image storage, disk node processors dedicated to the storage and processing of image parts, a server interface processor and a network interface. This contribution discusses how images can be partitioned into extents and efficiently distributed among disk nodes. It analyzes the performance of the system according to various parameters such as the number of cooperating disk nodes, the size of the image file extent and the type of available processing and communicating capabilities. Performance figures quoted hereafter refer to storing and accessing uncompressed images.

This contribution does not discuss the problem of disk crash recovery. However, RAID-5 redundancy schemes as proposed by Chen and Patterson (1990) could be incorporated into the proposed MPMD architecture.

The image server comprises a network interface, a server interface processor used for image assembly and processing, as well as an array of disk nodes (Figure 2.1).

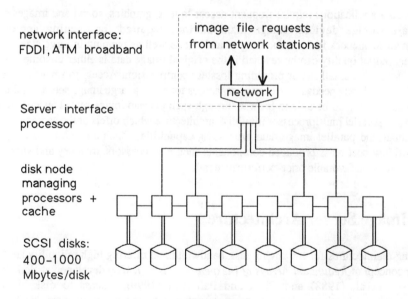

Figure 2.1. Image server architecture with 4 communication links to server interface processor

The server interface processor runs the image server master process receiving image access requests from the network and issuing image access calls to the parallel image file server. Image processing tasks required for image presentation such as resampling, filtering and adaptation of gray levels may be located on interface processors and on disk node processing units.

Image access performance is heavily influenced by how pixmap images are distributed onto a disk array. Image access characteristics are known: client workstations generally require rectangular portions of pixmap image files. Therefore, image file data is partitioned into rectangular extents. In order to simplify the file system which manages parallel storage of files on multiple disk nodes, extents are numbered sequentially from left to right and from top to bottom. The k disk nodes in the disk array selected for storing an image file are numbered from 0 to k-1. Image file extents are mapped sequentially one to one in modulo-k mode to disk nodes.

At image storage time, image size, extraction window size and number of disks are known. The image partitioning problem is reduced to the problem of finding a horizontal extent size which ensures that extents lying within the visualization window are distributed as uniformly as possible among the set of available disk nodes (Figure 2.2).

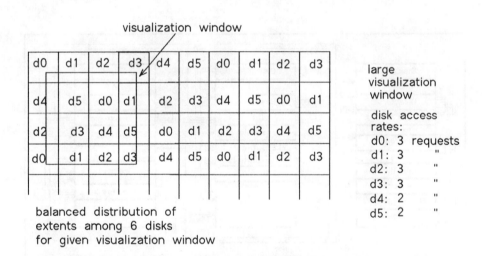

Figure 2.2. Example of extent distribution among disk nodes

The solution proposed by the author optimizes the disk number offset from one extent row to the next, depending on initial extent size, visualization window size and image size. The definitive extent width is computed so as to produce the required disk number offset (Hersch 1993).

2.3. Parallel File System Support

The *MPMD* architecture requires a parallel file system made up of a file system master process responsible for maintaining overall parallel file system coherence (directories, file index tables, file extent access tables) and extent serving processes running on disk node processing units. Extent serving processes are responsible for serving extent access requests, for maintaining the free block lists and for managing local extent caches.

The low-level file system support of one multiprocessor-multidisk cluster consists of a single directory containing all the files stored on one MPMD cluster. Files are accessed through a directory entry which points to the *distribution information block (DIB)*. This *DIB* contains information relative to the file size, the file extension in x and y dimensions, the extent width and height, the number of continuous extents per disk, the number of disks, a table with the successive disk numbers contributing to this file, and for each disk, a pointer to the *file local extent index table (FLEIB)* containing the local pointers to the data extent blocks (Figure 2.3). At file opening time, the file system renders part of the *DIB* content as the file information block.

Directories and *DIBs* have a fixed, maximal size. For safety reasons, they are duplicated on each of the disks in the cluster.

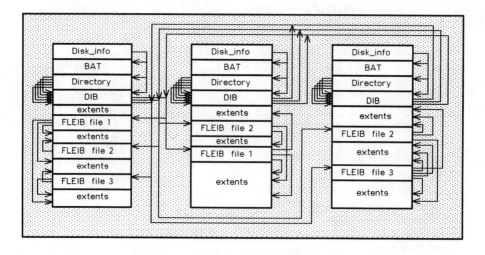

Figure 2.3. File system support in a disk cluster

At file opening time, each extent process reads the *file DIB* and the *FLEIB* from its disk. Once *DIB* and *FLEIB* are stored in memory, read and write operations on a given file can be executed at the rate of one disk access per extent. With an optimal extent size between 12Kbytes to 48Kbytes (see section 2.4), the throughput between disk and extent server is close to the maximal disk transfer rate.

2.4. Performance Characterization

Windowing systems offer visualization windows of variable sizes: a typical window size may be 512×512 pixels. Such a window may be enlarged to 1024×1024 or reduced to 256×256 pixels.

We will consider an architecture where the server interface processor is linked by two or four communication channels to a variable number of interconnected disk nodes. In the present contribution, we are interested in the behavior of an intelligent disk array in which disk node processors execute local processing operations in combination with disk accesses. For the purpose of image presentation, the following two image file access operations are supported: panning in large images by defining and placing at image access time a suitable visualization window at the required image location and zooming large-sized images onto normal sized visualization windows by specifying a subsampling factor (reduction factor).

In order to obtain detailed information about the performance of the proposed multiprocessor-multidisk architecture, a simulation program written in *Mathematica* is used. Basic performance parameters taken for the simulation such as message transfer speed over communication links and byte block transfer speed have been measured on a prototype multiprocessor-multidisk T800 transputer-based system. For the recently announced T9000 transputer, performance parameters for message and byte block transfers have been obtained from the data sheets. The simulation takes into account the time needed to compute extent distribution requests to disk nodes, communication time between server interface processor and disk node processors, SCSI (Small Computer System Interface) disk block access times, two-dimensional block copies including possible image size reduction for extracting visualized image parts from extents, transfer of resulting image parts through two or four communication links, receipt and assembly of image parts by the server interface processor.

Simulation parameters assume that the channel throughput of a T800-based system is identical to the effective throughput of T800 transputer communication links (~1.6 Mbytes/s) (Chardonnens et al., 1990) and that disks have a raw transfer rate of 2.4 Mbytes/s, a track to track access time of 4 ms and an average rotation time of 8.3 ms. Since multiple extents of the same image located on the same disk are generally stored on adjacent disk locations, we assume that mean seek time (15 ms) and average rotational delay (8.3 ms) are only applied to the first extent of an image on every disk. For consecutive extents of the same image, only track to track head displacement and transfer time are taken into account. T9000 transputers offer twice as much memory transfer throughput and 10 Mbytes/s data transfer bandwidth on their communication links as well as a crossbar switch for high-speed packet routing (Inmos 1991).

Images are accessed using a fixed-sized visualization window of 512×512 full-colour pixels. We will consider different extent sizes, between 1 and 20 interconnected disk nodes and four communication links between the server interface processor and the disk nodes. For the simulations, only uncompressed full colour (3 bytes/pixel) images were considered. Image size is much larger than visualization window size (for example: total image size is 2200×2200 pixels).

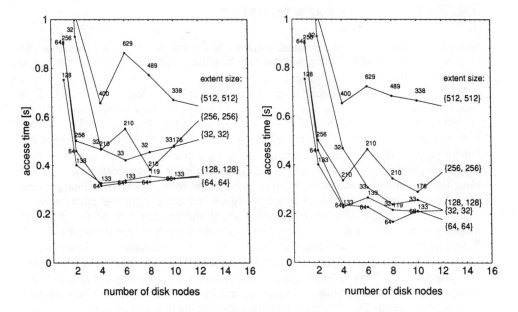

Figure 2.4. Image access times for 512 × 512 visualization window, on the left with two and on the right with four communication links between server interface processor and disk nodes

Figure 2.4 shows that performance depends heavily on available communication bandwidth. With two communication links, only two nodes provide close to linear speedup for image access. With four communication links, 4 nodes provide linear speedup. Optimal extent sizes for initial extent size are either 64 × 64 or 128 × 128 pixels. When not mentioned specifically, we assume that extent size is 128 × 128 pixels.

In Figure 2.5, performance of the proposed MPMD architecture is compared to the performance of an *ideal disk array (IDA)*, composed of a large array of disks connected by SCSI buses in direct memory access to the image server interface processor's main memory. We assume that the performance of the IDA system is ideal: SCSI channels, SCSI controllers and the image server's main memory have an infinite bandwidth. We also assume that its server interface processor is based on the same transputer-based technology as the MPMD server. The IDA's system bandwidth is therefore only limited by the throughput of the disks (disks of the same technology as the ones used in the MPMD system) and the processing capabilities of its single server interface processor. Figure 2.5 illustrates the fact that the MPMD T800 based-system is bounded by limited communication throughput: due to unlimited communication throughput, the ideal disk array performs 30% better. The IDA is bounded by the limited processing capabilities of its single server interface processor, which has the task of reassembling image parts originating from the different disks into one single image. Due to its improved communication bandwidth and processing power, the T9000-based MPMD system is not bounded by communication, but by disk access speed. Therefore, one obtains significant speedups with up to 10 disks hooked in parallel to access a 1024 × 1024 pixmap image. For a smaller size 512 × 512 image, only 8 disks can work efficiently in parallel. Both the IDA and the MPMD systems have similar performance, since they are not bounded by communcation bandwidth, or by processing power.

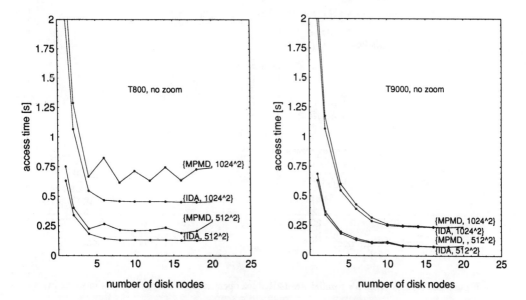

Figure 2.5. Image access times for 512 × 512, respectively 1024 × 1024 visualization windows, either with an MPMD system having four communication links between server interface processor and disk nodes or with an ideal disk array

Disk node processors can use their processing power for image data extraction while at the same time, thanks to direct memory accesses, executing SCSI transfers and communicating with the server interface processor. When disk accesses are combined with local processing operations, parallelization becomes very efficient and high speedups can be obtained with a relatively large number of disk nodes. Figure 2.6 illustrates the performance of a multiprocessor-multidisk array when disk node processors combine SCSI disk transfers and zooming out operations (integer subsampling by a factor of two). The server interface processor issues a Read&Reduce request in order to receive from the disk array a 256 × 256, (or 512 × 512) visualization window taken from a 512 × 512 (1024 × 1024) frame of the original image. Due to its parallel processing capabilities, the MPMD T800-based system offers for a large number of disk nodes up to twice the performance of an ideal disk array. On T9000-based systems, the difference between MPMD and IDA is less pronounced, since the single T9000 server interface processor associated with the ideal disk array is capable of reducing and assembling image parts at high speeds. With faster disks however, the difference between T9000-based IDA and MPMD systems will again become more significant, as it is in the case of the T800-based systems. Let us note that both for T800 and for T9000 systems, up to 16 disk nodes can be efficiently hooked in parallel.

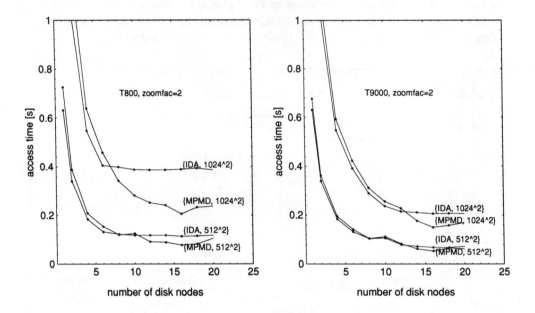

Figure 2.6. Access times for parallel Read&Reduce operations, in the same access mode as in Figure 2.5

2.5. Conclusions

Browsing through large sets of pixmap images requires the segmentation of images into rectangular facets, which are fetched on demand and in parallel from an array of disk nodes. Due to communication throughput bottlenecks of the current generation of disk node processors (T800 transputers), parallelization efficiency limits the number of useful parallel disk nodes. Without local processing operations, and for access to large image parts, a multiprocessor-multidisk system with limited communication throughput (6.4 Mbytes/s) between the disk nodes and the image server interface processor behaves 30% worse than an ideal disk array system connected by infinite bandwidth SCSI buses to a single image server interface processor. However, when intelligent disk nodes of the multiprocessor-multidisk system can be used to apply to their image extents local operations such as image size reduction (zoom-out), the MPMD architecture offers twice as much performance as an ideal disk array. This contribution shows that a multiprocessor-multidisk array composed of mass produced state of the art processors, communication channels and disks is highly efficient for single image access requests when using up to 16 intelligent disk nodes.

References

Chardonnens B, Hersch RD, Kolbl O (1990) Transputer based distributed Cartographic Image Processing, *Proceedings Joint Conference on Vector and Parallel Processing*: VAPP IV, Compar 90, (H. Burkhart, Ed), ETHZ, September 1990, Springer-Verlag, LNCS 457, 336-346.

Chen PA, Patterson DA (1990), Maximizing Performances in a Striped Disk Array, *Proceedings IEEE International Symposium on Computer Architecture*, Seattle, 322-331.

Hersch RD (1993), Parallel Storage and Retrieval of Pixmap Images, *12th IEEE Symposium on Mass Storage Systems*, Monterey, Calif, Digest of Papers, IEEE Computer Press, 1993.

Inmos (1991), *The T9000 Transputer Products Overview Manual*.

Patterson DA, Gibson G, Katz RH (1988) A Case for Inexpensive Disks (RAID), *Proceedings of the ACM SIGMOD Conf*, pp. 109-116.

Wilkes J (1991) DataMesh, Parallel Storage Systems for the 1990's, *11th IEEE Symposium on Mass Storage Systems*, Monterey, Calif, Digest of Papers, IEEE Computer Press, 131-136.

3

A Ternary Tree Representation of Generalized Digital Images

Hanspeter Bieri, Denise Mayor
Institut fur Informatik und angewandte Mathematik
Bern, Switzerland

3.1. Conventional Digital Images and Hyperimages

d-dimensional conventional digital images consist of pixels which are often conceived as d-dimensional *closed* unit cubes in the Euclidean space $\mathbf{R}^d$. This implies that different pixels are not disjoint, in general, as they may have boundary points in common. Hence, the pixels of a digital image form a division of the whole image extent only, but not a *partition*. As a consequence, anomalies may arise and certain algorithms in image analysis which are strictly additive are complicated. To conceive pixels as *open* unit cubes is no improvement because now the pixels of an image do not cover the whole image extent.

In (Bieri 1990) the pixels of a d-dimensional digital image are proposed to be *relatively open* unit cubes of dimensions $0, \ldots, d$. That is, there are pixels of different dimensions within the same image. Now, the pixels of an image do form a partition of the image extent, and the connection between (closed) "old" pixels and (relatively open) "new" pixels is very simple, as is easily seen in Figure 3.1 for $d = 2$.

In order to distinguish digital images composed of "new" pixels from those composed of "old" pixels, we will speak, as in (Bieri 1990), of *generalized digital images* or *hyperimages* on the one hand and of *conventional digital images* on the other hand. It is easily seen that every conventional digital image may be interpreted as a hyperimage, but not vice-versa. It will be practical to work with *normalized hyperimages* which are open cubes of edge-length 2^k ($k \geq 0$). Figure 3.2 shows a 2-dimensional conventional digital image and its embedding into a normalized hyperimage.

Virtual Worlds and Multimedia Edited by Nadia Magnenat Thalmann and Daniel Thalmann
© 1993 John Wiley and Sons Ltd

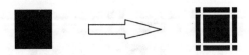

Figure 3.1. An "old" pixel is the partition of 9 "new" pixels

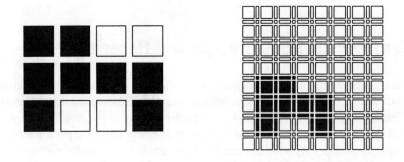

Figure 3.2. A conventional digital image of resolution 3×4 and its associated normalized hyperimage of resolution 8×8

For any d-dimensional hyperimage, the set of all its ("new") pixels can be provided with the topology induced by the natural topology of $\mathbf{R}^d$. This *digital topology is* examined in (Bieri 1990) and, from more theoretical points of view, already in (Khalimsky 1969) and more recently in (Kovalevski 1989). It has also been applied to computer graphics in (Khalimsky et al. 1990; Kopperman and Kong 1991; Françon 1991), for instance. Françon (1991) calls it *topology of Khalimski and Kovalevski* or, in short, *KK-topology*.

3.2. A Ternary Tree Representation of Hyperimages

From now on we only consider normalized binary hyperimages. The set of all pixels of a hyperimage can be represented as a regular grid of points in essentially the same way as in case of a conventional digital image (Bieri 1990). Therefore, disregarding space considerations, binary arrays are natural data structures for implementing hyperimages. In order to improve efficiency, it may be advantageous to convert these binary arrays to 2^d-trees (quadtrees, octrees, etc.) or bintrees, using standard procedures (Bieri and Metz 1991). But somehow more "natural" seems a *ternary tree representation,* for the following reason: We get the simplest partitioning of a relatively open rectangle into smaller relatively open pieces by intersecting the rectangle with a straight line such that 2 identical rectangles and an open segment result. All 3 resulting pieces allow the same kind of partitioning, so a simple finer partitioning of the given rectangle can be achieved by just applying this process repeatedly. It is obvious that this procedure works for a given relatively open box of any dimension d and that the corresponding partitioning can be represented every time in a straightforward way by a *ternary tree.* We will implement hyperimages like this (which explains why we assume them to be normalized). In this case, the process of partitioning terminates every time when each of the three resulting boxes consists of "new" pixels which are all "black" or all "white". The intersecting hyperplanes are most simply chosen to be perpendicular to the edges $l,...,d$, in sequence. Figures 3.3 and 3.4 illustrate the process of partitioning as well as the resulting ternary tree for a small hyperimage ("gray" boxes are bordered by dotted lines). This representation of a hyperimage by a ternary tree is quite similar to the representation of a conventional digital image by a bintree, apart from the important difference that the bintree only defines a subdivision of the conventional digital image and not a partition (Samet 1990a; Bieri 1987). A similar ternary tree structure to represent point data has been proposed in (Overmars and van Leeuwen 1982).

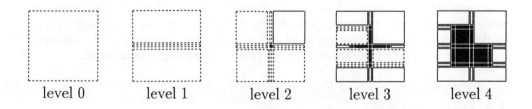

level 0   level 1   level 2   level 3   level 4

Figure 3.3. The process of partitioning a hyperimage

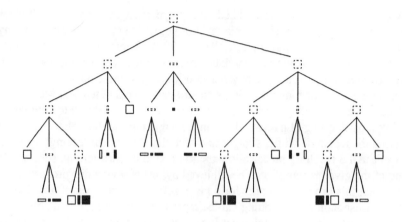

Figure 3.4. The ternary tree corresponding to the partitioning shown in Fig.3.3

3.3. Reflections on the Data Structures for Ternary Trees

We implement the ternary trees in a very conventional way using the common pointer technique. The main reason for this choice is that we wanted to program in C++ which only allows fixed-length arrays (as most similar programming languages do). So, all kinds of array implementation were unsuitable. Simulating dynamic arrays by linked linear lists would have made searching very inefficient, and simulating them by trees in order to implement other trees would not have made much sense either,. Hence, we implement our ternary trees using nodes linked by pointers. Figure 3.5 shows a node of a ternary tree and its definition in C++. The dimension of the node, i.e. the dimension of the subimage represented, is not stored but deduced from the position of the node within the tree.

3.4. Operations on Hyperimages

As in (Bieri 1990) we call the set union of all black pixels of a hyperimage its *figure*, the set union of all white pixels its *background* and the set union of all pixels its *extent*. The figure, background and extent of a *d*-dimensional hyperimage are always - fairly simple - subsets of the Euclidean space R^d, such that a number of elementary topological, geometrical and set operations may be applied to them in a reasonable way. Applying any of the following operations to hyperimages actually means applying it to their figures, and the result is always a hyperimage.

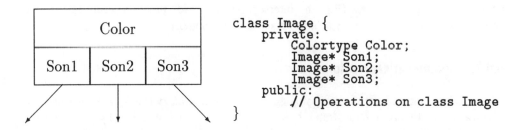

```
class Image {
    private:
        Colortype Color;
        Image* Son1;
        Image* Son2;
        Image* Son3;
    public:
        // Operations on class Image
}
```

Figure 3.5. The data structure of a ternary tree in our implementation

3.4.1. Set Operations

We have implemented the four most basic set operations, i.e. *union (U)*, *intersection (∩)*, *difference (\)*, and *complement (¬)*. Figure 3.6 shows some simple examples, starting from two conventional images. The figure of ¬ X is equal to the set difference extent(X) \ figure(X), of course.

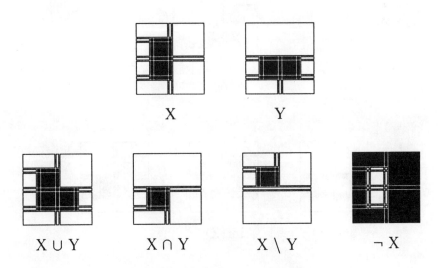

Figure 3.6. The 4 set operations

For each of these four operations our algorithm traverses the input tree(s) in preorder and constructs the corresponding output tree in parallel (i.e. simultaneously) to this traversal. As these algorithms are very similar to those for conventional digital images (Samet 1990a), we will not discuss them here in detail. Rather we would like to restate the important fact that set operations on hyperimages never result in *anomalies* as is often the case with conventional digital images. (E.g. the intersection of 2 "old" pixels meeting in just one corner is not empty but correctly a "new" pixel of dimension 0.)

3.4.2. Topological Operations

We have implemented the three topological operations *boundary* (bnd), *interior* (int), and *closure* (clos). Figure 3.7 illustrates how they create the output image by replacing the figure of the input hyperimage by the boundary, the interior or the closure, respectively, of the input figure. Figure 3.8 shows a conventional image of resolution 64×64 and the hyperimage resulting from applying the operation *boundary*.

As before, each algorithm traverses the input tree in preorder and constructs the output tree simultaneously. But now not only the actual input node has to be considered in order to determine the color of the corresponding output node, but also certain of its neighbors. We only present the details for $d = 2$. For every node of the input tree we use its dimension and color to access the proper lookup table (cf. Tables 3.1-3.3). Directly or via recursion the new color of the input node is returned, and iff it is black the node belongs to the figure of the output image. The following subroutines in pseudocode indicate the processing which has to be done for each input node and which depends on the dimension of the node:

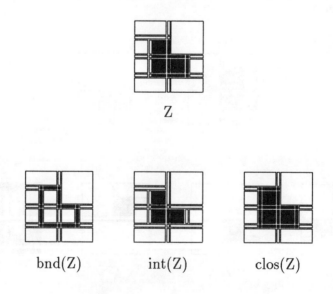

Figure 3.7. The 3 topological operations

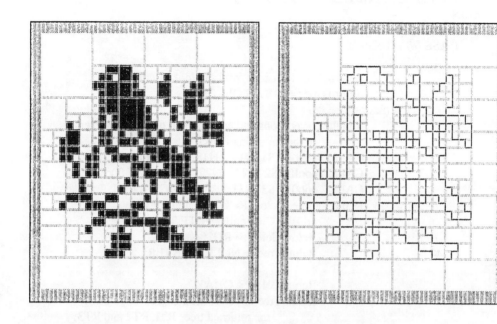

Figure 3.8. A bird and its boundary

- PROC Topo0D
        (Node, Neighbor1...Neighbor8: POINTER to
        NodeType;
        VAR ReturnColor: ColorType;
        VAR ReturnTree: POINTER to NodeType;
        LookupTable: POINTER to LookupTable0D);
  BEGIN
        FOR *each neighbor node Neighbor1 . . . Neighbor8*
            WHILE *the node is GRAY*
                replace it by the correct one of its sons;
        BlackNeighbors := *number of BLACK neighbor*
            nodes;
        ReturnColor := *take it from the lookup table;*
        ReturnTree := NULL POINTER;
        END

- PROC Topo1D
        (Node, Neighbor1, Neighbor2: POINTER to NodeType;
        VAR ReturnColor: ColorType;

```
        VAR ReturnTree: POINTER to NodeType;
        LookupTable: POINTER to LookupTableID );
BEGIN
        WhatToDo := take it from the lookup table;
        CASE WhatToDo OF
                End:
                        ReturnColor := take it from the lookup table;
                        ReturnTree := NULL POINTER;
                Rec(ursion):
                        find the correct sons and neighbors to use as parameters
                                in the following calls;
                        CALL Topo0D (S1, N11 ...N18, RC1, RT1, LT);
                        CALL Topo1D (S2, N21 ...N22, RC2, RT2, LT);
                        CALL Topo0D (S3, N31 . . . N38, RC3, RT3, LT);
                        IF the returned colors RCI, RC2 and RC3 are
                                all BLACK or all WHITE THEN
                                ReturnColor := RC1;
                                ReturnTree := NULL POINTER;
                ELSE
                        ReturnColor := GRAY;
                        ReturnTree := construct a GRAY node using
                                the returned trees RT1, RT2 and RT3;
END
```

* PROC Topo2D

```
        ( Node: POINTER to NodeType;
        VAR ReturnColor: ColorType;
        VAR ReturnTree: POINTER to NodeType;
        LookupTable: POINTER to LookupTable2D );
BEGIN
        WhatToDo := take it from the lookup table;
        CASE WhatToDo OF
                End:
                        ReturnColor := take it from the lookup table;
                        ReturnTree := NULL POINTER;
                Rec(ursion):
                        find the correct sons and neighbors to use as parameters
                                in the following calls;
                        CALL Topo1D (S1, N11 ...N12, RC1, RT1, LT);
                        CALL Topo2D (S2, RC2, RT2, LT);
                        CALL Topo1D (S3, N31 ...N32, RC3, RT3, LT);
                        IF the returned colors RCI, RC2 and RC3 are
                                all BLACK or all WHITE THEN
                                ReturnColor: = RC 1;
```

```
                              ReturnTree := NULL POINTER;
               ELSE
                              ReturnColor := GRAY;
                              ReturnTree := construct a GRAY node using the
                                            returned trees RT1, RT2 and RT3;
END
```

In order to start these programs for a given 2-dimensional hyperimage we only have to call Topo2D with the proper table as the last argument.

color of node	BOUNDARY		INTERIOR		CLOSURE	
	return color	what to do	return color	what to do	return color	what to do
WHITE	WHITE	End	WHITE	End	WHITE	End
BLACK	WHITE	End	BLACK	End	BLACK	End
GREY	-	Rec	-	Rec	-	Rec

Table 3.1. Lookup tables for nodes of dimension 0

color of node	color of neighbors	BOUNDARY		INTERIOR		CLOSURE	
		return color	what to do	return color	what to do	return color	what to do
WHITE	WHITE/WHITE	WHITE	End	WHITE	End	WHITE	End
WHITE	WHITE/BLACK	BLACK	End	WHITE	End	BLACK	End
WHITE	BLACK/BLACK	BLACK	End	WHITE	End	BLACK	End
WHITE	GREY/ANY	-	Rec	-	Rec	-	Rec
BLACK	WHITE/WHITE	BLACK	End	WHITE	End	BLACK	End
BLACK	WHITE/BLACK	BLACK	End	WHITE	End	BLACK	End
BLACK	BLACK/BLACK	WHITE	End	BLACK	End	BLACK	End
BLACK	GREY/ANY	-	Rec	-	Rec	-	Rec
GREY	WHITE/WHITE	BLACK	Rec	-	Rec	-	Rec
GREY	WHITE/BLACK	-	End	WHITE	End	BLACK	End
GREY	BLACK/BLACK	-	Rec	-	Rec	-	Rec
GREY	GREY/ANY	-	Rec	-	Rec	-	Rec

Table 3.2. Lookup tables for nodes of dimension 1

		BOUNDARY	INTERIOR	CLOSURE
color of node	# of BLACK neighbors	return color	return color	return color
WHITE	0	WHITE	WHITE	WHITE
WHITE	1-8	BLACK	WHITE	BLACK
BLACK	0-7	BLACK	WHITE	BLACK
BLACK	8	WHITE	BLACK	BLACK

Table 3.3. Lookup tables for nodes of dimension 2

3.4.3. Geometric Properties

In (Bieri and Nef 1984) it has been shown how some important geometric properties of d-dimensional conventional digital images, in particular volume, surface and Euler number, can be easily found by just determining the number mj of i-dimensional black pixels ($i = 0, ...,$ d). In the most important case $d = 2$ we have (Bieri and Kohler 1991):

$$A = m_2 \qquad \text{(area, = 2-dimensional volume)}$$

$$C = 2m_1 - 4m_2 \qquad \text{(circumference, = 2-dimensional surface)}$$

$$E = m_0 - m_1 + m_2 \qquad \text{(Euler number)}$$

A simple traversal of the given ternary tree is enough, of course, to determine $m_0, ..., m_d$ - and subsequently **A**, **C** and **E**. Our three geometric algorithms *area*, *circumference* and *Euler number* work according to this method.

3.4.4. Connected Components

The connected components of a hyperimage are just the connected components of its figure with respect to the natural topology of $\mathbf{R}^d$ (Bieri 1990). They are determined by means of two traversals of the given ternary tree in practically the same way as in case of a conventional digital image represented by a bintree or a 2^d-tree (Samet 1990b).

3.5. Performance Considerations

As in case of conventional digital images, worst-case time complexities of algorithms for hyperimages are of rather limited use. Worst-case examples in many respects are the "checkerboard-like" hyperimages where e.g. a pixel is black iff its dimension is even. The ternary tree of such a hyperimage of resolution $(2^k)^d$ has $(2^{k+1} - 1)^d = \Theta(2^{kd})$ leaves, $0.5(3(2^{k+1} -1)^d -1) = \Theta(2^{kd})$ nodes, and its depth is kd.

Our algorithms for the set operations, the geometric properties and the connected components are linear with respect to the number n of nodes, which is usually considered the input size. The algorithms for the topological operations are $O(nkd)$ (worst-case), because Topo0D searches for each node of dimension 0 the neighboring leaf nodes which may be $O(kd)$ further down in the tree. Whereas the size of the array implementing a given hyperimage is completely determined by the resolution, n may depend in a complex way on the shape of the figure of the image. In order to experiment with more or less "practical" inputs, we chose the letters of the alphabet and represented them as hyperimages of resolution 32 × 32 (cf. Figure 3.9). Table 3.4 shows for some of these letters how much space the array implementation and the ternary tree implementation require as well as the corresponding running times (on a PC) of our C++-program for the complement. The - probably more relevant - comparison between the ternary tree and bintree implementations shall be accomplished in another study.

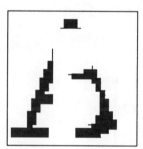

Figure 3.9. The letters A and B of the alphabet dataset and their intersection A ∩ B

In order to analyze experimentally the time complexity of our topological algorithms for "average-case" input, we made use of alphabet ternary trees of resolution 32 × 32 *(k = 5)* and 16 x 16 *(k = 4)*. Figure 3.10 shows results in the case of the algorithm *boundary* which confirm the expected linearity.

	SPACE (bytes)		TIME (seconds)	
letter	array	ternary tree	array	ternary tree
A	7938	8000	0.0461	0.0969
B	7938	11288	0.0460	0.1371
C	7938	8336	0.0461	0.1003
D	7938	8216	0.0460	0.0989
A∩B	7938	7520	0.0463	0.0888
A∩C	7938	3824	0.0461	0.0476
A∩D	7938	4904	0.0462	0.0624
B∩C	7938	8144	0.0463	0.0961
B∩D	7938	9416	0.0461	0.1207
C∩D	7938	6512	0.0460	0.0769
A∩B∩C	7938	3656	0.0459	0.0443
A∩B∩D	7938	4952	0.0461	0.0606
A∩C∩D	7938	3656	0.0461	0.0441
B∩C∩D	7938	7760	0.0462	0.0948
A∩B∩C∩D	7938	3656	0.0461	0.0447

Table 3.4. Space requirements and running times for the complement

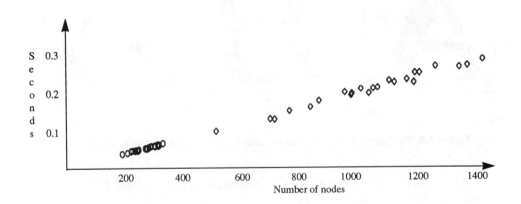

Figure 3.10. Measured times for the operation *boundary* for dimension d = 2 and resolution 2k ×
2k where k = *4 (o)* or k = *5 (o)*

References

Bieri H, Nef W (1984) Algorithms for the Euler characteristic and related additive functionals of digital objects, *Computer Vision, Graphics, and Image Processing,* Vol.28, pp.166-175.

Bieri H. (1987) Computing the Euler characteristic and related additive functionals of digital objects from their bintree representation, *Computer Vision, Graphics, and Image Processing,* Vol. 40, pp.115-126.

Bieri H (1990) Hyperimages - an alternative to the conventional digital images. In C.E. Vandoni and D.A. Duce, editors, *Proceedings of EUROGRAPHICS '90,* North-Holland, pp.341-352. .

Bieri H.; Kohler A (1991) Computing the area, the circumference, and the genus of a binary digital image. In J. Arvo (Ed.), *GRAPHICS GEMS II.* Academic Press, pp.107-111.

Bieri H., Metz I. (1991) Algorithms for generalized digital images represented by bintrees. In U. Eckhardt et al. (Eds.). Geometrical problems of image processing. *Research in Informatics,* Akademie Verlag, Vol. 4, pp.72-77.

Françon J (1991) *Topologie de Khalimski et Kovalevski et algorithmique graphique,* Université Louis Pasteur, Strasbourg, Département d'informatique, R91/10.

Khalimsky ED (1969) On topologies of generalized segments, *Soviet Math. Doklady,* Vol.10, pp.1508-1511.

Khalimsky E, Kopperman R, Meyer PR (1990) Computer graphics and connected topologies on finite ordered sets, *Topology and its Applications* Vol.26, pp.1-17.

Kopperman R., Kong Y (1991) Using general topology in image processing. In U. Eckhardt et al. (Eds.). Geometrical problems of image processing, *Research in Informatics,* Akademie Verlag, Vol. 4, pp.66-71.

Kovalevsky VA (1989) Finite topology as applied to image analysis, *Computer Vision, Graphics, and Image Processing,* Vol.46, pp.141-161.

Overmars M., van Leeuwen J (1982) Dynamic multi-dimensional data structures based on quad- and k—d trees, *Acta Informatica,* Vol.17, pp.267-285.

Samet H (1990a) *The Design and Analysis of Spatial Data Structures,* Addison-Wesley.

Samet H (1990b) *Applications of Spatial Data Structures,* Addison-Wesley.

4

An Overview of HDTV Systems

Murat Kunt
*Signal Processing Laboratory, Swiss Federal Institute of Technology
Lausanne, Switzerland*

4.1. Introduction

This chapter will discuss a few of the main issues related to recent developments in high
definition television (HDTV) systems, including a brief description of selected systems from
Europe, USA and Japan. It has previously been presented at various conferences (Kunt
1992a, 1992b, 1992c, 1993). Before discussing high definition, let us have a look to our
good old regular TV system. Doubtless, the best tool man ever made for mass education is
television. It is also the most successful commercial product: there are more than 1 billion
TV sets on the earth (more than telephones!) using a 50-year-old design. The main issue in
TV is that of programs. Instead of putting all the necessary effort into high-quality programs
for better education, look at the mess we have made of it. We broadcast greed, violence, hate,
injustice, religious crookery, Hollywood bad taste and, if there is time left, superficial and
biased information. Our good old TV system is undergoing important changes to improve its
technical quality, and what may happen is that we shall end up with much better images
showing poorer quality programs. It may well be another example of improving technicality,
but decreasing global quality. Some other well-known cases are fast-foods, 8 mm films
which become super 8 and then become video with increased practicality but poorer quality,
without forgetting publishing and book writing. Today everybody writes, nobody reads,
and the same is true for scientific papers as well. 'Cut & paste' helps proliferation and kills
quality. Nowaday, films are still edited by mechanical cut and paste, which is rather time
consuming. If ever this becomes electronic and more efficient, imagine how many cheap and
bad-taste films one can produce per week to pollute all the TV channels around the world.

Virtual Worlds and Multimedia Edited by Nadia Magnenat Thalmann and Daniel Thalmann
© 1993 John Wiley and Sons Ltd

4.2. Short History of TV

The first attempt to try to convert a visual scene into an electrical signal was made by Nipkow in 1884. From improvement to perfection, we move to the iconoscope of Zworkin in 1923, and then to the black and white TV tubes in 1941, and finally to color in 1950. Let us summarize in a few words how a TV system works. It is a typical communication system including a transmitter, a channel and a receiver. To be more specific, consider Figure 4.1, where such a system is shown. The first fact is that the 4-D space we are living in (three space variables and one time variable) is compressed in the system to a 1-D signal which is transmitted in the channel, and then expended to a 3-D signal which is displayed in front of the viewer. One dimension is lost by projecting the real world into an image plane, and the remaining 3-D space is sampled in time (thirty images per second in the US or 25 images per second in Europe). 2-D image space is scanned line by line producing a signal called a video signal. If the line by line scanning and the time sampling are repeated fast enough, one creates the illusion of continuity to fool the eye.

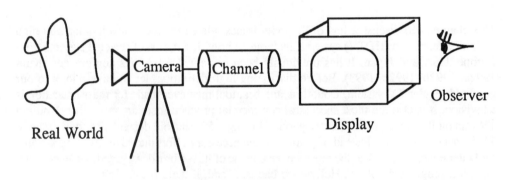

Figure 4.1. TV as a communication system

4.3. Video Signal

Since we are transmitting the video signal over the channel, it is interesting to determine its bandwidth. Assuming a square screen to display the image of size $N \times N$ points refreshed every F seconds, the highest frequency we can have is $N(N/2)F = N^2F/2$. For example, for 25 frames per second and 625 lines per screen, the base bandwidth of the video signal is around 5 MHz. Note that so far there is no NTSC (current US and Japan analog video format), PAL (current European analog video format) or SECAM (current French and

Eastern analog video format). The previous bandwidth represents a black and white image. Color was introduced through 3 primaries. There are either additive primaries like red, green and blue (RGB), or subtractive primaries, like yellow, magenta and cyan. A combination of either group of primaries may reproduce any desired color. Furthermore, there is no necessity to work just with these primaries. Any reversible three by three transformation is acceptable. For example, from the three additive primaries, R, G, B, we can obtain three other components, called Y, I, Q, (used in the NTSC system) or another set D,H,S corresponding to the intensity, hue and saturation, respectively. We can also have another transformation leading to one luminance and two chrominance signals. Accordingly, we can have a color TV by using three different video signals, one for each basic color primary. Why one should change the basis of color representation from basic primaries to any other transformation? The main reason was that of compatibility. To make the new color television, compatible with the existing black and white TV system, it was preferable to convert the RGB primaries into one luminance and two chrominance signals. Thus, the black and white receiver can receive only the luminance component, and allowed the viewer to watch a color program in black and white, or a black and white program can be broadcast and received with both black and white and color TV sets. If the base-band of a black and white video signal is 5 MHz, one may think that for color signal requiring three such signals, the bandwidth should be 15 MHz. In fact, because of the line repetition or frame repetition, a video signal is a quasiperiodical signal having a line spectrum. Thus, it is possible to include in the original base-band two more color components without increasing the bandwidth. Different TV systems, such as NTSC, PAL and SECAM, are in fact various ways of modulating the basic signal for transmission without increasing its bandwidth. In modulation, a parameter of a transmissible signal is varied as a function of the instantaneous value of the signal we want to transmit. There are three such parameters: amplitude, frequency or phase. If amplitude modulation is used, then the bandwidth of the transmitted signal is increased by factor of 2 with respect to the base-band of the video signal. It is possible to use single-side-band type modulation, but because of the very important DC component in the video signal, the preferred modulation scheme is the so-called vestigial side band modulation. Figure 4.2 shows the spectrum of the luminance signal modulated for transmission with the main carrier and audio carrier corresponding to the European system. In NTSC, the two chrominance signals I and Q modulate in amplitude and phase a secondary carrier situated in the upper part of the band at a frequence which interleaves various frequency components. The PAL system tries to remedy the NTSC inconvenience of being sensitive to phase distortions, so that the phase of one of the chrominance signals is alternated every two lines. In 625 line systems, the frequency of the chrominance carrier is higher by 4.4 MHertz than that of the main carrier. The SECAM system assumes that the chrominance signal does not need the same spatial resolution as the luminance signal. Chrominance resolution is divided by a factor of two. Thus, at each line of the luminance video signal, one transmits only one of the two chrominance signals which alternates with the other chrominance signal at the next line. At the receiver, one of them needs to be delayed (64 ms) to recombine them. In contrast with PAL and NTSC, SECAM uses frequency modulation for chrominance signals with two carriers situated around 4.2 MHz.

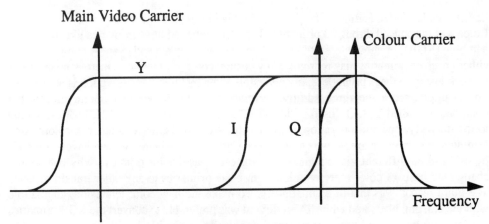

Figure 4.2. The NTSC Spectrum

4.4. What is Wrong with the Existing TV System ?

The first point is the synchrony. Because of the nonavailability of image memories in the early years of television, the present-day system, all the way from the camera to the display in front of the viewer, is a synchronous system. It requires high rates for motion rendition, but wastes bandwidth for transmission. The second point is unbalanced resolutions. For a given bandwidth, the gross video signal trades off time resolution with space resolution. Today's systems for motion rendition at 50 or 60 fields per second are rather poor on vertical resolution. Endless experience at the movie theater shows that higher space resolution is preferable at the price of lower temporal resolution (24 frames per second). Yet another point is related to the frequency multiplex. Frequency multiplex was well mastered at least in theory at the turn of the century. Although selective filters can be built, frequency multiplex led to the so-called composite signal, which with cheap filters in the receivers are at the origin of luminance used as chrominance and vice versa. Another point of criticism could be made on interlace. Introduced for better motion rendition, at the expense of poorer vertical resolution, interlace creates more problems than it solves. It does not perform as well as expected, emphasizes interline flicker, has poorer vertical motion definition, and complicates transcoding. With image memory in receivers, interlace should not survive in the future. Another point is related to the vestigial side band modulation, an obsolete technique leading to a larger RF bandwidth than the base bandwidth. Vestigial side band modulation should be replaced either by quadrature modulation or frequency division multiplex. Gamma correction is a measure of the deviation from an ideal input/output characteristic at the gray level of the entry signal. This correction is introduced prior to encoding. It violates the constant luminance principle mixing luminance and chrominance. Today's TV with the aspect ratio of 4/3 gives the viewer a quite different viewing experience than of the movie theater. A more rectangular screen (aspect ratio 16/9) will close this gap. Surprisingly, this point seems to be the only one on which there is a planetary consensus. There are many more wrong points one could list. However, since there are other consequences of the same basic principles, we shall not pursue the list. There are many improvements we can think of that could be incorporated into a new system. For example, receivers may have storage, avoiding interlace and relating frame rate to the motion rendition. We can do better signal processing (VLSI). One may introduce and expand programmability, which facilitates transcoding and upgrading. Frequency multiplex could be replaced by time multiplex avoiding cross talk. More contemporary modulation techniques could be used to avoid increase of bandwidth between the base-band and radio frequency. Modern vision knowledge may be introduced in the design of a new system. We may pay attention to respect the constant luminance principle and many more small improvements could be added to such a list. Anyway, a TV system should not be viewed as the one going from the camera to the display. It obviously includes the real world before the camera and the viewer before the display. Accordingly, such a system should be investigated end to end including the real world and the viewer. Because multimedia services have a foreseeable future, attention should be paid to them, emphasizing programmability and thus flexibility. Furthermore, technological updates should not affect the functions and should keep an extremely user-friendly receiver.

4.5. Elements of Vision

Let us now summarize some basic properties of human vision that could be incorporated into the design of a new system. The first important point is the sensitivity of the visual system to brightness. Between the sun at noon on a summer day (100,000 lux, lux being the unit of illumination) and the full obscure night (0.0003 lux), the dynamic range human eye is exposed to is extremely great. Physical systems, such as photographic paper, film or TV screen, are unable to reproduce such a dynamic range. Furthermore, by observing an image, its quality is assessed through the transmittance or the reflectance of small elementary surfaces. These are influenced by the immediate surroundings of the point observed, as well as wider areas. In addition, the subjective luminance of a region does not only depend on the effective luminance (physical luminance), but also on the illumination. It is absolutely necessary to distinguish between the effective luminance (measurable objective quantity) and the apparent luminance (subjective quantity). The latter is the response of the human visual system to the illumination received. The old Weber-Fechner experiment emphasizes this difference in a very simple way. The experimental set up shown in Figure 4.3 is just a screen having 2 different luminances. In the lower part, the luminance is L, and in the upper part the luminance $L+L'$. The set up is so that the observer may change the value of L'. At the beginning, it is set to zero, and it is increased until the border between these two areas is noticed by the observer. The experiment is repeated for other values of L. The ratio L'/L remains constant for a very large luminance interval of about four decades. If we repeat the same experiment by taking into account the surrounding luminance, as shown in the same Figure 4.3b, then the interval where the ratio L'/L is constant is reduced drastically. This is more pronounced whenever the difference between the surround and L is large. For example, if the surround is too bright, then the inner square appears as dark and no border is visible.

In the opposite case, the central square appears as a light source. In other words, for the human visual system to function, luminance differences on a small surface, small with respect to our visual field, need to be compressed. The reason why movie theaters and TV rooms are dark is to bring the surrounding luminance close to the actual luminance on the screen, so that luminance variations can best be seen. This property can for example be used in establishing quantizers for luminance or gamma correction systems for a video signal. Another interesting behavior of the human visual system is the variation of this sensitivity to luminance as a function of spatial resolution or the spatial frequency.

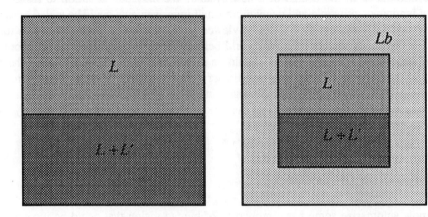

Figure 4.3. Weber-Fechner experiment

There are many ways to measure this interesting curve and a general result is shown on Figure 4.4. Interpreted in loose terms, this curve tells us that the human visual system may detect very small faults on uniform surfaces much more easily than on surfaces where the luminance has a large variation. Furthermore, beyond a certain spatial resolution, we cannot distinguish any variation. The first part of the curve is the differentiating behavior of the visual system whereas the second part is the integrating behavior. The first part has not so far been used in any TV system. The second part determines the distance at which one should watch the TV screen, still avoiding the lines structure. The similar situation may also give the number of lines we should have for a given observation angle. For a 625 line system, a TV display whose height is 50 cm should be watched at a distance of 2 meters. Another interesting sensitivity of the human visual system is the sensitivity to motion. If 2 light bulbs are turned on and off, one after the other, the human visual system senses a motion back and forth between them. If the switching rate is increased beyond a certain threshold, then the 2 light bulbs appear as permanently lit. If the sensitivity is measured as a function of cycles and sequence, typical curves that are obtained are shown on Figure 4.5. The general behavior is similar to the previous curve. There is a differentiating part for low frequencies and an integrating part in the high frequencies. This curve indicates that the human visual system can sense slow flickering motion more easily than fast flickering motion, and that beyond a certain temporal precision no motion is sensed. Flickering is very high at 25 Hz (25 images per second). For very bright images, it still exists even at 50 frames per second. In order to avoid flickering in the worst case, the sampling frequency should be increased at least 70 Hz or more. The last important point which is worth mentioning is that these two sensitivity curves discussed above are not independent. The spatiotemporal sensitivity cannot be decomposed into separable spatial and temporal sensitivity variations. Complete analysis of this behavior shows that the spatial resolution can be treated with the temporal resolution. It turns out that the human visual system is not very sensitive to a bad motion rendition in a high spatial frequency area, then of a rather flat shape.

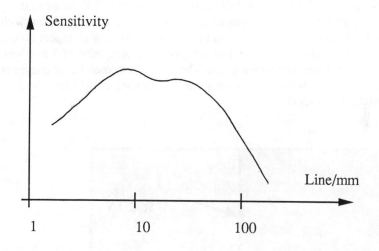

Figure 4.4. The spatial frequency response of the visual system

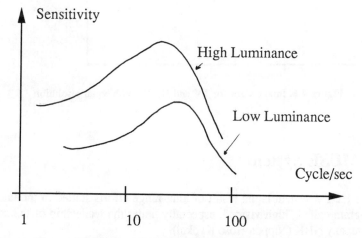

Figure 4.5. The time-frequency response of the visual system

4.6. High Definition Television

Let us move now to high definition television. It has become such a hot political and industrial topic that one can find it in the newspapers almost almost every day. Three regions, Japan, Europe, and the United States, are competing to establish a world standard for the next generation of TV system. A standard is necessary whenever there is more than one solution competing for the same problem. In the case of television, there will very likely be standards on production, transmission, recording, copying, and so forth. Figure 4.6 shows the size of the actual TV image and the new high definition TV image with equal space resolution. In figure 4.7, the two systems are shown for equal surfaces, but with different aspect ratios. The new TV screen will be more rectangular with an aspect ratio of 16 to 9. The essential parameters of a new system are given as a succession of 3 numbers. The first one is the number of lines per screen height. The second is the number of images per second, and the third is the number of frames per second. For example, the European proposition is characterized by 1250-50-50.

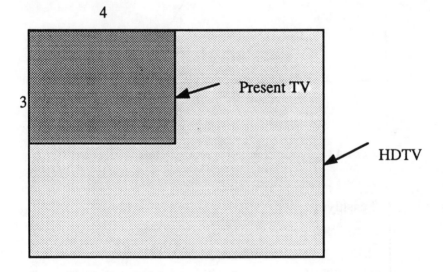

Figure 4.6. Image sizes for TV and HDTV with equal resolution

4.7. The MUSE System

The Japanese HDTV system is the result of long-range efforts started in the late seventies within a program called "high vision", especially under the leadership of the state owned broadcast company NHK (Nippon Hoso Kyokai).

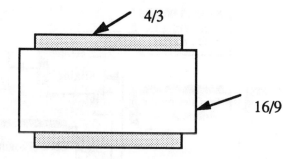

Figure 4.7. Image shapes for TV and HDTV with equal surface

The first prototype demonstration was available around 1986. It was almost a world standard as proposed at the CCIR meeting in Dubrovnik. The sample-minded compression scheme gives the name of the system MUSE, standing for multiple sub-Nyquist sampling encoding. This system has been designed for satellite broadcasting in the bands of 12 GHz. The transmission system adopted is analog frequency modulation requiring a transmission bandwidth of 27 MHz for a base-band within 8 MHz. The video signal of the MUSE system has 1125 lines, 30 frames and 60 fields per second. It is an interlaced scan. The video signal is processed component by component, chrominance signals being compressed through the so-called time compressed integration. Compression by a factor of 4 is used to fit the chrominance signal in the line blanking interval. The digital sound is inserted in the field blanking interval. Figure 4.8 shows the block diagram of the MUSE transmitter. The time compressed integrated signal is sampled at 64.8 MHz and processed to determine fixed areas and mobile areas. Each type of area is a sub-sample adjusted to fit the global signal within the 8 MHz bandwidth. Fixed areas are sub-sampled by a factor of 4 so that 4 fields are needed to reconstruct the full resolution of scene. For mobile areas, this type of sub-sampling cannot be used because during 4 fields the motion can be very important and may lead to blur. For mobile areas, the motion is transmitted field by field, but with much less spatial resolution. Figure 4.9 shows the spatial resolution of this system, as well as the overlaps induced by sub-sampling. Because of the poor motion rendition of this basic system, it has been improved by reducing the spatial resolution, so that the time compressed integration is not sampled at 64.8 MHz, but for the 8.6, reducing the sub-sampling to a ratio of 3 instead of 4. Figure 4.10 summarizes various processing steps of this system for mobile and fixed areas. The transmissible luminance information corresponding to this new scheme and its spectrum before and after sub-sampling is shown in Figure 4.11. Probably the greatest merit of the MUSE system is its existence. In 1991, they already had daily broadcasts for about one or two hours a day, which has been increased to 8 hours since January 1992. Its second merit is that it triggered an international competition between Europe, Japan and the US, for the development of a new television system.

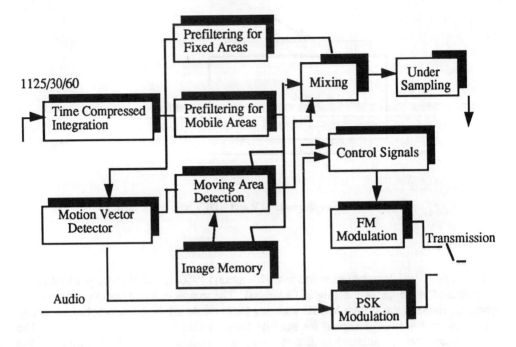

Figure 4.8. The MUSE transmitter

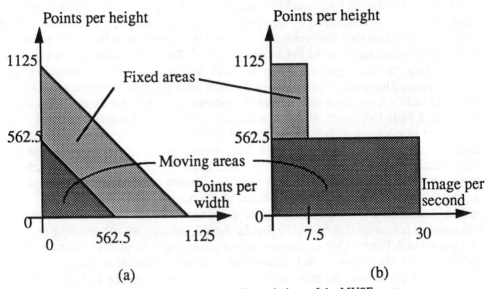

(a)   (b)

Figure 4.9. Space (a) and time (b) resolutions of the MUSE system

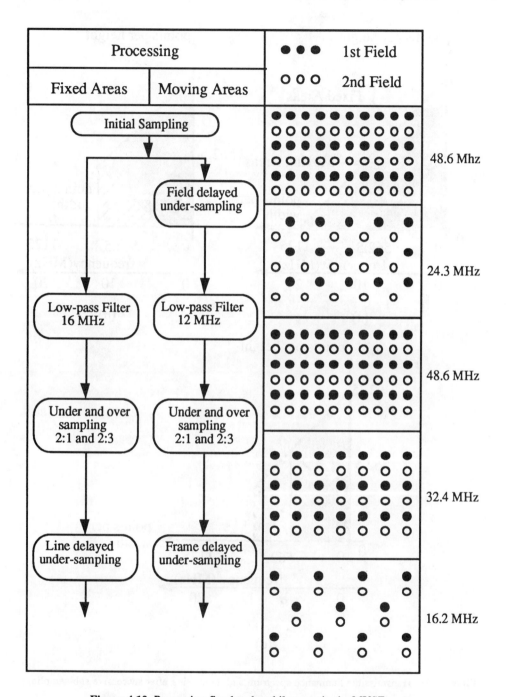

Figure 4.10. Processing fixed and mobile areas in the MUSE system

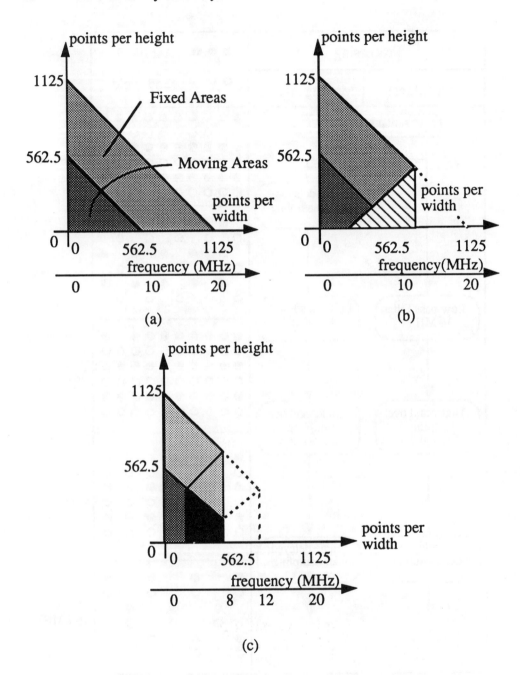

Figure 4.11. Transmissible luminance spectrum and its aliasing after successive sub-samplings

4.8. The HD-MAC System

The European answer to the MUSE system was the setting up of a European project called EUREKA 95, which came up with an equivalent system called HD-MAC. In contrast to the MUSE system, which is not compatible with existing TV systems, like NTSC, PAL or SECAM, HD-MAC was introduced in 1988 with the argument of compatibility. It refers to compatibility with a nonexisting D2-MAC system, which is even today not yet fully operational. The D2-MAC system is a component system, in which luminance and chrominance signals are sampled and time-compressed to fit within 64 μs of one video scanline, including audio and data. Because of time compression, the initial bandwidths of 5.6 MHz and 1.6 MHz for luminance and chrominance, respectively, increase to 8.4 and 4.8, requiring a global sampling frequency of 20.25 MHz. The D2-MAC system is the result of an evolution lasting for about ten years, starting with A-MAC, B-MAC, etc. The HD-MAC system is so-to-speak an upscaled version of D2-MAC. Accordingly by under-sampling a high-resolution video signal one can bring it down to D2-MAC format. The input to the HD-MAC system is a video signal with 1250 picture lines, interlaced, scanned with 50 fields and 25 frames. This signal is sampled in a quincuncial manner as shown in Figure 4.12a. Then the resulting picture point set is decimated into 4 subsets using odd and even numbered lines and columns. After some special arrangement, this subset became the fields of the D2-MAC system, which could be recombined to make the interlaced HD-MAC frames. This scheme is for the still picture case, where there is no motion. The initial signal is processed to determine three categories of areas in each picture: fixed areas, slowly moving areas and moving areas. Each area is analyzed according to these three hypotheses and processed for compression using a trade-off between time resolution and space resolution. The results are then compared with the original area and a decision is made to put the appropriate level where the similarity is the highest. Figure 4.13 shows the space and time resolution of the HD-MAC system. Compared to MUSE, the HD-MAC system reveals similarities as striking as those between the Tupolev and Concorde supersonic airplanes! The 1992 winter and summer Olympic Games were broadcast to some viewpoints through HD-MAC system. Although there are not yet regular daily broadcasts, one may consider HD-MAC as close to existence. Both MUSE and HD-MAC systems have very simple-minded data compression schemes and obsolete analog transmission modes.

4.9. American Systems

At the first stages of the competition between Japan and Europe, America was a careful observer. The Federal Communication Commission, better known as the FCC, fix the rules of the game. It is required that American high definition TV, HDTV, should be based on terrestrial transmission and should fit within the 6 MHz bandwidth as presently used for regular NTSC, with no interference to the existing NTSC system. In early 1989, there were many systems being developed in the US. We can mention the so-called Advanced Compatible Television or AC TV developed by the David Sarnoff Center and Thomson Consumer Electronics.

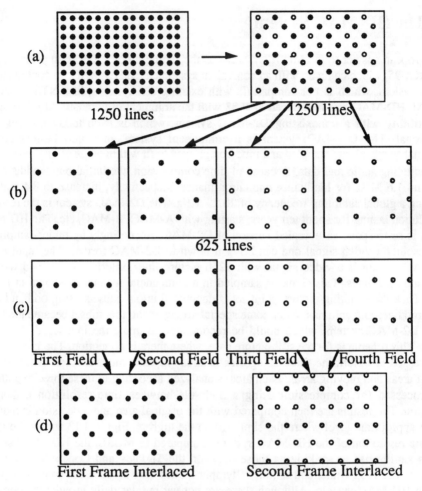

Figure 4.12. Frame and field processing in the HD-MAC system

The North American Philips firm developed another system based on NTSC, as well as the GLEN system. Both of these systems were using NTSC in one channel and an augmentation signal in the next one. The Zenith system was yet another candidate. Professor Schreiber designed two systems at MIT. Finally let us mention two versions of the MUSE system, one being incompatible and the other one compatible with NTSC receivers. These systems were mainly hybrid, combining some analog and some digital signal processing and modulation. Probably the most up-to-date system was the early MIT CC system, as proposed by Schreiber, based on subband coding. The FCC opened a competition which will be closed sometime in 1993, to find the best HDTV system for American needs. While the entire world was hesitating over various hybrid schemes, engineers from the General Instrument Corporation courageously came up with the first all-digital HDTV system. Then, three more opponents followed. Out of 6 systems competing today for FCC, four of them are all-digital.

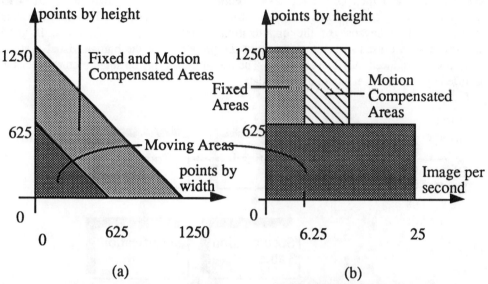

Figure 4.13. Space (a) and time (b) resolutions of the HD-MAC system

The space in this chapter is not enough to describe in detail all these four systems. Luckily, they share many common principles that we can summarize, mentioning briefly their specificities, which make them unique. Important points on these systems are data compression and channel coding. Data compression is important to reduce the number of bits necessary to transmit, to represent faithfully the original data, i.e. the original scenes. Because compressed data is much more sensitive to noise existing in the transmission channel, compressed data must be protected against such disturbances. This is done with the channel coding. The use of digital techniques in both areas allows flexibility and efficiency. The data compression can be subdivided into spatial data compression and time data compression. The first refers to the removal or the attenuation of the spatial correlation existing between picture points of the same frame, whereas the second one refers to the redundancy existing from one frame to the next. Although we know in theory that these two types of redundancy should not be processed independently for the best efficiency, as a good engineering practice, they will be processed independently. There are some old techniques to remove spatial correlation within a single image. Introduced some 20 years ago, the so-called linear transform coding techniques allow us to compact the energy of the image signal in two specific areas of a transform domain and then, assigning bits to each transform coefficient in a very specific manner, compressions around 10 to 1 or 15 to 1 are easily obtained with good quality reconstructed pictures. Since its early years, this technique has been continuously improved by intensive fine tuning, so that today recommendations from international standardization bodies exist on the label of JPEG (Joint Photographic Expert Group),. The JPEG coder is shown in Figure 4.14. Basically, the input image is subdivided into blocks of 8 by 8 pixels. Each block is transformed by the so-called discrete cosine transform (DCT). The transform coefficients are quantized according to some specifications and then coded for transmission. The decoder shown in Figure 4.15 implements the inverse operations to reconstruct the picture. The JPEG scheme involves information loss because of the quantization of transformed coefficients. If good specifications are used to take into account the properties of the human visual system, distortions introduced may be very small. The use of transforms on small picture blocks is justified by the statistical nature of image data.

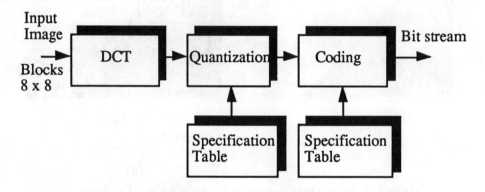

Figure 4.14. The JPEG coder

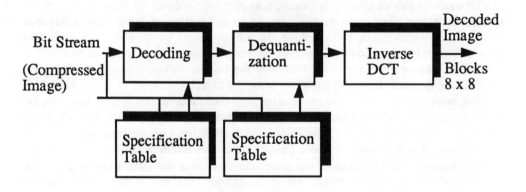

Figure 4.15. The JPEG decoder

To reduce temporal redundancy, it is easy to realize that from one frame to the next, there are great similarities since they are only 16 or 20 ms apart. In such a case, there is no need to code each frame independently from the preceding one. The common principle used is to fully encode the first frame and then code only the changes appearing in the forthcoming frames with respect to the first one. These changes are best described if the objects moving in the scene are identified. Such an identification, however, is a very difficult task even for today's most developed computer vision systems. Again, a good engineering approximation of this problem is to trace the motion of small image blocks, for example 8 by 8 from one frame to the next. Figure 4.16 shows the subdivision of a given frame with numbered blocks and the previous frame showing the corresponding position of each block. It is possible to go one step further by taking into account the previous situation, to predict where the given block will be in a third frame. If the prediction is good, there is no need to transmit additional information. If there is a slight prediction error, then it is sufficient to transmit this small error with a very reduced number of bits, to recover fully the position of this block in the third frame. This technique is known as motion compensation. A better description would be the coding of the prediction error. Accordingly, using the previous techniques, one can produce a sequence of error images containing the prediction error of block motions from one frame to the next. This is called the displaced frame difference sequence. A common procedure is to view each frame of this new error sequence as an image and apply the spatial decorrelation technique previously discussed, using for example a discrete cosine transform. A recommendation called MPEG (Moving Picture coding Experts Group) is issued by the International Standardization Organization for video coding at about 1.5 Mbit per second. The comment one can make is that the statistics of the displaced frame differences do not behave like those of a real image. So applying a technique which is suitable for one does not necessarily mean that it is also suitable for the other. As far as the transmission is concerned, digital modulation allows the protection of the messages so that transmission errors can be detected and even corrected at the receiver.

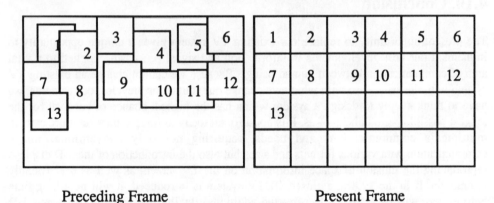

Preceding Frame   Present Frame

Figure 4.16. Block matching motion estimation

Among the competing American systems, the Zenith AT & T consortium designed a system which uses the previous principles. It has a very elaborate motion detection scheme, which uses hierarchy so that a coarse motion analysis is made in all cases and then depending on the bit available for transmission, more refined motion analysis is implemented where such a precision is needed. The spatial redundancy is attenuated using the discrete cosine transform. A rather large number of different quantizers are designed to quantize and code the transformed coefficients. The selected quantizer is indicated to the receiver through vector quantization. The coded data is modulated in the system, using 2 types of vestigial side band modulation with 4 or 2 levels. The main motivation for such a double scheme is to introduce graceful degradation of the transmitted data as a function of the distance from the emitter. The so-called Digicypher system proposed by the General Instruments Corporation also uses similar principles. One level straightforward motion compensation reduces the time redundancy followed by a discrete cosine transform for spatial redundancy reduction. Quantized coefficients are then encoded prior to quadrature amplitude modulation. The advanced television research consortium (ATLC) brings together Philips, Thomson, NBC and the David Research Center of Stanford Research International. This system uses the MPEG recommendation adapted to the high definition picture format. They call it MPEG++. An interesting originality of this system is the introduction of priorities to the data to be transmitted. Very important data receives high priority and is coded with high security as opposed to low priority data which is less protected for transmission, against transmission error. In this scheme, the modulation used is again quadrature amplitude modulation. Among all digital HDTV systems, let us mention finally the new system proposed by MIT. This system also uses the same general principles. It is mentionned that in a newer version of the system, a subband analysis will be introduced to reduce the spatial correlation of the data.

4.10. Conclusion

The present opportunity to replace our existing TV system gives a unique opportunity to implement our best developments in information and signal processing applied to a vital area of communication between human beings. Because we cannot change an existing TV system with the same ease with which we change our shirts, our bicycles, our cameras, we have to think deeply to design a system which has the highest chance of survival for the longest possible period ahead of us. It is not difficult today to foresee important progress in multimedia communications and needs, requiring not only conventional image communication with various formats and sizes but also the introduction of the 3-D displays reproducing the illusion of space information on the TV screen, as well as user friendly interaction. If in the 1990's, a closed HDTV system is introduced, it will be a long time before there will be a chance to offer the additional flexibilities of multimedia and 3-D systems to the consumer. It is the author's opinion that priority should be given to the HDTV system which has the most open architecture and design, so that future developments can be easily incorporated into the existing system.

References

Kunt M (1992a) HDTV, *IEEE Information Theory Society Newsletter*, N. Mehravari (Ed), vol. 42, No. 3, pp. 1-15.

Kunt M (1992b) Recent HDTV Systems, *Signal Processing* VI, Theories and Applications, J. Vandewalle et al. Eds, North-Holland, Amsterdam, pp. 83-89.

Kunt M (1992c) An Overview on Current HDTV efforts, *Proc. of Canadian Conference on Electrical and Communications Engineering*, 13-16 September, Toronto, Canada, pp. TA5.16.1-TA5.16.7.

Kunt M (1993) Recent HDTV Systems, In G. Vernazza (Ed) *Image Processing: Theory and Applications*, Elsevier Science Publishers, Amsterdam.

5

Progressive Image Transmission for Multimedia Applications

Martin J. Dürst
Multi-Media Laboratory, Institut für Informatik der Universität Zürich
Switzerland

5.1. Introduction

Multimedia databases and applications in the emerging world-wide network will rely on storing and transmission schemes that limit resource use while assuring the fast availability of the desired information. Besides basic mechanisms applicable to all kinds of media, for each type of data specific measures will have to be taken. Here particularly the case of gray scale image data is discussed. After examining the requirements for image coding and transmission, we present BCQ-coding (Dürst 1990), an efficient method for the progressive transmission of images. Based on theoretical considerations and experimental results, BCQ-coding is compared to the nowadays predominant JPEG standard (Wallace 1991). This leads to a better understanding of the problems and solutions for image storage and transmission in the context of multimedia applications.

5.1.1. World-wide Networks

Progress in hardware and software networking technology has made possible the world-wide integration of computing and storage resources. The emerging global network will contain huge amounts of information in various forms. But without careful planning of this network, obtaining the desired information in a timely fashion will only be possible, but not at all probable.

Virtual Worlds and Multimedia Edited by Nadia Magnenat Thalmann and Daniel Thalmann
© 1993 John Wiley and Sons Ltd

To take advantage of globally available data, two closely intertwined problems have to be solved: the performance problem and the abstraction problem. Performance is of importance for the following reasons: larger volumes of data and the higher functionality offered to the end-user consume the greater part of the ever-improving hardware performance. The global network will never be homogeneous; large performance gaps and mismatches appear anew with each step ahead in the technological progress.

The primary solution to the performance problem is the use of data caching and replication to trade communication performance (bandwidth) against storage space. Replication heuristics consider the balance between storage and bandwidth availability and the probability of future accesses to the various data entities (see (Mullender 1989) part IV).

However, being able to obtain sufficient information is not enough. To obtain the *desired* information is much more important. This leads to the abstraction problem. Selecting the desired information, either automatically or manually, is only possible if it is adequately abstracted. In addition, abstraction can also reduce raw information and therefore alleviate the performance problem.

Abstraction can be carried out manually. Categories (directory names), file names, titles, keywords, abstracts, and the like, are mostly manually prepared abstractions of documents of any kind. Automatically produced abstractions tend to be more media-specific. Text can be abstracted mainly with index terms, tables of contents, and plain text from fully formatted documents. Abstraction for structured graphics is still mostly domain-dependent. For images, video, and sound, automatic abstraction is possible by reducing resolution. Other methods are again very domain-dependent and in addition require huge amounts of computation.

Using these abstractions, data is accessed incrementally. The coarsest representation is obtained. Then some items are selected. For these items, the next finer representation is transmitted. This representation is again used for selection. The process is continued until the desired information is reached. For most media, this has to be done in rather coarse steps. Text, as well as sound and video, have to be scanned sequentially. Rescanning has to be done at a significantly coarser level to reveal enough new information per time unit. On the other hand, graphics and especially images are perceived instantaneously. Therefore the time dimension can be fully used for refinement.

5.1.2. Image Transmission

Among all media types, only still images combine straightforward abstraction by resolution reduction with continuous refinement along the time dimension. This means of image transmission has been termed *progressive transmission* since its first description in (Tanimoto 1979). Since then, many different algorithms and applications have been proposed (see (Tzou 1987) or (Dürst 1990) for references). The prototypical application consists of scanning an image database. Adapted to the high screen resolutions and transmission speeds common today, it may look as follows: first, the set of possible images is reduced based on descriptors and key words. Then transmission of the images themselves is started; several images are refined in parallel. The viewer can select or reject any image as soon as it is displayed with enough detail. These images are immediately replaced by others that have not yet been scanned. The rejected images are discarded; the selected ones might be refined to full resolution off line.

The resolution of an image has three dimensions, gray scale resolution and two dimensions of spatial resolution. We will not consider color images, which pose some very specific problems. Progressive transmission can be easily simulated using analog devices. Spatial resolution can be increased by gradually adjusting the focus of a lens system. Gray scale resolution can be increased by turning the contrast knob on a monitor screen.

When implementing the refinement of digitally coded images with digital algorithms, absolute smoothness can no longer be achieved. Additional compromises have to be made to limit the amount of calculation and of information transmission. However, a digital representation makes it easier to distribute the resolution increase unevenly among the different areas of the image, adapted to the human visual system. Also, trying to transmit the most important information in an image first automatically leads to compression. Indeed, the relation between progressive transmission algorithms and image compression algorithms is of considerable importance for the development of both (Dürst and Kunii 1991).

5.2. Requirements for Image Coding

Based on the preceding general discussion, we now analyze the requirements for compression and progressive transmission algorithms in the context of world-wide hybrid multimedia systems. The requirements comprise the following points (Dürst 1990; Wallace 1991):

1. Progressive increase of image quality in small incremental steps. Small incremental steps are important to fully use the time dimension for replay. The size of the incremental steps should not be measured in bits and bytes, but in terms of a quality function. For the same amount of information, image quality increases much more in the initial parts of the transmission than later.
2. Good compression rate over the whole quality range. Many algorithms for compression and progressive transmission are engineered towards a certain image quality. An ideal algorithm should be easily applicable for very low rates, with barely visible image contents, up to lossless transmission of images.
3. Low requirements for calculation and possibility for hardware implementation.
4. No dependence on the type of image. A single method should be applicable to all types of image. Adaptation to certain kinds of images or to particular areas in an image should occur automatically.
5. Single mode of operation. There should be only one way of coding an image for all storage and transmission purposes, so that conversions are avoided.

The above requirements will be used later to evaluate various progressive transmission algorithms.

5.3. BCQ-Coding

Here we present BCQ-coding as an image coding method that is very well suited to the above requirements of hybrid multimedia systems. BCQ-coding is based on the binary condensed quadtree (BC-Quadtree). When BCQ-coding is used for compression or transmission, the terms BCQ-compression or BCQ-transmission are also used.

5.3.1. The Binary Condensed Quadtree (BC-Quadtree)

The BC-quadtree (Dürst and Kunii 1989) is an efficient combination of the quadtree as a two-dimensional spatial hierarchy (Samet 1984; Samet and Webber 1988) with the binary gray scale hierarchy. These two hierarchies allow for a stepwise increase of both spatial and gray scale resolution (Dürst and Kunii 1991).

The BC-quadtree can best be explained using an example. Figure 5.1 shows a small example image (left) and its corresponding BC-quadtree (right). The root node at the top of the BC-quadtree corresponds to the whole image. Nodes on the next level correspond to two-by-two subimages, arranged left to right and top to bottom. Nodes on the lowest level of the BC-quadtree correspond to individual pixels, again arranged in the same sequence within the respective subtrees. The entries in each node consist of actual bit values (0 or 1), subscripts indicating the bit position (for reference only; 1 for the most significant bit, 3 for the least significant bit), and parentheses indicating where a node has to be split up.

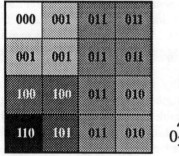 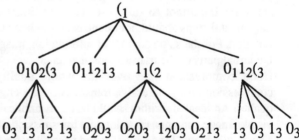

Figure 5.1. An example image with its BC-Quadtree

Compared to the traditional raster quadtree (Samet 1984), the BC-Quadtree condenses pixels bitwise, starting with the most significant bit. It is therefore very well suited to natural gray scale images, where adjacent pixels mostly have similar values, but rarely exactly the same ones.

5.3.2. Image Transmission

The symbols '(', '0', and '1' can now be transmitted in sequence like the Depth First Expression of Kawaguchi et al. (Kawaguchi and Endo 1980). The '0' and '1' contain the information about the values of the individual bits, whereas the '(' is used to transmit the structure of the BC-quadtree. In variants of the BC-quadtree, additional symbols are used to express uncertainty (Dürst and Kunii 1992). As long as sender and receiver agree on the way to determine the sequence of the symbols, any sequence which sends more significant symbols before the less significant symbols of the same pixel or subimage can be used.

To determine the exact symbol sequence for progressive transmission, it proved particularly useful to divide all the symbols of an image into components according to their spatial resolution (size of the corresponding subimage) and to their gray scale resolution (bit position). As an example, for an image of 256 by 256 pixels with 8 bits per pixel, the size of all the images later used, there are altogether 56 components.

The components with lower spatial resolution in general are smaller because there are just not as many subimages of the corresponding size as for higher spatial resolution. Also, the components of lower gray scale resolution in general are smaller because better condensation is possible in the more significant bits. As the components are transmitted from low to high resolution, this nicely fits requirement 1 above.

The simplest transmission sequences are the lexical orderings of the components with either spatial resolution or gray scale resolution being more significant. This results in uniquely increasing spatial resolution (see Figure 5.2) or gray scale resolution (see Figure 5.3). The images have been obtained from the Japanese Standard Image Database (Onoe et al. 1979). However, increasing spatial and gray scale resolution is also possible by adequately ordering the components, for example by the sum of their spatial and gray scale resolution (see Figure 5.4). See (Dürst 1990) and (Dürst and Kunii 1991) for more details on the actual algorithms and the implementation.

Figure 5.2. Increasing spatial resolution (bytes transmitted: 125, 250, 500, 1000, 2000, 4000, 8000, 16000; full image: 65536)

But not only does BCQ-coding allow us to increase spatial and gray scale resolution in a balanced way suited to the human visual system, it also does this adaptively. For each subimage or pixel, only a small part of all the components are actually transmitted. In areas of an image that are relatively flat, these components have more gray scale resolution than spatial resolution. In areas with high peaks and low valleys, on the other hand, more spatial resolution will be transmitted. This is exactly what the human visual system sees best in the respective areas. Adaptation to the specific properties of certain areas of the image is therefore obtained automatically with BCQ-coding, whereas it needs special consideration in most other coding methods (see e.g. (Lohscheller 1984)).

Figure 5.3. Increasing gray scale resolution (bytes transmitted: see Figure 5.2)

Figure 5.4. Balanced increase of spatial and gray scale resolution (bytes transmitted: see Figure 5.2)

5.3.3. Variants

Besides the variation of the sequence of resolution components as explained above, BCQ-coding offers other ways to vary coding, transmission, and display of an image. Additional compression can be achieved by entropy coding the symbol sequence, for example using arithmetic coding (Witten et al. 1987). Another possibility is to optimize the gray scale hierarchy by using a dynamic programming algorithm (Dürst and Kunii 1989).

Most of the time during transmission, only the leading bits of subimages or pixels are known. Therefore, there exist several variants for deciding the exact gray values. This gives some flexibility to the receiver that is of importance in a heterogeneous environment, for example if repainting large parts of the screen takes some time.

Using the central value of the allowed gray scale interval is most straightforward. It has been used in Figures 5.2 to 5.4. However, it can lead to strange aliasing effects (see (Dürst 1990)). Using the lowest gray scale value of an interval, i.e. starting transmission with a black picture, reduces the number of accesses to the frame buffer by a factor of two on the average.

Painting the unknown bits based on a predefined random pattern distracts the viewer from the absolutely flat subimages and their sharp boundaries, leading to a perceived increase in quality especially in the first stages of the transmission. However, the best solution found so far for determining the missing bits is to calculate and transmit the actual average for every component and interval.

5.4. Face Recognition Experiment

To evaluate the practical use of progressive transmission and to compare BCQ-coding with other methods, we here summarize an interesting face recognition experiment described in (Dürst 1990). Recognizing faces is an activity for which the human visual system is particularly trained; also, many applications for progressive transmission deal with facial data.

5.4.1. Setup

A group of 30 students was each presented with simulated transmissions of 40 facial images. The images included both their colleagues and famous personalities (politics, sports). The size of the images was 256×256 pixels, with 8 bits per pixel. The participants had to enter a code number from a list with 62 names as soon as they had recognised the image. The number of transmitted bits necessary to recognize a face was measured. Only correct results were considered for later processing.

For each participant, eight transmission methods or variants were used, each with five images. The sequence of the images and the method assignment was randomized. The simulation speed of the slower methods was increased to let most transmissions terminate within 50 seconds. The eight methods were as follows (see also Fig.5.5):

a) *Line-by-line transmission.* This method was chosen to show the advantage of progressive transmission over raw image transmission. It includes one-dimensional predictive encoding.

b) *Uniform spatial resolution increase.* A uniform variant of Dreizen's method, described under c), was chosen, because the increase of spatial resolution with BCQ-coding is not uniform.

c) *Dreizen's method* (Dreizen 1987). This method comes closest to BCQ-coding in terms of general aims and computational complexity. Based on the quadtree, it increases spatial resolution in several passes, each time splitting only those subimages where the change in gray value is stronger than a given threshold. Fully quantized gray values are transmitted for each of the subimages.

d) *BCQ-transmission starting with a black background*, with component sequence *o4*. In component sequences *o2*, *o3*, and *o4*, both spatial and gray scale resolution is increased, but with different weights: 3:2 for *o2*, 1:1 for *o3*, and 1:2 for *o4*. In addition, the lowest (pixel) spatial resolution level was treated with even lower priority because the human visual system is less sensitive to high frequencies (Mannos and Sakrinson 1974).

e) *BCQ-transmission increasing gray scale resolution* only, with central representative (as already displayed in Figure 5.3).

f) *BCQ-transmission* with average representative and arithmetic coding, using component sequence *o2*. For arithmetic coding, a sequential model was used that resulted in an additional compression of about 5%. Models that rely on neighborhood relations, as in (Knowlton 1980) are expected to lead to even better performance.

g) *BCQ-transmission* as in f), but with component sequence *o3*.

h) *BCQ-transmission* as in f), but with component sequence *o4*.

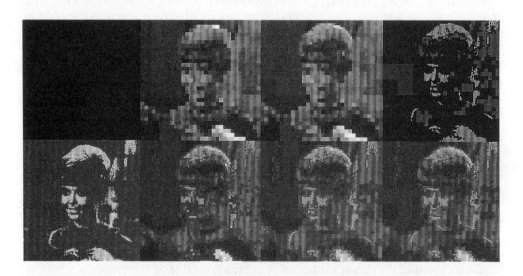

Figure 5.5. Facial image transmitted with eight different methods (bytes transmitted: 8000)

	Method	bits transmitted
a)	Sequential	177031
b)	Dreizen (homogeneous)	16641
c)	Dreizen	13107
d)	*o4*, black to white	14982
e)	gray scale resolution, centre	11561
f)	*o2*, average, arithmetic	8917
g)	*o3*, average, arithmetic	7914
h)	*o4*, average, arithmetic	10158

Table 5.1. Average number of bits necessary to recognize a face

5.4.2. Results

The number of bits needed on average to recognize a face are given for each method in Table 5.1. Progressive transmission, in any form, is more efficient than sequential transmission by a factor of about 20. Also, the benefits of a simultaneous and balanced increase of spatial and gray scale resolution, as easily possible with BCQ-coding, are obvious when comparing the results for different transmission sequences and for the method of Dreizen. Only somewhat less than one kilobyte is necessary to transmit a face up to recognizability with the best variant of BCQ-coding.

5.5. Comparison with JPEG

5.5.1. General Considerations

It is particularly interesting to compare BCQ-coding to the presently most popular image compression standard, JPEG (Wallace 1991). JPEG is based on transform coding, specifically the DCT (discrete cosine transform), widely accepted as the best orthogonal transform available. The problems of JPEG discussed below are in theory solvable with other implementations of transform coding; the restrictions taken in JPEG are due to careful practical considerations.

The first problem of JPEG is that it uses different modes for basic image compression, progressive encoding, and lossless encoding. This means that either each image has to be stored several times for different purposes or it has to be transformed before transmission. Also, if after some previewing, the lossless version of an image is desired, transmission has to begin anew. Lossless compression is difficult to integrate into transform coding because of the rounding errors incurred during transformation (Wang and Goldberg 1988).

When examining progressive encoding in JPEG more closely, it turns out that there are two transmission sequences offered, called *spectral selection* and *successive approximation*, which correspond to increasing spatial and gray scale resolution. Balancing both increases is not provided. This simplifies data organization. Also, it reduces the number of times the inverse transform has to be calculated at the receiver. Although some savings are possible (Takigawa 1984), the fact that the inverse transform has to be calculated every time a new component arrives makes too small refinement steps infeasible.

5.5.2. Face Recognition Experiments

Using the DCT for progressive transmission has been investigated particularly by Lohscheller (1984). His dissertation (Lohscheller 1982) also contains some results on face recognition. Comparison with these results provides an additional way to evaluate JPEG and BCQ-transmission.

The description of the experiments in (Lohscheller 1982) is not very detailed, but overall, the setup was very similar to that described above. The number of experiments was considerably smaller, using seven portraits and between 10 and 15 viewers. The smaller number suggests that the faces presented were better known to the subjects than in our case.

A seemingly important difference between the two experiments is the size of the images used. 512·512 in the case of Lohscheller, and 256×256 here. However, the minimal amount of information necessary to build up an image that allows us to identify a person can be expected to be independent of the resolution of the original image, provided that the original resolution is not extremely low. The results of both experiments can therefore be well compared in terms of the number of bits necessary for the recognition.

The results obtained by Lohscheller (1982, p.89) are given in Table 5.2 for the different transformation block sizes he used. For a block size of 32·32 pixels, these results come close, but still lie above those of BCQ-coding; for the more practicable block sizes of 16·16 and 8·8, the results fall way behind those presented in this chapter.

Block size	8·8	16·16	32·32
Bit average	33840	19827	10512

Table 5.2. Number of bits for person recognition using DCT (from [Lohscheller 1992])

That the transform coding approach, which requires much more computation than BCQ-coding, does not perform better, is mainly due to the following: first, the fixed block size inhibits a transmission of very low spatial resolution only. Second, a balance of spatial and gray scale resolution increase, due to its high cost, was neither used by Lohscheller, nor is it provided in JPEG. So transform coding and JPEG fail to provide appropriate compression for very low-quality reproduction (which never was an aim for JPEG) and for lossless encoding (unless a special mode is used). On the other hand, it has to be admitted that for intermediate to high-quality reproduction, JPEG performs better than BCQ-coding. We are currently investigating possibilities of improving the performance of BCQ-coding in these quality ranges.

5.6. Conclusions

A very simple coding method, BCQ-coding, based on the BC-quadtree (bitwise condensed quadtree), was reviewed and compared with the well-known JPEG standard in the framework of world-wide multimedia networks. Thereby BCQ-coding performed very well as an abstraction tool for natural images in the low-quality reproduction range.

BCQ-coding shows that a high factor of content abstraction can be obtained by using straightforward data structures and algorithms. This is due to its hierarchical nature both in the spatial and in the gray scale dimension. Obviously, better abstraction is possible with methods based on computer vision and object recognition. However, these methods are very domain-dependent and mostly not yet ready for practical use. On the other hand, a simple progressive coding and transmission algorithm can greatly improve the performance of the emerging world-wide multimedia network.

Acknowledgments

I would like to thank Prof. T.L. Kunii of the University of Tokyo and Prof. P. Stucki of the University of Zürich for providing fruitful research environments.

References

Dreizen HM (1987) Content-driven progressive transmission of gray-scale images. *IEEE Trans. Commun.*, vol. 35, pp. 289-296.

Dürst MJ, Kunii TL (1989) Error-free image compression with gray scale quadtrees and its optimization, in *Proceedings of the International Workshop on Discrete Algorithms and Complexity*, Fukuoka, Japan, pp. 115-121.

Dürst MJ (1990) A New Method for Image Compression and Progressive Transmission. Dissertation, University of Tokyo, Japan.

Dürst MJ, Kunii TL (1991) Progressive transmission increasing both spatial and gray scale resolution, in *International Conference on Multimedia Information Systems '91*, McGraw-Hill, Singapore, pp. 175-186.

Dürst MJ, Kunii TL (1992) Methods for the efficient storage and manipulation of spatial geological data, in *Three-Dimensional Modeling with Geoscientific Information Systems*, A.K. Turner, Ed., NATO ASI Series C, Vol. 354, Kluwer Academic Publishers, Dordrecht, NL, pp. 189-214.

Kawaguchi E, Endo T (1980) On a method of binary-picture representation and its application to data compression. *IEEE Trans. Pattern Anal. Machine Intell.*, vol. 2, pp. 27-35.

Knowlton K (1980) Progressive transmission of gray-scale and binary pictures by simple, efficient, and lossless encoding schemes. *Proc. IEEE*, vol. 68, pp. 885-895.

Lohscheller H (1982) Einzelbildübertragung mit wachsender Auflösung. Dissertation, Fakultät Elektrotechn., RWTH Achen, Germany.

Lohscheller H (1984) A subjectively adapted image communication system, *IEEE Trans. Commun.*, vol. 32, pp. 1316-1322.

Mannos JL, Sakrinson DJ (1974) The effects of a visual fidelity criterion on the encoding of images. *IEEE Trans. Inform. Theory*, vol. 20, pp. 525-536.

Mullender S (1989) Ed., *Distributed Systems*, ACM Press, New York.

Onoe M, Sakauchi M, Inamoto Y (1979) *SIDBA Standard Image Data Base*. MIPC Report 79-1, Multidimensional Image Processing Centre, Institute of Industrial Science, University of Tokyo.

Samet H (1984) The quadtree and related hierarchical data structures. *ACM Comput. Surv.*, vol. 16, pp. 187-260.

Samet H, Webber RE (1988) Hierarchical data structures and algorithms for computer graphics, Part I: Fundamentals, and Part II: Applications. *IEEE Comp. Graph. and Appl.*, vol. 8, no. 3, pp. 48-68, May 1988, and no. 4, pp. 59-75.

Takigawa K (1984) Fast progressive reconstruction of a transformed image. *IEEE Trans. Inform. Theory*, vol. 30, pp. 111-117.

Tanimoto SL (1979) Image transmission with gross information first. *Comput. Graphics Image Process.*, vol. 9, pp. 72-76.

Tzou KH (1987) Progressive image transmission: a review and comparison of techniques. *Optical Engineering*, vol. 26, pp. 581-589.

Wallace GK (1991) The JPEG still picture compression standard. *Commun. ACM*, vol. 34, no. 4, pp. 30-44.

Wang L, Goldberg M (1988) Progressive image transmission by transform coefficient residual error quantization. *IEEE Trans. Commun.* vol. 36, pp. 75-87.

Witten IH, Neal RM, Cleary JG (1987) Arithmetic coding for data compression. *Commun. ACM*, vol. 30, pp. 520-540.

6

WEBSs: An Electronic Book Shell with an Object-oriented Scripting Environment

J. Monnard, J. Pasquier-Boltuck
Institute for Automation and Operations Research, University of Fribourg
Switzerland

6.1. Introduction

WEBSs (Woven Electronic Book System with scripts) is a hypermedia environment for the creation and consultation of Integrated Electronic Books (IEB). An IEB represents an organized gathering of knowledge on a given subject. It consists of a collection of documents (texts, graphics, logico-mathematical models) that can be interconnected with the help of semantic networks of blocks and links called webs. This information space may also be hierarchically structured with the help of specialized documents called browsers.

WEBSs also provides a scripting environment that relies on the same basic objects as an IEB (i.e. documents, blocks, links and sets), rendering it consistently integrated with the other components of the system. In its simplest form, a script is a list of commands which can be executed as though they had been entered one by one by the user. In addition, scripts may also include sequencing instructions such as loops and conditionals, as well as calls to special functions and to other scripts. Scripts enhance the application in two ways. First, the ability to combine basic WEBSs actions allows users to easily define new high-level functions like, for example, the automatic creation of tables of contents and indexes. Secondly, the behavior of the objects that constitute an electronic book can be enriched by writing scripts that will be automatically executed each time a triggering object performs a specific action.

Virtual Worlds and Multimedia Edited by Nadia Magnenat Thalmann and Daniel Thalmann
© 1993 John Wiley and Sons Ltd

Examples of related works include HyperCard (Goodman 1987), NoteCards (Trigg et al., 1987), the Scripted Documents system (Zellweger 1989), the Andrew Toolkit (Sherman et al. 1990), (Hansen 1990) and, relying on more formal models (respectively Petri-Nets and conceptual documents), χTrellis (Stotts and Furuta 1990) and MacWeb (Nanard and Nanard 1988).

This chapter, after a presentation of the key elements underlying the IEB concept supported by WEBSs (Section 6.2), focuses on the scripting capabilities of WEBSs (see also (Monnard 1992), (Pasquier-Boltuck et al.1988), and (Monnard and Pasquier-Boltuck 1992)). Section 6.3 discusses the rationale behind WEBSs scripts, provides a general definition of scripts and, together with the examples of Section 6.6, demonstrates some of their benefits. Sections 6.4 and 6.5 are more technically oriented: they describe respectively the syntax of WEBSs scripting language and the scripting environment. They are, however, indispensable in order to get a realistic grasp of what it takes to efficiently combine the features of a classical object-oriented hypermedia system such as WEBSs or Intermedia (Meyrowitz 1986) with those of a powerful scripting environment.

6.2. The IEB Concept

An Integrated Electronic Book represents an organized gathering of knowledge on a given subject. An IEB created with WEBSs is composed of **a collection of documents** containing information pertaining to the book's subject, that can be interconnected with the help of networks of **blocks** and **links**. **Sets** may also be created to regroup collections of objects. **Scripts** allow users to automate series of actions and to modify the behavior of specific objects. Finally, **an IEB database** allows for the integration of the above components within a meaningful unit or book. Figure 6.1 shows a Macintosh folder containing the WEBSs application and two IEBs (one called "Simulation" and the other "Markov"). Sections 6.2.1 through 6.2.3 describe more precisely these components, while Section 6.2.4 presents an example from an existing electronic book.

6.2.1. Documents

WEBSs supports four types of documents (see also Figure 6.3):

- **Textual documents.** These documents correspond to the text of the different chapters, sections, sub-sections and paragraphs found in classical books. They can be created with WEBSs own text editor, which allows for simple formatting operations: setting of font, size, style, color and justification for a piece of text. Alternately, documents created with a standard word processor and saved in "Text Only" format may also be transformed into WEBSs documents.

- **Graphic documents.** These documents correspond to the illustrations, figures and other graphics found in classical books. WEBSs does not offer a graphical editor, but pictures created with a drawing application and saved in PICT format can be transformed into WEBSs documents.

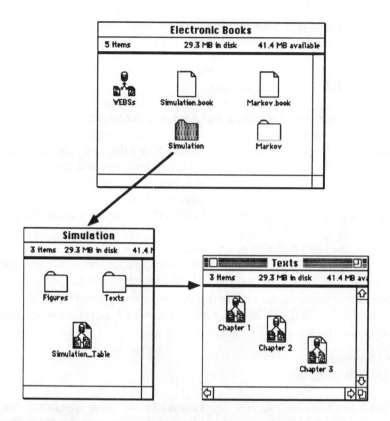

Figure 6.1. Two WEBSs IEBs viewed through the Macintosh desktop interface

- **Browser documents.** These documents can be compared to the tables of contents found in classical books. More precisely, a browser represents a tree-like structure, where each node can be associated with one or more documents. Browsers are used to hierarchically organize subsets of documents.

  The possibility to freely create browsers of this sort represents a powerful structuring tool, offering the potential for defining different ways of organizing the same original collection of documents. In fact, once activated, a browser defines a particular reading environment, permitting, for example, the use of special commands in order to achieve a sequential reading of the IEB. A browser can also be used in order to selectively print or search for a string in the documents associated with its nodes.

- **Logico-mathematical models.** These types of documents vary according to the particular subject, e.g. Markov chains or linear optimization models. An IEB on a complex subject may even offer several different types of models. It is possible to carry out complex calculations and manipulations on these logico-mathematical models, the results of which can usually be cut and pasted within regular textual or graphic documents. Due to their versatility, it is clear that the educational potential of these models extends far beyond the simple guided exercises available in classical textbooks, and constitutes one of the principal advantages of an IEB over its paper competition.

6.2.2. Blocks, Links, Sets and Scripts

A **block** simply represents a selection made inside a document (for example, a string of characters in a textual document or a rectangle in a graphical document). A **link** corresponds to the connection between two blocks which the user may choose to follow in order to jump from one location in a document to another (or even to another document).

A **set** represents a collection of (possibly heterogeneous) objects – documents, blocks, links, scripts or other sets. Sets play an important role in scripts.

A **script** is a program which is executed automatically by the system. Scripts have two main uses:

- First, they allow users to define new high-level functions by automating and sequencing any series of actions. By writing the appropriate script, a user can for example open all the documents that belong to a specific set with a single operation.
- Secondly, the behavior of the objects that constitute an electronic book can be enriched by creating scripts that will be automatically executed each time a triggering object performs a specific action.

6.2.3. The IEB Database

In the framework of WEBSs, **an IEB database is like any other Macintosh file**. This file automatically inherits the name of the IEB it represents with the extension ".book". Individual IEBs are always supported by a file of this sort (e.g. the "Simulation.book" and the "Markov.book" files of Figure 6.1).

At the higher conceptual level, an IEB database is composed of one public and zero or more private webs. A web is always made up of (1) a list of documents, (2) for each document, a list of its blocks, (3) a list of links, (4) a list of sets, (5) a list of scripts. The objects of the **public web** are created by the author of the IEB and they can be consulted in read-only mode. The objects of a **private web** are owned by a reader and are invisible to all other users.

6.2.4. The IEB Creation Process

The definition of an IEB within the WEBSs system follows a very flexible process which is described below and summarized in Figure 6.2 :

- A certain number of documents are created by an author inside a public web.
- The author can then define a large network of blocks and links between the documents and organize all or part of them with the aid of various browsers and sets, as well as enrich the behavior of his IEB with scripts.

- Readers can consult these public documents using the particular reading environment defined jointly by the links, sets and scripts created by the author and by the browser that the individual reader has chosen to activate.
- Finally, readers have at their disposal their own private webs, in which they can create documents, define a network of blocks and links through all of the documents which are accessible to them, and even create their own browsers, sets and scripts. We see, therefore, that it is possible for users of WEBSs to enrich the reading environment offered by the author with the aid of a group of personal elements.

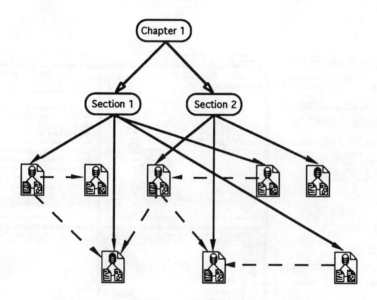

Figure 6.2. The documents of an IEB are hierarchically organized by the browsers (plain arrows) and further interconnected by the webs (dashed arrows)

6.2.5. Example

The WEBSs system is being experimented with an IEB on Markov chains (Pasquier-Boltuck and Collaud 1992), of which Figure 6.3 presents a sample screen shot:

- The document on the left is a browser, which offers a structured access to the other documents of the IEB. In the illustrated example, the user has clicked on node "4.2 Le générateur" and has opened a "tabletop" (Trigg 1988) of four documents that present the second example of the IEB.
- The two upper documents on the right present the problem underlying the example. More precisely, they both describe the states and the transitions of a simple emergency power

unit, the left one using the classical Markov graph notation and the right one a textual description. These two documents are strongly interconnected by links, that can be followed by double-clicking their markers (●). It is thus easy for the user to go back and forth between the graphical and the textual representation of the system.

- Finally, the two lower documents on the right are the corresponding logico-mathematical Markov model and a second graphic document, which contains the reliability function that was computed from the executable Markov model by selecting the appropriate item from the *Calculate* menu.

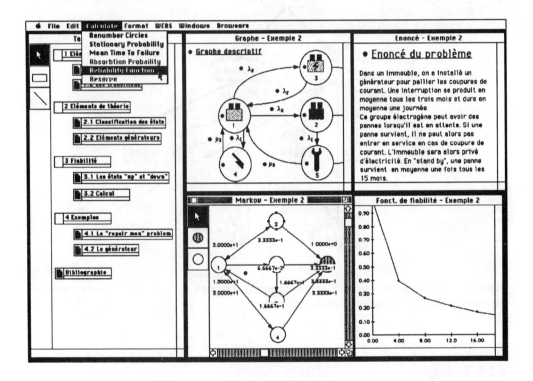

Figure 6.3. A screen shot from the "Markov chains" IEB

Note the interest of always having a judicious arrangement of the windows on the screen. WEBSs does not provide automatic layout algorithms for this task. An elegant solution to this kind of problem, however, is provided by scripts (see Section 6.6.1).

6.3. Key Ideas of Scripts

6.3.1. Rationale behind Scripts

Upon experimenting with the previous version of WEBSs (without scripts), we systematically analyzed the comments of users (Pasquier-Boltuck and Collaud 1992). We found the system to have two main shortcomings: (1) it did not provide enough support in the authoring process of an electronic book (the creation of many links and browsers is complex and at times a monotonous task); (2) users had no way to adapt the application to their needs. The need for active, or as Meyrowitz (Meyrowitz 1990) calls them, "responsive" documents that respond to user demands by executing actions was the third rationale that led us to include scripting facilities in WEBSs.

6.3.2. What is a Script?

In its simplest form, a script is a program (a list of commands) which is executed automatically by the system. Scripts may also include sequencing instructions such as loops and conditionals, as well as calls to predefined routines and other scripts. In WEBSs, there are two kinds of scripts: unbound scripts and triggered scripts.

6. 3.2.1. Unbound Scripts

Unbound scripts are launched directly by the user. They allow him/her to regroup a complex set of actions into a single command and to play it back at will in different contexts; they represent a kind of high-level macro facility, as is available in many applications. Such a script could for instance automatically create a glossary by searching for all occurrences of specific words in a group of documents and creating links to a document where their meaning is explained (see the sample script of Section 6.3). Unbound scripts can also be invoked by other scripts.

6.3.2.2. Triggered Scripts

The idea of triggered scripts is simple: a script writer can decide that a script will be automatically executed when a certain action is performed by a specific "target" Object, like the opening of a document. This enables him/her to affect the way an object reacts to a given action. For instance, the standard behavior when following a link is to show the link endpoint. But a script can be attached to a link named "Special Link #1" such that following it displays a message on the screen before going to the endpoint.

The main originality of our scripting model resides in the fact that a triggered script can be attached not only to an individual object, but also to all objects in a specific set, or to all objects of a certain class (see Figure 6.4). Thus, triggered scripts allow the author of an IEB to obtain a common behavior from a group (set or class) of objects with a minimal effort. For example, it is easy to write a script which adds any textual document when it is opened to a set named "Visited Text Documents". This set may later be used for miscellaneous purposes such as creating a history path of visited documents (see the sample script of Section 6.6.2).

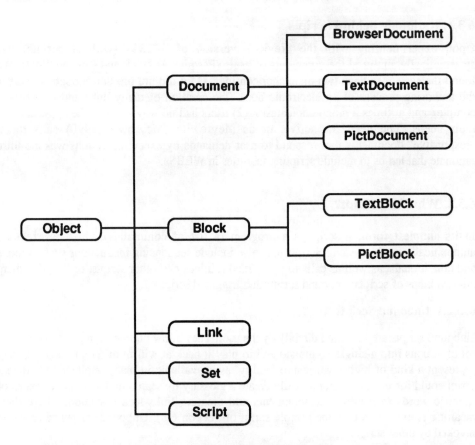

Figure 6.4. WEBSs hierarchy of classes. The class Object is the ancestor of all other classes. Note that the WEBSs system allows its users to add their own subclasses to this hierarchy (up to one level of depth) by editing the type attribute associated with any object of an IEB

6.4. Syntax and Contents of Scripts

The scripting language is very similar to Pascal, including variable declarations and statements, with a few additions such as dot notation to invoke methods on objects (as in Object Pascal). A WEBSs script consists of two parts:

- a header that defines the object(s) to which the script is attached and the method that will trigger its execution,
- a main block that contains declarations of variables and a list of statements to be executed when the script is invoked.

6.4.1. Script Header

6.4.1.1. Class-Bound Scripts

Header "ON" MethodIdentifier "OF" "ANY" ClassIdentifier [TypeSpec]
Example ON Open OF ANY TextDocument

A script beginning with this header will be triggered when any member of class *TextDocument* receives the *Open* message. If we specified *Document* as the class, then the script would be triggered by any member of a subclass of *Document* (e.g. *TextDocument* or *PictDocument*). More generally, every object that belongs to a subclass of the class mentioned in a script header can trigger a script (provided that the other conditions are met).

Interesting in this header is the optional *TypeSpec* specification. The type attribute of objects may serve as a selector in a header to assign a different behavior to distinct types of objects; if a type is specified in a script header, only objects of that type will trigger the script. For example, a script beginning with a header of the form *ON Open OF ANY Document of type Reference* will only be activated by documents whose type is *Reference*.

6.4.1.2. Set-Bound Scripts

Header "ON" MethodIdentifier "OF" "ANY" ClassIdentifier [TypeSpec]
         "IN" ObjectSpecifier
Example ON Open OF ANY TextDocument IN [ExampleDocuments]

This header means that any object from class (or a subclass of) *TextDocument* that belongs to a set named *ExampleDocuments* will activate the script.

6.4.1.3. Object-Bound Scripts

Header "ON" MethodIdentifier "OF" ClassIdentifier [TypeSpec] ObjectSpecifier
Example ON Follow OF Link [Example1]

With such a header, the script will be triggered when a member of class (or a subclass of) *Link* with name *Example1* receives the *Follow* message.

Note that scripts for individual objects are bound to object names and not to the objects themselves: a script can refer to a name even if no object with this name exists. This allows users to write a script in advance if they know the name of the future object. When an object is later created with the name mentioned in the header, the script will automatically be applicable.

6.4.1.4. Unbound Scripts

Header "ON" "Execute"["(" FormalParameterList ")"] [":" TypeIdentifier]
Example On Execute(theDoc : Document): Integer

The optional parameter list and result type indicate that the script accepts parameters and/or returns a result.

6.4.2. Main Block

The main block contains declarations of variables and a list of statements to be executed. The scripting language includes the types integer, string and boolean, as well as all the classes from Figure 6.4. Other characteristic elements of scripts are described below.

- A construct is provided to perform a group of statements on every object in a set.
- Objects can invoke methods, using a dot notation. Calling of inherited methods is supported. Object attributes are also accessed through methods (e.g. there are *SetName* and *GetName* methods); this solution facilitates the definition of read-only attributes.
- Scripts may call predefined functions – to, for example, display a message or activate a menu command – and other unbound scripts. Since scripts are objects, they are called by invoking their *Execute* method. In fact, unbound scripts, which can take parameters and return a result, can serve as user-defined global functions.
- To access an object by name, the notation [*objectName*] is used. When the script is executed, the system searches among all the objects in the active IEB for an object with the name *objectName* and generates an error if none is found. Statements within a script may also refer to the object that triggered the current execution with *current*.

6.5. WEBSs Scripting Environment

This section focuses on the main elements of the scripting environment that allow WEBSs users to work efficiently with scripts. They include a script browser, which provides rapid access to all the scripts in the active IEB, and facilities for viewing and editing object properties and sets.

The script browser, shown in Figure 6.5, is the main component of the scripting environment. This is where most script-related operations take place: creation, editing, syntax checking, etc. From the pop-up menu on the top left, users select the kind of scripts they want to visualize: unbound scripts, scripts for classes, sets or individual objects. Depending on this choice, the left pane shows a list of classes, sets or object names. By choosing an item in this list, the corresponding list of scripts is displayed in the right pane. The contents of the script selected from this list are displayed in the lower pane, where it can be edited. Commands for manipulating scripts and executing unbound scripts are available from a *Script* menu.

The symbols that appear next to a script name have the following meanings:

✓   A check mark indicates that the script is enabled and will automatically be executed when the triggering conditions defined by its header are met. Clicking on the check mark toggles its state, allowing users to easily turn on/off individual scripts. A command also exists for globally deactivating the automatic execution of scripts. It is intended for users who want to consult an IEB without triggering any scripts. This command, however, must be used with caution, because some important functionality may be disabled and the electronic book may not behave consistently.

?   A question mark is displayed if a script has not been compiled or contains errors.

✗   Public scripts (created by the author of an IEB) are indicated by a read-only icon. They cannot be modified by readers but can nonetheless be enabled or disabled.

Furthermore, since scripts may be attached to objects, the system provides a way for users to visualize and modify object properties (name, type, etc.). This is accomplished by means of a dialog box which can be invoked for any object in an IEB. Finally, WEBSs offers simple facilities for creating and editing sets.

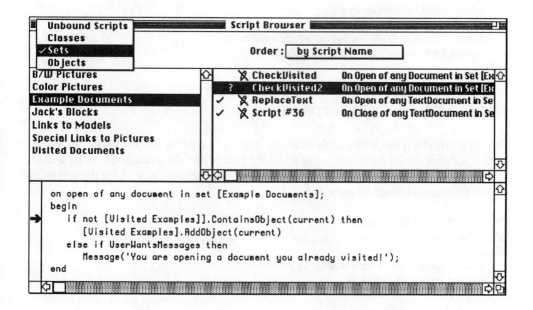

Figure 6.5. The script browser. A list of scripts for the set "Example Documents" is displayed in the right pane, and script "CheckVisited2" is currently being edited. The arrow on the left indicates a syntax error.

6.6. Examples of Scripts

The scripting environment described in this chapter has been implemented and is currently being tested on the "Markov chains" IEB introduced in Section 6.2.5. Our first experiments are quite positive and show that scripts are a real enhancement to WEBSs. This section briefly presents three sample scripts, which may facilitate the process of authoring and/or consulting an IEB.

6.6.1. Assigning a Predefined Window Location to a Document

The script presented below assigns to any document of type *MarkovExampleModel* the same window location as the document *ModelTemplate*. If the author of the IEB on Markov chains presented in Figure 6.3, (1) provides all the documents of his/her examples with appropriate types (e.g. *MarkovExampleGraph*, *MarkovExampleModel*, etc.), (2) defines all the corresponding template documents (e.g. *GraphTemplate*, *ModelTemplate*, etc.), and (3) creates all the corresponding class-bound scripts, he/she will have an elegant solution to the screen layout problem raised at the end of Section 6.2.5.

```
ON Open OF ANY Document of type MarkovExampleModel;
VAR left,top,right,bottom: Integer;
BEGIN
    [ModelTemplate].GetWindowLoc(left,top,right,bottom);
    current.SetWindowLoc(left,top,right,bottom);
END
```

6.6.2. Creating a Set of Visited Documents

This script checks if the set *Visited Document* exists and puts the current document into it. Such a script is useful for maintaining a history path of the documents visited by a user. More sophisticated versions of it might take into consideration the type of the document, as well as the date and length of each visit.

```
ON Open OF ANY Document;
VAR aSet : Set;
BEGIN
    aSet := GetNamedObject('Visited Documents');
    IF aSet = nullObject THEN
    BEGIN
        aSet := NewSet;
        aSet.SetName('Visited Documents')
    END;
    aSet.AddObject(current)
END
```

6.6.3. Creating a Glossary

The script presented below is an unbound script which proposes a simple but yet embryonic solution for automating the process of creating a glossary. In order to apply it, the user must (1) create a glossary document, (2) create a block for each entry in the glossary and give it the type *Glossary*, (3) put all the documents to be searched for in a set, and (4) call the script with the pertinent parameters (i.e. the name of the glossary document and the one of the set). This whole process could itself be automated by an appropriate script.

```
ON Execute(doc: TextDocument;theSet:Set);
VAR    index:          Integer;
       textDoc:        TextDocument;
       tBlock:         TextBlock;
       theString:      String;
BEGIN
    doc.Open;
    doc.Select;
    FOR EACH tBlock OF TYPE Glossary IN doc.GetBlocks DO
    BEGIN
       tBlock.SelectMarker; { Select the block marker and get its string }
       theString := tBlock.GetExtentString;
       FOR EACH textDoc IN theSet DO
       BEGIN
         textDoc.Open; { Open the document and put the cursor at the beginning }
         textDoc.Select;
         textDoc.DeselectAll;
         index := textDoc.FindString(theString,false); {Search for the string}
         WHILE index > 0 DO { While the string is found }
         BEGIN { Check if there is already a block to avoid creating duplicate blocks }
            IF textDoc.StringAt(index-1,1) = '•' THEN
                textDoc.SelectString(index-1,1)
            ELSE BEGIN { Create a block and select its marker }
                textDoc.SelectString(index,Length(theString));
                DoMenu('Create Block');
                textDoc.SelectString(index,1);
            END;
            DoMenu('Start Link'); {Create the new link and give it the right type }
            doc.Select;
            DoMenu('Complete Link'); { Create the link }
            lastLink.SetName('Glossary - ' + textDoc.GetName);
            lastLink.SetType(Glossary);
            textDoc.Select;
            textDoc.SelectString(index+Length(theString),0); { to advance the cursor,
                so that we don't find the same word again and again }
            index := textDoc.FindString(theString,false);
         END;
       END
    END;
{3} FOR EACH textDoc IN theSet DO
       textDoc.Close { to close all the documents in theSet }
END
```

In summary, the above script automatically builds up the glossary, by creating links between each block of type *Glossary* in the glossary document and the occurrences of the corresponding entry in the chosen set of documents.

6.7. Conclusion

Our experiments with electronic books have shown us that even a sophisticated parameterizable shell cannot anticipate the various and sometimes contradictory needs of all users. Therefore, since it is extremely difficult for those who are not the programmers of the system to immerse themselves in the intricacies of the application code, we are convinced that scripting environments such as the one described in this chapter present the best potentiality for future research.

Naturally, the programming of scripts like the one of Section 6.6.3 is not a trivial task and cannot be achieved by the typical end user of an IEB shell. We do not, however, consider this difficulty as a major problem: it will be the task of specialists to define well structured libraries of general purpose scripts, which the end users will tailor to their specific needs with a minimal effort. We are presently working on creating such a library.

Acknowledgments

Our research on "The Integrated Electronic Book" was sponsored, from December 1985 until November 1991, by the Swiss National Science Foundation, under grants No. 1.018-0.84 and 1.813-0.88.

References

Goodman D (1987) *The Complete HyperCard Handbook*, Bantam Books.

Halasz FG, Moran TP, Trigg RH (1987) NoteCards in a Nutshell, *Proceedings of CHI and GI '87*, Toronto, pp.45-52.

Hansen WJ (1990) Enhancing documents with embedded programs: How Ness extends insets in the Andrew ToolKit, *Proceedings of 1990 International Conference on Computer Languages*, IEEE Computer Society Press, pp.23-32.

Meyrowitz N (1986) Intermedia: The Architecture and Construction of an Object-Oriented Hypermedia System and Applications Framework, *OOPSLA '86 Proceedings*, Portland, OR, pp.186-201.

Meyrowitz N (1990) Responsive Documents – The Call of the 90s, *Technique et Science Informatique*, Vol.9, No.6, pp.473-474.

Monnard J (1992) *A User's Guide to the Woven Electronic Book System with Scripts*, Working Paper No 207, IAUF.

Monnard J, Pasquier-Boltuck J (1992) An Object-Oriented Scripting Environment for the WEBSs Electronic Book System, *Proceedings of the ACM ECHT'92 Conference on Hypertext*, ACM Press, 1992, pp.81-90.

Nanard J, Nanard M (1988) Conceptual Documents: a Mechanism for Specifying Active Views in Hypertexts, *ACM Conference on Documents Processing Systems*, Santa Fe, NM, pp.37-42.

Pasquier-Boltuck J, Grossman E, Collaud G (1988) Prototyping an Interactive Electronic Book System Using an Object-Oriented Approach, in G. Goos, ed., *Proceedings of the*

European Conference on Object-Oriented Programming ECOOP'88, Springer, pp.177-190.

Pasquier-Boltuck J, Collaud G (1992) Création de livres électroniques avec le système WEBS: rapport sur un premier groupe d'expériences, in J. Pasquier-Boltuck, ed., *Electronic Books and their Tools*, Peter Lang (Bern), pp.69-84.

Sherman M, Hansen W, McInerny M, Neuendorffer T (1990) Building Hypertext on a Multimedia Toolkit: an Overview of Andrew Toolkit Hypermedia Facilities, in A. Rizk, ed., *Hypertext: Concepts, Systems and Applications*, Cambridge University Press, 1990, pp.13-24.

Stotts PD, Furuta R (1990) Hierarchy, Composition, Scripting Languages, and Translators for Structured Hypertext, in A. Rizk, ed., *Hypertext: Concepts, Systems and Applications*, Cambridge University Press, pp.180-192.

Trigg RH, Moran TP, Halasz FG (1987) Adaptability and Tailorability in NoteCards, in H.-J. Bullinger, ed., *Human-Computer Interaction - INTERACT'87*, Elsevier Science Publishers, 1987, pp.723-728.

Trigg RH (1988) Guided Tours and Tabletops: Tools for Communicating in a Hypertext Environment, *ACM Transactions on Office Information Systems*, 6 (4), 398-414.

Zellweger P (1989) Scripted Documents: a Hypermedia Path Mechanism, *Hypertext'89 Proceedings*, Pittsburgh, PA, pp.1-14.

The current version of WEBSs can be obtained freely via ftp. Send an e-mail to one of the authors for more information (e-mail: monnardj@cfruni51.bitnet, pasquier@cfruni51.bitnet)

7

Virtual Reality in Architecture

Gerhard N. Schmitt
ETH Zürich, Swiss Federal Institute of Technology

7.1. Introduction

The advent of the first architectural drawing initiated a process in the art of architecture, design, and construction whose next logical step will be the use of virtual reality (VR) techniques. New possibilities for translating thoughts into simulated objects bring us closer to the goal of a more responsible architecture, in which many of the design consequences will be known and experienced *before* the construction of the actual building. We will describe VR's potential for enhancing: the design process, design exploration, as well as analysis and discovery in design practice.

VR in architecture requires substantial financial and intellectual investments. Although most of the basic components of VR are already known and tested, their combination offers almost unlimited options. We do not want to repeat the traditional procedure of translating known techniques into a new environment. The Department of Architecture at ETH Zürich has therefore initiated the implementation of an Architectural Space Laboratory (ASL) for research, educational and practical purposes. Goals and applications developed for the ASL will be discussed in detail..

7.2. Origins and Definition

Virtual reality is based on a model of reality whose representation is available in the computer and can be experienced directly and interactively. The computerized information, rather than being represented as a separate, two- or three-dimensional object for observation, suddenly surrounds the designer who finds himself directly inside the data space. This is one of the most characteristic properties of VR, which differentiates it from

Virtual Worlds and Multimedia Edited by Nadia Magnenat Thalmann and Daniel Thalmann
© 1993 John Wiley and Sons Ltd

other forms of representation (Novak 1992). VR models include aspects of reality which communicate with different human senses. In the past, a designer had to hold the representation of an entire design for a new building in her or his own imagination. The computer was mainly used as a means to externalize the design ideas. In advanced CAD applications, the architect is able to study specific aspects of a design by having separate programs perform calculations on certain properties (see Figure 7.1, left side). In a VR environment, the architect is entirely "inside" the design and influences it from within. Analysis thus becomes a more integral part of design (see Figure 7.1, right side).

The underlying procedure that makes these aspects visible is traditionally known as simulation. Examples of existing simulation tools include those that: calculate geometry or energy use (Schmitt 1983), perform structural analysis or determine the cost and maintenance requirements of a construction. VR provides the means for the interactive exploration of a data model based on various types of simulation and thus allows for a multitude of combined experiences. The boundaries between advanced simulation and VR explorations are indistinct.

Architecture is a natural application area for VR. Architectural plans and perspectives attempt, with the simplest and most effective means, to generate an illusion. The goal is to produce a sense of the completed architectural design. The problem is that laymen do not easily understand the language of two- and three-dimensional abstractions and therefore have difficulty using them as a basis for the evaluation of new projects. Their lack of understanding is even more critical when they must judge the interaction of form, function, behavior and cost, based on traditional representations only. A virtual model, shown in a high degree of reality, which integrates and considers all of those aspects, will be of enormous help to any architectural jury. The jury will be able to explore a design and its consequences more easily and thoroughly than ever before.

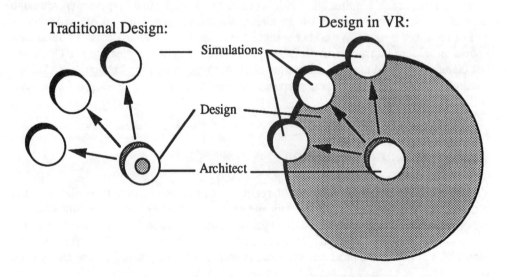

Figure 7.1. Traditional design versus design in VR.

To limit the scope of the discussion, we will concentrate on three distinct aspects of VR: virtual past, virtual analysis, and virtual design. They have special relevance for architecture and will therefore be discussed separately, before applications are presented.

7.3. Virtual Past

Representation and reconstruction of past architecture, be it as exact replicas in the form of drawings, watercolors or computer models, are well known. They form an important part of design education. Whereas in most cases the form of nonexistent or destroyed architecture can be regenerated, other known information and characteristics of the period are often unavailable or neglected. Making this information available in its most appropriate form is possible in a VR environment, with the incorporation of acoustic, color and atmospheric impressions. All historical reconstructions are impaired by the fact that we apply our own - and therefore time dependent - scales, political opinions and societal values to the artifacts, buildings or cities under consideration. Stenvert has attempted to study the effects of constructing the past with the aid of computers, which serves as an interesting approach to be used in VR as well (Stenvert 1992). In order to conduct a more realistic reconstruction, researchers should be able to step back into time. This requires the creation of a virtual environment, which must closely resemble conditions at the time the object was constructed. Examples are:

- *Design instruments.* Reconstruction could be supported by the simulation of original design and documentation instruments, for example clay tablets, papyrus rolls, circle construction tools, and antique measuring instruments.
- *Construction tools.* The original construction process could be supported by the simulation of contemporary instruments to carve stone, to construct scaffoldings, stone movement equipment, and others.
- *Construction techniques.* Material behavior, construction catastrophes and the influence of weather could be simulated to better understand the original construction techniques.
- *Human resources and socioeconomic conditions.* Size, strength and number of available workers, and some idea of their knowledge could improve the realism of the reconstruction. Information about religion and ideologies, power structures in society, zeitgeist, guilds and unions could be included as well.
- *Environmental conditions.* If available, knowledge on climatic and weather data, transportation modes, and energy considerations could increase the accuracy of a reconstruction.

Most of these conditions can be simulated directly as three-dimensional objects or be made available upon request as multi-media information. The goal is to equip the researcher with as much knowledge of the past as possible in order to reconstruct it. This may lead to interesting new discoveries and the explanation of unresolved questions.

With the reconstruction of the Roman town of Aventicum, we have begun to move into a virtual past (see Figure 7.2, Color Section). For the purpose of reconstruction of the entire city we developed knowledge-based modeling instruments which incorporate some of the architectural knowledge of the time of construction (Schmitt 1991). Nevertheless, we were, at that time, unable to fully exploit the computer model of Aventicum, because it only represented the geometric model of the city. In the Architectural Space Laboratory, a virtual model of this simulated Roman village will bring the extended experiences of a multi-media world to the viewer. It is now possible to add additional information to the model, in the form of sounds, short videos and bit mapped images, to strengthen the impression of being in a virtual past. Researchers will be able to compare the reconstruction with the newest excavations and apply necessary corrections.

7.4. Virtual Analysis

Analysis of design is more difficult than its generation, if a complete evaluation of an entire object is expected. A perfect analysis of a building almost requires to redesign it in order to understand its functioning. VR facilitates analysis, in that it lets the designer experience simultaneous views of a building and related analysis data. Analysis of only one aspect of a building can be performed efficiently by computers. Geometric analysis tools are most advanced. In the example in Figure 7.3 (see Color Section), a complex steel object, with a side length of 8 m, was to be placed in an existing villa as an artistic installation. For this purpose, a virtual model of the building was constructed to facilitate the exact placement of the sculpture. The artist moved and rotated the sculpture until it fit in the virtual building as he envisioned it. As the next step, the program produced the intersection points with the existing walls. These points were then marked in the actual building, drilled, and the steel sections of the sculpture installed.

A major source of problems in construction is the misinterpretation of two-dimensional working drawings. The projection of a true scale, laser "skeleton" of a building and all its parts could resolve most three-dimensional questions. In combination with a tele-surveying instrument, the designer and building realization team could follow the progress of the construction on their workstation and compare it with the simulated model.

In summary, virtual analysis is an appropriate tool for confirming or refuting design theories, be they of geometric, acoustic, energy, or of any other quantitative and computable nature. VR is a tool for visualizing and comparing otherwise invisible properties of a design.

7.5. Virtual Design

Virtual design is the application that will interest architects most. It requires the definition of a new working environment for architects. VR provides the physical and technical means to continue a well developed direction in architectural theory: futuristic scenarios. The designs of Sant'Elia and Bruno Taut in the first two decades of this century, as well as some projects by El Lissitzky (Bürkle and Oechslin 1991) are examples of this approach to design. These projects differ from futuristic film architecture or science fiction scenarios, in that they are strongly connected to architectural tradition in *content* and do not simply use geometry to evoke memories of architecture. In the example shown in Figure 7.4 (see Color Section), the design topic was a "tower of thought". The interpretations ranged from a constructivist approach to the de-materialization of support structures. Although physically not constructable, these objects offer insights into important new properties of a virtual architecture.

On a more modest scale, virtual design can be simulated in a VR environment using more design influencing information than is available today. The early design phase and the preparation of a building program may serve as an example. In that process, one of the first steps is a site visit. While many constraints usually restrict this important act to a minimum amount of time, tele-sensoring and tele-surveying could be of help (Balaguer and Mangili 1991). This involves the placement of an instrument on the site which will stay there during the design process. The instrument has the following purposes:

- *Data collection.* Temperature, atmospheric and lighting conditions, precipitation, wind, and insolation are monitored and compared with average data of this area. Differences are detected and used to define a more accurate microclimate of the site. The design workstation receives the data, which serve as a realistic framework for the design.
- *Visual control.* The instrument is equipped with a stereo camera which allows the designer to request particular views from the site. The views can be used to create simulations of the new building and the existing environment.

Ideally, the instrument would be movable, tele-operated from the designer's workstation. For client presentation purposes, as well as a means for constant evaluation of the new design in the given context, selected views of the site during different times of the day and the year are necessary. A pilot project of this type has been realized in Berlin, as one of the early activities of Art+Com.

7.6. Demonstration Centers for Virtual Reality in Architecture

Various centers in Europe, Japan, and North America are discovering the scientific and commercial value of VR. In Germany, the group Art+Com of Edouard Bannwart in Berlin is best known for its innovative use of VR in architecture and other fields. Art+Com has made various contributions to exhibitions and has its own production facilities. In the Netherlands, the Calibre Institute at the Technical University of Eindhoven has developed a platform for demonstrations of VR in architecture. Calibre has shown its capabilities at the CAAD futures '91 conference at ETH Zürich, and at the 1992 eCAADe meeting in Barcelona. In the United States, a number of universities are beginning to explore VR in architecture. The ACADIA organization dedicated its annual workshop in 1991 to this subject.

The Fraunhofer Institute for Graphical Data Processing in Darmstadt, Germany has established a demonstration center for virtual reality. The purpose of the center is to demonstrate VR technologies as well as VR applications. It is one of the early institutes which offers an integrated look at the scientific and commercial aspects of VR such as:

- VR infrastructure
- Translation of data for use in VR and generation of virtual worlds
- Application of special VR software for high quality presentations
- Execution of innovative VR applications
- Consulting for VR use in new application areas
- Presentation and testing of new VR equipment and techniques
- Education and training in VR systems
- Continuous workshop as an open information and communication forum

Targeted application areas are architecture, interior design, city and infrastructure planning, industrial design, construction, medical technology, education and training systems. The founders have recognized that realistic VR experience requires a new set of compatible computing instruments. The center has therefore developed a VR tool kit to cover the new requirements. A subset of VR techniques may be used by clients without previous knowledge in computing. Specially educated personnel are available to ensure competent operation of the equipment. The center hopes to attract clients interested in being able to walk through the data generated with their own CAD system. The center has shown the results of some of the first applications (Goebel and Huth 1992) at several trade fairs and exhibitions.

7.7. The Architectural Space Laboratory

A VR environment that can satisfy architects requires extremely fast hardware and intelligent software. The Department of Architecture at ETH Zürich has brought together the necessary components for such an environment. It will allow, both in research and teaching, the combination of such simulation tasks for new design-, planning- and construction projects which have previously not been possible. The goal of the *Architectural Space Laboratory* (ASL) is sensory simulation of architecture (see Figure 7.5 in Color Section). The ASL is an installation for testing valid scenarios for architectural practice of the next century, in which clients and architects can together explore various aspects of new buildings. Through its connection to international networks, the ASL is able to communicate with institutions in other countries and continents and to send and receive interactive simulations of building designs.

Research, teaching and practice - concerning virtual past, virtual analysis, and virtual design - are the most important tasks for the ASL. It is important to us that virtual design in architecture is not only an individual activity, but a team effort and experience. For this purpose, we need to develop a range of new instruments which allow the reuse of information generated with traditional CAD programs and their integration in a VR environment. Some of them are:

- *Diagrams.* From sketches and diagrams, a direct path to the generation of design alternatives is needed (Ervin 1992). A prototype system will be developed for practical purposes (Dave 1993).
- *Intelligent objects.* These are the building blocks out of which the virtual design models are constructed. Intelligent objects have physical properties like building elements or furniture as well as functional properties such as networks. The ASL will allow the simulation of intelligent objects containing information about energy, cost, structure and other properties, which are normally not visible.
- *Interfaces.* Designs not created with intelligent objects may be imported from other modelers. The interfaces are able to accept CAD and other data.
- *Modeling of physical attributes and behavior.* Examples such as: sound, 3D-interaction, object attributes and object behavior, will be represented in the VR environment.
- *Interaction.* Walk-throughs based on different user and maintenance requirements.
- *Presentation.* Tutorials for the use of trackers, large stereo screen projections, and stereo sound for simulation will be provided for teaching purposes.

These instruments will also become of increasing value for mainstream CAD modeling systems. With intelligent objects, for example, participatory design involving clients and architects becomes feasible. The ASL will not only be useful for representation tasks, but also be a means for validating designs (see Figure 7.6 in Color Section). In such an environment, it will be possible to walk into a concert hall and simultaneously check the audio system from any seat. Every space of a building model will be accessible for evaluation based on simulations of factors unique to any given day of the year including daylighting and temperature factors. Wall or window dimensions could be instantly manipulated to fit recommended energy standards. Plans for large construction projects which may involve severe environmental impact will be simulated in the ASL, precipitating possible changes in the planning and design stages. A large number of other applications wait to be tested with this new technology as well.

7.7.1. ASL Applications in Education

Architecture students traditionally display their design work as two-dimensional drawings, representing plans, sections, elevations, axonometric and perspective views. These static representations are the most important basis for design evaluation. Sometimes, physical models are included. Modeling design with computer aided architectural design systems increases the depth of representation. If modeled correctly, various abstractions of the same object are available, as well as different levels of detail. The capability for providing different views of the same design is one of the major strengths of CAAD.

For more than a decade, we have explored computer-based presentation and representation techniques. A major weakness we encountered is the physical size of the screen. The consequence of this limitation is that individual views must appear in sequence or be reduced to a very small size. The parallel view of different representations, which is possible in traditional design presentation, is not possible without an unrealistically large number of computers. There are two solutions to this problem: parallel screens and larger displays. Parallel screens pose a computational and a practical problem once the number rises beyond three or four. The resolution of large projections can be a problem, because the resolution does not grow in relation to the size of the projection. Nevertheless, it is preferable to provide large screen projections with a size of at least 3 by 5 m, rather than many small screens. For this reason, we chose large screen projection for the ASL.

At this scale, plans, elevations and sections will be visible and discernible for viewers from a distance typical of that used in traditional design reviews. The main advantage is that perspective views and walk-throughs approach the real scale of 1:1. This creates a different sensation and perception for the viewers than small screens or plots. The viewers are then "in" the building rather than merely looking at a projection of the building. This large screen projection also has advantages over head mounted projectors. This allows more than one person to participate in the design evaluation, which is otherwise less practical if each person is in his or her own virtual world. This applies to presentations and evaluations in the same space, as is typically the case in architecture schools. For interaction between different spaces and also for international cooperation, head-mounted displays are better, because they are able to create a feeling of virtual "togetherness".

7.7.2. ASL Applications in Research

Research results must be repeatable and quantifiable. With architectural research moving into new, computer-based and -assisted areas, visualization and verification of results cannot be achieved by traditional means. For this reason, the paper medium will lose much of its relative importance and will be increasingly supported, and later partially replaced, by digital media. Architectural research in CAAD began from two extreme ends of a spectrum. On one side it focused on the implementation of quantitative analyses methods and on software to support highly formalized activities, such as the production of working drawings. On the other hand, it started with high expectations of the formalization of the design process itself (Simon 1992). After more than two decades of CAAD research, it has become clear that quantitative methods alone are insufficient guarantees for better design and that it is neither possible, nor useful, to imitate or translate the human design process on a machine. In the process, however, new relations, facts and goals were discovered:

- *The building as an organism.* Although apparently a static artifact, buildings consist of thousands of interacting parts. Modeling a building must include a multitude of abstractions besides a geometric CAD representation, such as light, sound, cost, and energy. All of these abstractions are interrelated and need either a compatible representation or well functioning interfaces.

- *Visualizing the invisible.* Of all physical phenomena in a building, only light is actually not visible, but the effect of light can be visualized. The quality of a design depends on the relation and content of other physical attributes as well. An efficient way to evaluate the quality of the overall performance of a building is to present of all involved and measurable building properties in graphical form. This allows one to compare visible and nonvisible criteria and to judge the overall quality of a building.
- *Externalizing built-in knowledge.* Modeling buildings as completely as possible, including their design process, requires the formalization and externalization of assumptions and knowledge. While commonsense knowledge is especially evident in human interaction, human-computer cooperative work suffers from the absence of this knowledge in today's programs.

In the example in Figure 7.7 (see Color Section), a knowledge-based system generated a large number of different design solutions for medieval churches and monasteries. Using VR techniques, it will be possible to explore the actual spatial quality of the design. This aspect is usually neglected in fundamental research projects. Spatial and other design quality exploration will build an important link in the process generating practical results.

We have established that any building design process involves modeling in a virtual world. Virtual reality therefore comes as a welcome tool to support this process. In a virtual environment, a building can be seen as a diagram, as a geometric model, as a energy model, as a cost model, or any combination of these. The influence of each property on the others can be made visible and used as a valuable design feedback tool. Once these questions have been resolved at the research level, they will become available in education.

7.7.3. ASL Applications in Practice

Architectural design practice is the most immediate beneficiary of a virtual reality installation. Japanese kitchen design firms are already well known for letting their clients walk through virtual kitchens and simulate their usage. Clients may be impressed by speed and completeness of architectural models appearing on a computer screen. They will begin to demand to experience the space before the building has been built in order to make decisions that may influence cost or other factors. The example in Figure 7.8 (see Color Section) shows the end result of a practical design application for a competition. The computer was used from the beginning of the design process, the model evolved as the end result. The virtual model can be explored in the ASL.

In Switzerland, wooden or metal frames placed in 1:1 scale on the proposed building site, indicate the extents of planned construction projects. They represent a very simple, abstract simulation of the proposed building, which does not offer any information beyond size and positions such as material or other important architectural properties. Considering the fact that those scaffoldings are a basis for important decision making, the necessity for a realistic simulation of a new project in VR becomes evident. Even traditionally presented projects are, in some form, virtual architecture, in that they attempt to convince the client with every possible means of the quality of the idea. This fact is demonstrated in every architectural competition.

Construction projects normally involve discussions between all interested participants or parties . The simulation in Figure 7.9 (see Color Section) was executed to provide the basis for such a discussion between the architects and neighbors of the proposed large building. In post-industrial countries with a well developed infrastructure, space is densely populated. In such a setting, each new building has a strong impact on its neighborhood. It is therefore imperative that the consequences of such interventions be clearly shown before construction. VR allows realistic simulation of a new project in an existing context and will therefore show positive and negative aspects of the proposed building at a level that better facilitates discussions among professionals and lay people. Architects will use VR to demonstrate and prove their competence to participate in the creation of the built environment. VR will then help to bring forth more than mere formal-geometric aspects of new projects.

VR techniques are also needed to realize integrated building design processes, where different partners are involved in the design of one object. For project meetings, each design team will be able to present its model and superimpose it on the already existing models. In this way, conflicts, intersections and unwanted influences can be detected and corrected immediately. As in education, design practice needs new interaction and manipulation techniques with virtual models. It is not sufficient to merely display information, but essential to modify the objects in virtual reality. This complicates the already existing set of mappings between CAD models and different data models. Out of this requirement, a new research direction will develop.

7.8. Costs and Benefits

The costs of a powerful and visually satisfactory architectural VR environment are still the equivalent of an entire workstation cluster. This includes hardware, software, audio-visual equipment and the necessary changes in infrastructure. Therefore, few offices will be equipped with such facilities in the near future. Service bureaux or research institutions will offer VR services in a similar manner as they have offered CAD services in the past.

Cost options aside, the pre-construction exploration of an architectural project with this technology has fundamental advantages over the use of traditional drawings or models. Unwanted surprises will be reduced with simulations and VR. It is well known that mistakes have a drastically different cost consequence, depending on whether they are discovered and eliminated in the planning-, documentation- or construction phase. The estimates range between a relation of 1:10:100 to 1:100:1000 (cost elimination in the planning : documentation : construction phases). It is therefore evident that the search for mistakes and the correction of problems must, when possible, occur in the planning phase. VR techniques are ideal for accomplishing this task by instantly manipulating and evaluating the proposed design in ways which are not possible with a traditional medium. In this context we refer briefly to the field of medicine where it is common practice that facilities, in the same price range as high end VR environments, are installed as soon as the demand exists; patients are then burdened with the costs. A defendable cost : benefit ratio for VR installations in architecture is quickly reached once large projects undergo this simulation procedure and serious mistakes are detected in the early planning phase.

7.9. Chances and Dangers

VR in architecture is still a controversial topic. A VR environment is perceived as a high tech sensory stimulation, whose mastering is - like photography - an art which will become an integrated communication skill of any creative professional. The fear of practitioners, without access to this capital intensive equipment, is that it will be used to blind potential decision makers with technological gimmicks. This concern needs to be taken seriously, as the same fear surfaced with the introduction of photography - and has indeed, in some cases, proven to be well based. Each new technology is equipped with this negative potential. With the introduction of VR in universities and teaching environments, students must not only be educated in the technical aspects, but also in the ethical responsibilities involved in the use of VR. The main goal of VR in architecture should be clarification; that is the most complete simulation of a new condition with the best available modeling techniques.

The differences between reality and simulation are greatly reduced with the introduction of VR, as is the level of abstraction of architectural representations. The consequence will be that laymen have a better chance to understand and judge a proposed building. It will also expand the architect's degree of freedom and require a higher degree of responsibility.

7.10. Possible Effects

With the introduction of VR, the architectural workplace will become more cost intensive. Previous investments made in CAD are protected through VR and might even gain in value, if three- or multi-dimensional models were produced before. In the teaching environment of the near future, only a fraction of all students will be able to design their buildings in VR. Most of them will only hear about this new technology in lectures and demonstrations. The first phase will consist of developing an extensive library of past and future architecture to create a database of excellent examples of built architecture. The second stage will be the experimentation with and the integration of VR in the design process.

In the process of planning architecture in practice, VR will become indispensable. From the many possible applications, the evaluation of proposed buildings in existing contexts by laymen and professionals will be the first to be realized. Emerging conflicts, weaknesses or the absence of intended effects such as transparency can be detected, explored and corrected. The testing of a project in virtual space by architects or engineers will help guarantee that functional, construction and performance standards are met. The need for time intensive drawing exchange can be minimized or eliminated with common sessions using VR equipment.

In developing countries where housing problems are prevalent, VR could quickly find its niche as well. Structural qualities of various constructions could be tested for resistance against earthquakes, tempests or flooding. Simulations of strength, strain or weathering could be performed. Models exist for the simulation of traffic development, dispersion and accumulation of emissions and city growth. They will become important instruments in an integrated VR environment.

7.11. Towards a Virtual Architecture

Continuing with this vision to its final consequence, the question arises whether real architecture will not become obsolete, if a virtual architecture offers qualities which are difficult to build physically. It will be possible for residents of simple apartments to select and generate desirable and enjoyable interiors with VR. In a time when the abstraction and rationalization of spaces for living and working have peaked, the probability that VR will be used as a time machine back to "safe" virtual Biedermeier, Rococo or Roman environments is growing. Such developments are underway. Hardware such as the Silicon Graphics Reality Engine, connected to the appropriate periphery, generates a quality of space, color, and interaction that is highly seductive. The image in Figure 7.10 (see Color Section) is one frame from such an interactive travel through a new virtual architectural space, in which traditional physical properties have lost most of their meaning. But more important than being able to create this experience, is the fact that the new freedom in modeling and integrated evaluation possibilities will certainly lead to new inventions and architectural expressions. My hope is that virtual architecture will not become self-centered, but rather that it will be an important step towards an architecture which will become more responsible in its entirety.

7.12. Conclusions

Within two years, at the beginning of the 1990s, virtual reality in architecture has moved from the theoretical to the implementable stage. As was the case in the early days of artificial intelligence, the possibilities of the new technology appear abundant and all-encompassing. As was the case in the more mature days of artificial intelligence, some useful techniques will crystallize and find their way into mainstream CAAD applications; others may continue to be out of reach.

VR will make architecture an even more capital intensive profession. If successful, VR will change the educational profile of a typical architect. VR will also increase the need for high quality third party service institutes where CAD models and traditionally designed buildings can be experienced in a virtual world. VR improves the chances of providing an integrated model for the simulation of architecture - from initial design to facility management. The introduction of CAAD has shown that the geometry of design is only one form of representation. VR will strengthen the argument that the reduction of computers to mere electronic drawing devices is a dead end. Instead, a building must be seen as an organism whose parts are interacting sensibly.

The most critical question, whether or not architecture will improve with the use of VR, cannot be answered at this point. VR does encourage and facilitate the more responsible use of information and the application of feedback knowledge early in the design process.

Acknowledgments

I want to thank my colleagues who have helped to implement some of the ideas on VR in architecture, in particular Eric van der Mark, Florian Wenz, David Kurmann and Werner Riniker, as well as Sharon Refvem and Maia Engeli for the development of critical software. Special thanks to the Vice President Research of ETH, Prof. Ralf Hütter and the Director of Computing Services, Dr. Walter Seehars, for their financial support in the establishment of the Architectural Space Laboratory.

References

Balaguer F, Mangili A (1991) Virtual Environments, in NM Thalmann and D Thalmann (ed.), *New Trends in Animation and Visualization*, John Wiley & Sons, New York, pp.91-106

Bürkle C, Oechslin W (1991) *El Lissitzky - Der Traum vom Wolkenbügel*, GTA Institute, ETH Zürich, Switzerland

Dave B (1993) A Diagramming System Ph.D. Dissertation, ETH Zürich, Switzerland

Ervin S (1992) Intra-Medium and Inter-Media Constraints, in Schmitt G (ed.) *CAAD Futures '91*, Vieweg Verlag, Wiesbaden, Germany

Goebel M, Huth M (1992) CADArt Virtual Design, *Computer Graphic topics*, Vol.4, No.4, pp.19

Novak M (1992) Liquid Architectures in Cyberspace, in M Benedikt (ed.), *Cyberspace: First Steps*, MIT Press, Cambridge, MA, pp.225-254

Schmitt G (1991) Computer Graphics in Architecture, in NM Thalmann (ed.), *New Trends in Animation and Visualization*, John Wiley & Sons, New York, pp.153-163

Schmitt G (1983) Auswirkungen des Energieproblems auf die Architektur unter besonderer Berücksichtigung von Computersimulationen und Computer-Aided-Design als Entscheidungshilfen im Entwurfsprozeß, Ph.D. Dissertation, Technische Universität München, Germany

Simon H (1992) People and computers: their roles in creative design, Keynote Lecture, *Second International Conference on Artificial Intelligence in Design*, Carnegie Mellon University, Pittsburgh, PA

Stenvert R (1992) Constructing the Past: Computer-Assisted Architectural-Historical Research, Ph.D. Dissertation, Rijksuniversiteit te Utrecht, The Netherlands

8

Virtuality Builder II: On the Topic of 3D Interaction

Jean-Francis Balaguer, Enrico Gobbetti
Computer Graphics Laboratory
Swiss Federal Institute of Technology, Lausanne

8.1. Introduction

Most of today's user interfaces for 3D graphics systems still predominantly use 2D widgets, even though current graphical hardware should make it possible to create applications in which the user directly manipulates aspects of three-dimensional synthetic worlds. The difficulties associated with achieving the key goal of immersion has led the research in virtual environments to concentrate far more on the development of new input and display devices than on higher-level techniques for 3D interaction.

It is only recently that interaction with synthetic worlds has tried to go beyond straightforward interpretation of physical device data (NSF 1992), (Balaguer and Mangili 1992). The design space for 3D interaction tools and techniques remains mostly unexplored, while being far larger than in standard 2D applications. Moreover, as stated by Myers, "the only reliable way to generate quality interfaces is to test prototypes with users and modify the design based on their comments" (Myers 1989, p.15). The creation of complex interactive applications is an inherently iterative process that requires user interface tools, such as toolkits or frameworks.

The lack of experience in 3D interfaces makes it extremely difficult to design 3D interface toolkits or frameworks. We believe that offering the possibility to rapidly prototype and test novel interaction techniques should be the primary goal of such tools. It is therefore more important for these tools to provide a wide range of interaction components, than to enforce a particular interface style.

Virtual Worlds and Multimedia Edited by Nadia Magnenat Thalmann and Daniel Thalmann
© 1993 John Wiley and Sons Ltd

In this chapter we present the *Virtuality Builder II* (*VB2*) framework developed at the Swiss Federal Institute of Technology for the construction of 3D interactive applications. First, we shall give an overview of the design concepts of *VB2*. Next, we shall concentrate on how users interact with dynamic models through direct manipulation, gestures, and virtual tools. More details on the rendering and modeling clusters are found in (Gobbetti et al. 1993a), and more detailed explanations of the dependency maintenance algorithms, as well as on their use to implement tools behavior, are found in (Gobbetti et al. 1993b).

8.2. Design Concepts

VB2 is an object-oriented framework designed to allow rapid construction of applications using a variety of 3D devices and interaction techniques. As shown in Figure 8.1, *VB2* applications are composed of a group of processes communicating through inter-process communication (IPC). A central process manages the model of the virtual world, and simulates its evolution in response to events in the form of IPC messages coming from the processes that encapsulate asynchronous input devices. Sensory feedback to the user can be provided by several output devices. Visual feedback is provided by real-time rendering on graphics workstations, while audio feedback is provided by *MIDI* output and playback of prerecorded sounds.

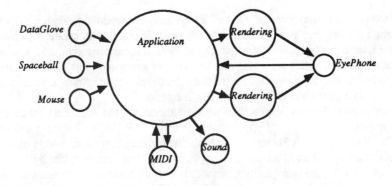

Figure 8.1. Overall structure of *VB2*

In order to obtain animated and interactive behavior, the system has to update its state in response to changes initiated by sensors attached to asynchronous input devices such as timers or trackers. The virtual world can be seen as a network of interrelated objects whose behavior is specified by the actions taken in response to changes in the objects on which they depend.

To model this kind of behavior, three different aspects have to be considered:

- the *state* of the system;
- the *long-lived relations* that have to be maintained between the different components of the state;
- the *sequencing relations* between states.

In *VB2*, each one of these aspects is modeled using different primitive elements: *active variables* are used to store the state of the system, *reactions* to maintain object's properties, *hierarchical constraints* to declaratively represent long-lived multi-way relations between active variables, and *daemons* to react to variable changes for imperatively changing between different system states. A central state manager is responsible for adding, removing, and maintaining all active constraints as well as managing the system time and activating reactions and daemons. This way, imperative and declarative programming techniques can be freely mixed to model each aspect of the system with the most appropriate means, much as in the programming language *Kaleidoscope* (Freeman-Benson 1990).

8.2.1. Information Modules

All *VB2* objects are instances of classes in which dynamically changing information is defined with active variables related through hierarchical constraints. Grouping active variables and constraints in classes permits the definition of information modules that provide levels of abstraction that can be composed to build more sophisticated behavior.

8.2.2. Active Variables

Active variables are the primitive elements used to store the system state. An active variable maintains its value and keeps track of its state changes. Upon request, an active variable can also maintain the history of its past values. A variable's history can be accessed using the variable's local time, which is incremented at each variable's state change, or using the system's global time, which is incremented at each atomic constraint operation. This simple model makes it possible to elegantly express time-dependent behavior by creating constraints or daemons that refer to past values of active variables.

8.2.3. Reactions and Transactions

In *VB2*, modifying some active variables of an information module requires that a *transaction* on this module has been opened. Transactions are used to group changes on active variables of a same module. *Reactions* register themselves with a set of active variables and are activated at the end of a transaction. They are used to enforce object invariants as well to maintain any kind of relation between a set of active variables. The reaction code is imperative and may result in the opening of new transactions on other modules as well as in the invalidation of the value of modified variables. All the operations performed during a transaction are considered as occurring within the same time slice.

8.2.4. Hierarchical Constraints

Multi-way relations between active variables are specified in *VB2* through *hierarchical constraints*, introduced in *ThingLab* (Borning et al. 1987) for the construction of two-dimensional user interfaces.

Constraint objects are composed of a declarative part, which defines the type of relation that has to be maintained, together with set of concerned active variables, and an imperative part, which is a list of possible methods that could be used to maintain the constraint. Constraint variables are located either directly or through *symbolic paths*. A symbolic path is an indirect reference to a variable described by the sequence of names of the active variables that have to be traversed to reach the referenced variable. Constraint methods are general procedures of any complexity that ensure the satisfaction of the constraint after their execution by computing certain of the constrained variables as a function of some of the others. A priority level is associated with each constraint to define the order in which constraints need to be satisfied in case of conflicts: this way, both required and preferred constraints can be defined for the same active variable.

A central constraint solver is activated each time a constraint is added to the graph or removed from it, and each time an active variable changes its value. Its goal is to maintain symbolic paths, and to decide which constraints should be satisfied, which method should be used for each constraint, and in what order these methods should be invoked. All the operations that the constraint manager performs to address these needs are considered as occurring at the same time and do not modify the system time.

We based our solver on the *DeltaBlue* algorithm (Freeman-Benson and Maloney 1989), which we extended to perform lazy evaluation and deal with constraints composed of methods having multiple outputs. Constraints using symbolic paths are handled by transforming them to fixed reference constraints that are automatically removed from the network and reconnected to the correct variables each time a component of a symbolic path changes, as in the user-interface toolkit *Multi-Garnet* (Sannella and Borning 1992).

8.2.5. Daemons

Daemons are the imperative portion of *VB2*. They are the objects which permit definion of the sequencing between system states. Daemons register themselves with a set of active variables and are activated each time their value changes. The action taken by a daemon can be a procedure of any complexity that may create new objects, perform input/output operations, change active variables' values, manipulate the constraint graph, or activate and deactivate other daemons. The execution of a daemon's action is sequential and each manipulation of the constraint graph advances the global system time. A priority level is associated with each daemon to define the activation order.

8.3. Interaction Techniques

In most typical interactive applications, users spend a large part of their time entering information, and several types of input devices, such as 3D mice and *DataGloves*, are used to let them interact with the virtual world. Using these devices, the user has to provide at high speed a complex flow of information, and a mapping between the information coming from the device sensors and the actions in the virtual world has to be devised.

The definition of this mapping is crucial for interactive applications, because it defines the way users communicate with the computer. Ideally, interactive 3D systems should allow users to interact with synthetic worlds in the same way they interact with the real world, thus making the interaction task more natural and reducing training.

8.3.1. Direct Manipulation

In most systems, the interaction mapping is hard coded and directly dependent on the physical structure of the device used (for example, by associating different actions with the various mouse buttons). This kind of behavior is obtained in *VB2* by attaching constraints directly relating the sensors' active variables to variables in the dynamic model, as in the example of Figure 8.2. These constraints define the interaction metaphor, and their activation and deactivation are triggered by daemons.

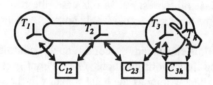

Figure 8.2. Graphical objects grabbed by user with constraints

Such a direct mapping between the device and the dynamic model is straightforward for tasks where the relations between the user's motions and the desired effect in the virtual world is mostly physical, as in the example of grabbing an object and moving it, but needs to be very carefully thought out for tasks where user's motions are intended to carry out a meaning. In this latter case, hardwiring virtual world actions to specific sensor values forces commitments that risk reducing device expressiveness and can make applications difficult to use (Fels and Hinton 1990).

In order to overcome these problems, *mediator* objects can be interposed between sensors and models to transform the information accordingly to interaction metaphors. Two major types of mediators are used in *VB2*:

- *adaptive pattern recognizers*, to enhance sensor data with classification information, hence increasing the expressive power of the input devices;
- *virtual tools*, encapsulations of visual appearance and behavior, to present selective views of models' information and offer the interaction metaphors to control it.

Information transformation is obtained by propagation through the mediators' internal constraint networks. Multiple mediators can be simultaneously active to allow manipulation of several models at the same time or of a single model with different interaction metaphors.

8.3.2. Hand Gestures

VB2 uses a gesture recognition system linked to the *DataGlove*. The gesture recognition system has to classify, on the basis of previously seen examples, movements and configurations of the hand in different categories. Once the gesture is classified, parametric information for that gesture can be extracted from the way it was performed, and an action in the virtual world can be executed. This way, with a single gesture, both categorical and parametric information can be provided at the same time in a natural way (Rubine 1991). A visual and an audio feedback on the type of gesture recognized and on the actions executed are usually provided in *VB2* applications to help the user understand the system's behavior.

VB2's gesture recognition is subdivided into two main portions: posture recognition, and path recognition (e.g. Fig.8.3). The type of gesture chosen is compatible with Buxton's suggestion (Buxton 1986, 1990) of using physical tension as a natural criterion for segmenting primitive interactions: the user, starting from a relaxed state, begins a primitive interaction by tensing some muscles and raising the state of attentiveness, performs the interaction, and then relaxes the muscles. In our case, the beginning of an interaction is indicated by positioning the hand in a recognizable posture, and the end of the interaction by relaxing the fingers.

The posture recognition subsystem is continuously running and is responsible for classifying the user's hand finger configurations. Once a configuration has been recognized, the hand data is accumulated as long as the hand remains in the same posture. This data is then passed to the path recognition subsystem to classify the path. A gesture is therefore defined as the path of the hand while the hand fingers remain stable in a recognized posture.

The gesture recognition system is a way to enhance the data coming from the sensors with classification information and thus provides an augmented interface to the device. The ability to specify the mapping through examples makes applications easier to adapt to the preferences of new users, and therefore makes them simpler to use.

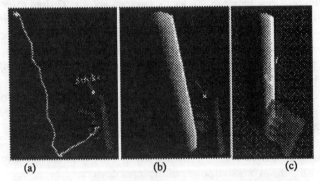

(a)   (b)   (c)

Figure 8.3. a,b. Creating a cylinder by gestural input; **c.** Grabbing the cylinder through posture recognition

8.3.3. Virtual Tools

The amount of information that can be controlled on a three-dimensional object and the ways that could be used to control it are enormous. Gestural input techniques and direct manipulation on the objects themselves offer only partial solutions to the interaction problem, because these techniques imply that the user knows what can be manipulated on an object and how to do it. The system can guide the user to understand a model's behavior and interaction metaphors by using mediator objects that present a selective view of the model's information and offer the interaction metaphor to control this information. We call these objects *virtual tools* (see examples in Figure 8.4).

Figure 8.4. Examples of simple virtual tools

VB2's virtual tools are first class objects, like the widgets of *UGA* (Unified Graphics Architecture) (Conner et al. 1992), that encapsulate a visual appearance and a behavior to control and display information about application objects.

The visual appearance of a tool must provide information about its behavior and offer semantic feedback to the user during manipulation. In *VB2*, the visual appearance of a tool is described using a modeling hierarchy. In fact, most of our tools are defined as articulated structures that can be manipulated using inverse kinematic techniques, as tools can often be associated with mechanical systems.

The tool's behavior must ensure the consistency between its visual appearance and the information about the model being manipulated, as well as allow information editing through a physical metaphor. In *VB2*, the tool's behavior is defined as an internal constraint network, while the information required to perform the manipulation is represented by a set of active variables (Figure 8.5).

In *VB2*, virtual tools are fully part of the synthetic environment. As in the real world, the user configures its workspace by selecting tools, positioning and orienting them in space, and binding them to the models he/she intends to manipulate (Figure 8.6). Multiple tools may be attached to a single model in order to simultaneously manipulate different parts of the model's information, or the same parts using multiple interaction metaphors.

Instances   *Constraints and active variables*

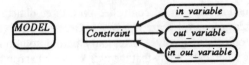

Figure 8.5. Notation

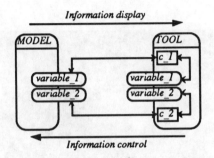

Figure 8.6. Model and virtual tool

8.3.3.1. Virtual Tool Protocol

The user declares the desire to manipulate an object with a tool by *binding* a model to a tool. When a tool is bound, the user can manipulate the model using it, until he/she decides to *unbind* it.

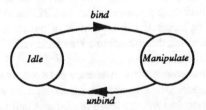

Figure 8.7. Tool's state transitions

When a *bind* message is sent to a tool, the tool must first determine if it can manipulate the given model, identifying on the model the set of public active variables requested to activate its binding constraints. Once the binding constraints are activated, the model is ready to be manipulated. The binding constraints being generally bidirectional, the tool is always forced to reflect the information present in the model even if it is modified by other objects.

When a tool is bound to a model, the user can manipulate the model's information through a physical metaphor. This iterative process composed of elementary manipulations is started by the selection of some part of the tool by the user, resulting in the activation of some constraint like, for example, a motion control constraint between the 3D cursor and the selected part. User input motion results in changes to the model's information through propagation of device sensor values through the tool's constraint network, and so until the user completes the manipulation, deselecting the tool's part. Gestural input techniques can be used to initiate and control a tool's manipulations, for example by associating selection and deselection operations to specific hand postures.

The *unbind* message is sent to a tool to detach it from the object it controls (Figure 8.7). The effect is to deactivate the binding constraints in order to suppress dependencies between the active variables of the tool and model. Once the model is unbound, further manipulation of the tool will have no effect on the model. Figure 8.8 shows an example.

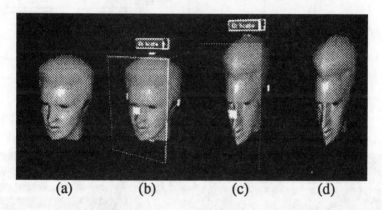

$$(a) \qquad (b) \qquad (c) \qquad (d)$$

Figure 8.8 a. Model before manipulation; **b.** A scale tool is made visible and bound to the model; **c.** The model is manipulated via the scale tool; **d.** The scale tool is unbound and made invisible

8.3.3.2. Composition of Virtual Tools

Since virtual tools are first class dynamic objects in *VB2*, they can be assembled into more complex tools much in the same way as simple tools are built on top of a modeling hierarchy. The reuse of abstractions provided by this solution is far more important than the more obvious reuse of code.

An example of a composite tool is *Dr. Map*, which is a virtual tool used to edit the texture mapping function of a model by controlling the parallel projection of an image on the surface of the manipulated model. The tool is defined as a plane on top of which is mapped the texture and a small arrow icon displays the direction of projection (Figure 8.9). In order to compute the mapping function to be applied to the model, the tool needs to know the texture to be used, the position and orientation of the model in space, and the position and orientation of the tool in space. The textured plane represents the image being mapped, and a *Dr. Plane* tool allows manipulation of the plane in order to change the aspect ratio of the texture's image. Pressing the grabber button allows the user to position and orient the tool in the 3D space, hence specifying the direction and origin of the texture projection. Figure 8.10 shows views of *Dr. Plane* and *Dr. Map*.

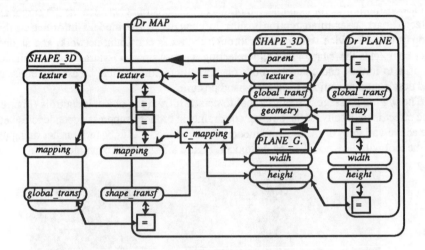

Figure 8.9. *Dr. Map*'s simplified constraint network

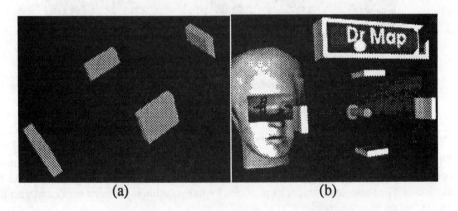

Figure 8.10. a. View of *Dr. Plane*; **b.** View of *Dr. Map*

Similarly, the material editing tool is built out of color tools and the light tool is built out of a cone tool. By reusing other tools we enforce consistency of the interface over all the system, allowing users to perceive rapidly the actions they can perform. Building tools by composing the behavior and appearance of simpler objects is relatively easy in *VB2*: for example, *Dr. Map* tool was built and tested by one person in about a couple of hours. The fast prototyping abilities of the system are very important for a framework aimed at experimenting with 3D interaction.

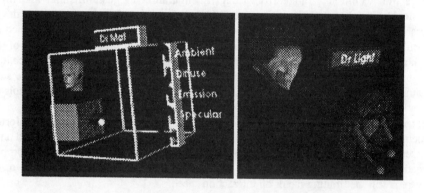

Figure 8.11. View of some other tools

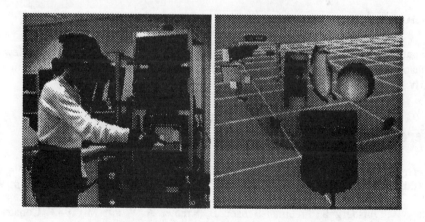

Figure 8.12 . Synthetic environment

8.4. Conclusions and Further Work

We have presented the *VB2* framework for the construction of three-dimensional interactive applications. In *VB2*, multiple devices can be used to interact with the synthetic world through various interaction paradigms. *VB2* is implemented in the object oriented language *Eiffel* (Meyer 1992) on *Silicon Graphics* workstations, and is currently composed of over 300 classes.

Interaction techniques range from direct manipulation to gestural input and three-dimensional virtual tools. Adaptive pattern recognition is used to increase input device expressiveness by enhancing sensor data with classification information. Tools, which are encapsulations of visual appearance and behavior, present a selective view of the manipulated model's information and offer the interaction metaphor to control it. Since tools are first class objects, they can be assembled into more complex tools, much in the same way simple tools are built on top of a modeling hierarchy. New three-dimensional tools are easily added to the system, and their number is rapidly growing.

Hierarchical constraints, active variables, reactions and daemons are used to uniformly represent system state and behavior. The use of an incremental constraint solver based on an enhancement of *DeltaBlue* makes it possible to run, at interactive speeds, complex applications composed of thousands of variables and constraints. The redraw time of the hardware is still the limiting factor on interaction speed.

We believe that *VB2* provides a good platform for prototyping and integrating a large variety of three-dimensional interaction metaphors to control all the different aspects of synthetic environments. We are currently extending the framework with time-varying constraints and tools for animation control in order to build a virtual reality animation system.

Acknowledgments

We would like to thank Michel Gangnet, Geoff Wyvill and Russell Turner for reviewing this chapter, and Angelo Mangili for his participation to the implementation and design of an early version of *VB2*.

References

Balaguer JF, Mangili A (1992) Virtual Environments. In Thalmann D, Magnenat-Thalmann N (Editors) *New Trends in Animation and Visualization*, John Wiley and Sons, pp.91-105.

Borning A, Duisberg R, Freeman-Benson B, Kramer A, Woolf M (1987) Constraint Hierarchies, *Proc. OOPSLA*, pp.48-60.

Buxton WAS (1986) Chunking and Phrasing and the Design of Human-Computer Dialogues. In *Information Processing*. North-Holland. Elsevier Science Publishers, pp.475-480.

Buxton WAS (1990) A Three-state model of Graphical Input. In Diaper D, Gilmore D, Cockton G, Shackel B (Editors) *Human-Computer Interaction: Interact, Proceedings of the IFIP Third International Conference on Human-Computer Interaction*, North-Holland, Oxford.

Conner DB, Snibbe SS, Herndon KP, Robbins DC, Zeleznik RC, Van Dam A (1992) Three-Dimensional Widgets. *SIGGRAPH Symposium on Interactive Graphics*, pp.183-188.

Fels SS, Hinton GE (1990) Building Adaptive Interfaces with Neural Networks: The Glove-Talk Pilot Study. In Diaper D, Gilmore D, Cockton G, Shackel B (Editors) *Human-Computer Interaction: Interact, Proceedings of the IFIP Third International Conference on Human-Computer Interaction*, North-Holland, Oxford, pp.683-687.

Freeman-Benson BM (1990) Kaleidoscope: Mixing Objects, Constraints, and Imperative Programming, *Proc. ECOOP/OOPSLA*, pp.77-87.

Freeman-Benson BM, Maloney A (1989) The DeltaBlue Algorithm: An Incremental Constraint Hierarchy Solver. In *Proceedings of the Eighth Annual IEEE International Phoenix Conference on Computers and Communications*, March, pp.561-568.

Gobbetti E, Balaguer JF, Thalmann D (1993a) VB2: A Framework for Interaction in Synthetic Worlds. Submitted for publication.

Gobbetti E, Balaguer JF, Mangili A, Turner R (1993b) Building an Interactive 3D Animation System. In Meyer B, Nerson JM (Editors) *Object-Oriented Applications*, Prentice-Hall (to be published).

Meyer B (1992) *Eiffel: The Language*. Prentice-Hall.

Myers BA (1989) User-Interface Tools: Introduction and Survey. *IEEE Software*, Vol.6, No.1, pp.15-23.

NSF (1992), Research Directions in Virtual Environments, *NSF Invitational Workshop*, UNC at Chapel Hill, pp.154-177.

Rubine DH (1991), The Automatic Recognition of Gestures, PhD Thesis, CMU-CS-91-292, Carnegie Mellon University.

Sannella M, Borning A (1992) Multi-Garnet: Integrating Multi-way Constraints with Garnet, TR-92-07-01, Dept. of Computer Science, University of Washington.

Figure 7.2. Aventicum in Roman times. Reconstruction using architectural prototypes

Figure 7.4. Design study using types and instances: towers of thought

Figure 7.5. A simulated view of the ASL at ETH Zürich. Model Florian Wenz, rendering Sharon Refvem

Figure 7.6. Student design of a library for an architectural historian. Without a virtual model, the geometry and use of the library are difficult to understand   Zoran Sladoljev, chair for Architecture and CAAD, 1992

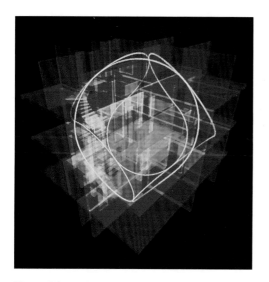

Figure 7.3. Kraftstrasse Zürich. Artist
Christoph Rütimann, model Florian Wenz

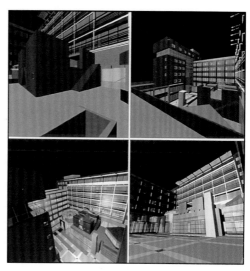

Figure 7.8. Competition model for a bank in Granada.
The virtual model was produced using types and
instances by Leandrano Madrazo

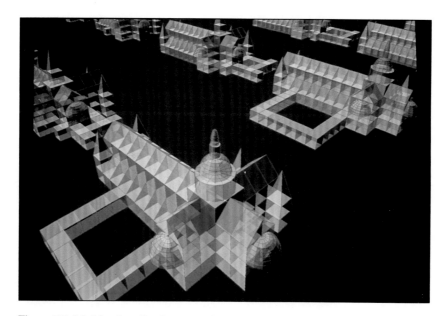

Figure 7.7. Models of medieval monasteries generated with a knowledge-based system.
Program Shen-Guan Shih

Figure 7.9. Extension of ETH Hönggerberg. Architects Mario Campi and Franco Pessina. Simulation of the new chemistry building. Model Sharon Refvem, rendering Eric van der Mark

Figure 7.10. Exploration of new data and design spaces. Model Florian Wenz

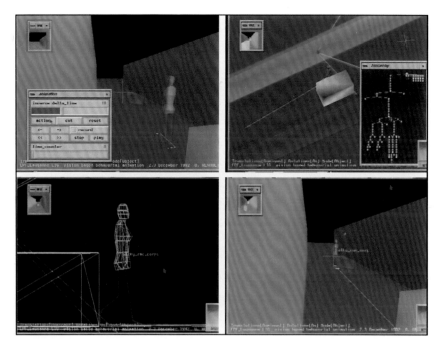

Figure 9.4. Vision-based navigation

Figure 9.6. Synthetic actor with hair, beard and skin texture

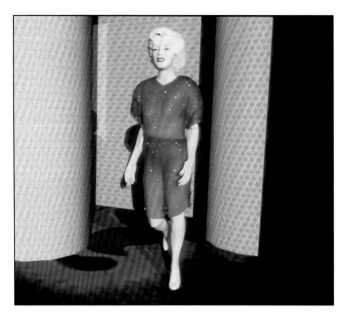

Figure 9.9. A dressed synthetic actress

Figure 9.10. A dressed synthetic actress

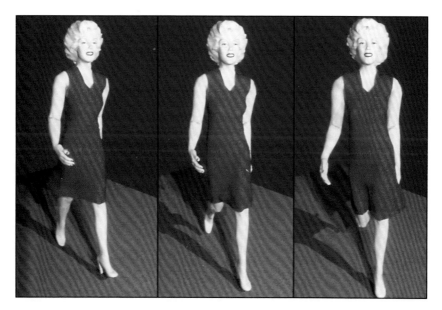

Figure 9.11. A synthetic actress walking with clothes

Figure 9.12. A synthetic actress with hair and fur coat and skin texture

4

Figure 10.1. Frame from Racoon, RENAULT DESIGN

Figure 10.2. Production of Racoon, RENAULT DESIGN

9

The World of Virtual Actors

Nadia Magnenat Thalmann
MIRALab, CUI, University of Geneva
Switzerland

Daniel Thalmann
Computer Graphics Lab, Swiss Federal Institute of Technology
Lausanne, Switzerland

9.1. Introduction

The long-term objective of our research is the visualization of the simulation of the behavior of realistic human beings, called **synthetic actors**, in a given environment, interactively decided by the animator. The ultimate reason for developing realistic-looking synthetic actors is to be able to use them in virtually any scene that re-creates the real world. However, a virtual scene -- beautiful though it may be -- is not complete without people.... Virtual people, that is. Scenes involving synthetic actors imply many complex problems we have been solving for several years (Magnenat-Thalmann and Thalmann 1991).

Behavioral techniques make possible the automating of high-level control of actors such as path planning. By changing the parameters ruling this automating, it is possible to give a different personality to each actor. This behavioral approach is a major step relatively to the conventional motion control techniques. Another complex objective is modeling human facial anatomy exactly, including movements to satisfy both structural and functional aspects of simulation. In order to improve the realism of synthetic actors, there are two important features to render: hair and clothes. Realistic hair has long been an unresolved problem because the great number of geometrical primitives involved and the potential diversity of the curvature of each strand of hair make it a formidable task to manage. Dressing synthetic actors with complex clothes is also a challenge. It is somewhat difficult to realistically

Virtual Worlds and Multimedia Edited by Nadia Magnenat Thalmann and Daniel Thalmann
© 1993 John Wiley and Sons Ltd

animate complex objects consisting of many surface panels like trousers or jackets without proper dynamic constraints. Problems include seaming the surface panels together, attaching them to other rigid objects, and calculating collision responses when they self-collide or collide with rigid objects.

In Section 9.2, we discuss the problem of controlling synthetic actors. It presents the development of a general concept of autonomous actors reacting to their environment and taking decisions based on perception systems, memory and reasoning. Section 9.3 explains the specific problem of facial animation and communication. In Section 9.4, we will review techniques for rendering fur and hair and modeling hairstyle. We emphasize a method based on pixel-blending for generating images completely free of aliasing artifacts. In the last section, we present methods for designing and animating clothes. Deformable models provide a powerful approach to this problem.

9.2. Animation System with Autonomous Actors

Most of the computer-generated films have been produced using traditional computer animation techniques like keyframe animation, spline interpolation, etc. Automatic motion control techniques (Wilhelms 1987) have been proposed, but they are strongly related to mechanics-based animation and do not take into account the behavior of characters. In fact, there are two ways of considering three-dimensional computer animation (Magnenat Thalmann and Thalmann 1990) and its evolution. The first approach corresponds to an extension of traditional animation methods. The animator uses the computer to assist in the creation of keyframes and simple motions and deformations like stretching and squashing. The second approach corresponds to simulation methods based on laws of physics, physiology or even psychology. The purpose is not the same: traditional methods allow us to create three-dimensional characters with exaggerated movements while simulation methods are used to try to model a human behavior accurately. High-level animation involving human beings and animals may be produced in this way.

Many authors have proposed methods to implement motion of articulated bodies. Some methods come from robotics like inverse kinematics and dynamics. Inverse kinematics permits direct specification of end point positions (e.g., a hand or foot). There are two major problems in inverse kinematics: finding any solution that will achieve the desired goal and, finding the most desirable solution. Inverse kinematics can be used as constraints with dynamic simulations (Isaacs and Cohen 1987). Dynamics has been used to automatically generate realistic motion (Armstrong and Green 1986; Wilhelms and Barsky 1985) that successfully animates the motion of chains, waves, spacecraft, and automobiles. The problem is that force/torque control is not intuitive. The course of a simulation is completely determined by the objects' initial positions and velocities, and by forces applied to the objects along the way. It just solves the initial value problems. How to return some level of control to the animator is one of the most difficult issues in dynamic simulation.

In task-level animation (Badler et al. 1989; Zeltzer 1989), the animator specifies what the synthetic actor has to do, for instance, "jump from here to there". For example, Witkin and Kass (1988) describe a spacetime constraint system in which constraints and objectives are defined over spacetime, referring to the set of all forces and positions of all of a creature's degrees of freedom from the beginning to the end of an animation sequence. Cohen (1992) takes this concept further and uses spacetime windows to control the animation interactively. But, task-level animation raises a problem: how to introduce individual differences into the generic activities which are generated automatically ? In the task of walking, everybody walks more or less the same way, following more or less the same laws. It is the "more or less" which is difficult to model. Even the same person does not walk the same way everyday. If he is tired, or happy, or has just received some good news, the way of walking will appear somewhat different. As in traditional animation, an animator can create a lot of keyframes to simulate a tired character walking, but this is a very costly and time-consuming task.

To individualize human walking, we have developed (Boulic et al. 1990) a model built from experimental data based on a wide range of normalized velocities (see Figure 9.1). The model is structured on two levels. At a first level, global spatial and temporal characteristics (normalized length and step duration) are generated. At the second level, a set of parameterized trajectories produce both the position of the body in space and the internal body configuration, in particular the pelvis and the legs. This is performed for a standard structure and an average configuration of the human body. The experimental context corresponding to the model is extended by allowing continuous variation of the global spatial and temporal parameters for altering the motion to try to achieve the effect desired by the animator. The model is based on a simple kinematics approach designed to preserve the intrinsic dynamic characteristics of the experimental model. But what is important is that this approach allows individualization of the walking action in an interactive real-time context in most cases.

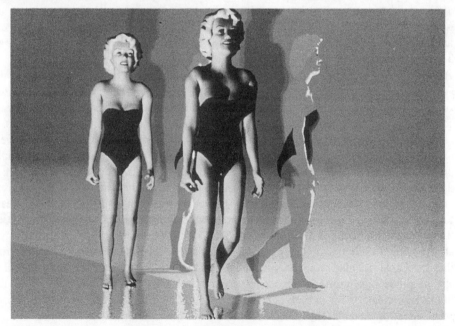

Figure 9.1. Biomechanics walking

Virtual humans are not only visual. They have a behavior, perception, memory and some reasoning. Behavior is often defined as the way animals and humans act, and is usually described in natural language terms which have social, psychological or physiological significance, but which are not necessarily easily reducible to the movement of one or two muscles, joints or end effectors. In fact the behavior of any living creature may be simulated. Reynolds (1987) introduced the term and the concept of behavioral animation in order to describe the automating of such higher-level animation. Behavior is not only reacting to the environment but should also include the flow of information by which the environment acts on the living creature as well as the ways the creature codes and uses this information. Reynolds studied in detail the problem of group trajectories: bird flocks, herds of land animals and fish schools.

A typical human behavioral animation system is based on the three key components:

- the locomotor system
- the perceptual system
- the organism system

A locomotor system is concerned with how to animate physical motions of one or more actors in their environment. This is the control part of the system. A perceptual system is concerned with perceiving the environment. According to Gibson (1966), we may consider five perceptual systems: basic orienting system, auditory system, haptic system, taste-smell system, and visual system. The organism system is concerned with rules, skills, motives, drives and memory. It may be regarded as the brain of the actor.

Our main purpose is the development of a general concept of autonomous actors reacting to their environment and taking decisions based on perception systems, memory and reasoning. With such an approach, we should be able to create simulations of situations such as actors moving in a complex environment they may know and recognize, or actors playing ball games based on their visual and touching perception.

Although many techniques have been developed for the control of articulated bodies, they are generally applied to much simpler systems than humans. For a general **locomotor system**, only a combination of various techniques may result in a realistic motion with a relative efficiency. Consequently, our locomotor system is based on several integrated methods. As we have already developed several techniques: keyframe, inverse kinematics, direct/inverse dynamics (Figure 9.2) and biomechanics-based walking, we integrate them using a blending approach. Production of a natural looking motion based on the integration of all parts of body using different types of motion control methods is certainly a challenge. In our case, a blending module is associated with the coach-trainee correction method that we have created in the context of walking. This method allows the kinematics correction of joint-space based motion with respect to Cartesian constraints (Boulic and Thalmann 1992). In such a way, it is still possible to modify the keyframe sequence, a low-level description of motion, for a higher level goal-oriented requirement. We believe that this approach will greatly extend the scope of predefined motions (rotoscopy, specialized model, keyframed etc..). A new methodology emerges for motion conception and editing which is centered on the coach-trainee correction method. The functional diagram in Figure 9.3 organizes the composition of the input motions around the blending module prior to the coach-trainee correction module.

Figure 9.2. Dynamics-based motion

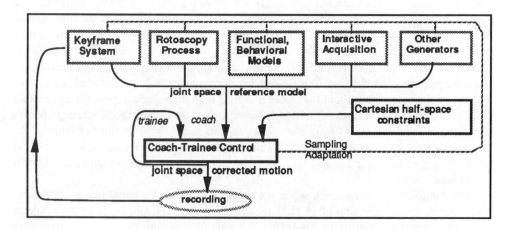

Figure 9.3. Functional diagram of motion blending

A **perceptual system** is concerned with perceiving the environment. The most important perceptual subsystem is the vision system. The originality of our approach in this wide research area is the use of a synthetic vision as a main information channel between the environment and the actor (Renault et al. 1990). We model the actor brain with a memory (essentially visual) and a limited reasoning system allowing the actor to decide his motion based on information. The movement decision procedure is the central coordinator to determine further movement. Our approach is based on the use of Displacement Local Automata (DLA), which is similar to the concept of script introduced by Schank (1980) for natural language processing. For vision, a DLA is a black box which has the knowledge allowing the synthetic actor to move in a specific part of his environment. Examples are the DLA *displacement-in-a-corridor*, the DLA *obstacle-avoidance*, the DLA *crossing-with-another-synthetic-actor* , the DLA *passage-of-a-door* etc. This concept of DLA has the advantage of being able to increase or decrease the description level. The DLA system allows for the creation of a kind of assemblage game where, using simple and modular elements, it is possible to react to a lot of everyday simple situations. It should be noted that our DLAs are strictly algorithmic; they correspond to reflexes which are automatically performed by the adult and they only use vision as the information source.

The controller is the thinking part of our system or the **organism system**. It makes decisions and performs the high-level actions. In an unknown environment, it analyzes this environment and activates the right DLA. In the simpler case of a known environment (i.e. already used), the controller directly activates the DLA associated with the current location during the learning phase. This controller also has to handle the DLA end, the DLA errors and other messages coming from the DLAs. In particular, a DLA may be in a situation where it does not know what to do and the controller should solve the problem. In any known environment, the controller should be able to activate the DLA associated with the current location. This means that an environment description has to be stored somewhere. This is the role of the navigator. From information provided by the controller (information that can come itself from DLAs), the navigator builds step by step a "map" of the environment. The navigator then gives to the controller the location of the synthetic actor in the map, and of course, it should plan the path from a known location to another known location (at a high level: e.g. go to the kitchen). Another function of the navigator is to allow the controller to change the initialization of some DLAs (e.g. changing the attention level in the corridor) and anticipate the DLA changes. This description of the navigator functionalities emphasizes the role of the map which should be more a logical map than a geographical map, more a discrete map than a continuous map. In fact, human beings only remember discrete properties like *the tree is on the right of the car*. This suggests that to give to the behavior of the synthetic actor a maximum of believability and a maximum of developing possibilities, it is essential to give the actor a world representation similar to the representation that human beings have.

More complex problems come when the actor is supposed to know the environment, which means the introduction of an actor memory. Using his vision, the actor sees objects and stores them into his memory. Thereafter, the actor may use this memory for a reasoning process. Our actor visual memory is defined using an octree, which has to represent the visual memory of an actor in a 3D environment with static and dynamic objects. Objects in this environment can grow, shrink, move or disappear. A recursive algorithm allows a path to be found from the actor to any position avoiding the obstacles based on his memory. The actor should also be able to remember if there is no path at all or if there are loops as in a labyrinth. This requires implementation of a backtracking mechanism. Once an actor has found a good path, he may use his memory/reasoning to take the same path. However, as new obstacles could have been added on the way, the actor will use the current synthetic vision to decide the exact path, reacting to the new obstacles. Figure 9.4 (see Color Section) shows an example of vision-based animation.

9.3. Face, Skin, Hair and Beards

Computer modeling and animation of synthetic faces has attained a considerable attention recently. Because the human face plays the most important role for identification and communication, realistic construction and animation of the face are of immense interest in the research of human animation. The ultimate goal of this research would be to model exactly the human facial anatomy and movements to satisfy both structural and functional aspects. However, this involves many problems to be solved concurrently. The human face is a very irregular structure, which varies from person to person. The problem is further compounded with its interior details such as muscles, bones and tissues, and the motion which involves complex interactions and deformations of different facial features.

For our facial deformations, we have extended the concept of Free Form Deformations (FFD) introduced by Sederberg and Parry (1986), a technique for deforming solid geometric models in a free-form manner (Kalra et al. 1992). More details may be found in Chapter 14.

To improve the "Barbie-like" aspect of virtual humans, we propose a technique based on texture mapping of photos of real faces (Kalra and Magnenat Thalmann 1993). A separate tool for matching the 3D facial topology on a given picture/photo of a face is developed. Only a few feature points are selected from the 3D model to exactly match the corresponding points on the picture. Delaunay triangulation is used to connect these points. These points can be moved and displaced on the picture interactively. An interpolation scheme in a triangular domain is used to get the desired texture coordinates. As a result the picture is deformed and mapped on the 3D model. In order to map the entire head, multiple views are needed. These pictures are projected on a cylinder. Then the corresponding matching is performed between the cylindrical projected 3D model points and cylindrical projected pictures. By using texture mapping the quality of rendering improves considerably. In addition, it allows us to put a picture of a specific person on a given 3D model.

In the field of human animation, hair presents perhaps the most challenging rendering problem and therefore has been one of the least satisfactory aspects of human images rendered to date. The difficulties of rendering hair result from the large number and detailed geometry of the individual hairs, the complex interaction of light and shadow among the hairs, and the small scale of the hair width in comparison with the rendered image. The rendering of hair therefore constitutes a considerable anti-aliasing problem in which many individual hairs, reflecting light and casting shadows on each other, contribute to the shading of each pixel.

Several researchers have published methods for rendering fur and human hair. Gavin Miller (1988) modeled hair with triangles to form a pyramid, using oversampling to avoid aliasing. Watanabe and Suenaga (1989) modeled human hairs as connected segments of triangular prisms and were able to render a full head of straight human hair in a reasonably short time using a hardware Z-buffer renderer with Gouraud shading. Perlin and Hoffert (1989) employed volume densities, controlled with pseudo-random functions, to generate soft furlike objects. Perhaps the most impressive rendering of fur to date was achieved by Kajiya and Kay (1989) for a teddy bear using a generalization of 3D texturing known as texels. Rosenblum et al. (1991) presented hair animation methods using a mass spring model. Anjyo et al. (1992) proposed methods using one-dimensional projective differential equations and pseudo-force fields. Both methods neglect the effect of collision between hairs for simplicity. Kurihara et al. (1993) proposed a simplified collision detection method using cylindrical representation.

To create hairstyles, our program offers, in the special module HairStyler, some interactive facilities. First, the three-dimensional curved cylinder is composed of straight cylindrical segments connected by points. The "in-between" points can be moved in the space to be adjusted, modified, deleted, or added. Just one type of individual hair can be assigned to each triangle in the scalp mesh. However the same hair can be assigned to various triangles. In order to adjust the hair orientation on the curved scalp surface, its direction can be modified by rotating the hair around the normal of its triangle. After defining each hair format and applying it to the respective triangle, the final style can be defined. The same hairstyle can have different lengths, by making it grow or shrink using a multiplication factor. A hairstyle generally has between 100,000 and 150,000 hairs, but this density can be regulated either for individual triangles or the entire scalp. Initially all the hairs placed in the triangle have the same length, orientation and symmetrical position. To make hairstyles look more natural, all these parameters can be changed interactively. A random length, orientation and position can be assigned to each triangle hair set.

Rendering an image of hair with our system involves several steps:

- creating a database of hair segments
- creating shadow buffers from all lights
- rendering the hairless objects using all shadow buffers
- composing the hair on the hairless image

In our system, hair rendering is done by raytracing using a modified version of the public domain Rayshade program. An implementation module of the shadow buffer algorithm (Williams 1978) has been added to a raytracing program, based on an earlier version of hair rendering based on pixel blending (Leblanc et al. 1991). The process is step by step. First, the shadow of the scene is calculated for each light source, as well as for the light sources for the hair shadows. The hair shadows are calculated for the object surface and individually for each hair. Finally the hairstyle is blended into the scene, using all shadow buffers. The result is an image with a three-dimensional realistic hairstyle rendering where complex shadow interaction and highlight effects can be seen and appreciated. Figure 9.5 shows an example of a synthetic actress with a hairstyle. Figure 9.6 (see Color Section) shows an example of a synthetic actor with hair, beard and skin texture.

Figure 9.5. Synthetic actress with hairstyle

9.4. Clothes

Cloth animation in the context of human animation involves the modeling of garments on the human body and their animation. In our film "Rendez-vous à Montréal" (Magnenat Thalmann and Thalmann 1987) featuring Humphrey Bogart and Marilyn Monroe, clothes were simulated as a part of the body with no autonomous motion (see Figure 9.7). For modeling more realistic clothes, two separate problems have to be solved: cloth animation without considering collisions (only the basic shape and the deformations due to gravity and wind are considered), and collision detection of the cloth with the body and with itself.

In a geometric approach, the shape of flexible objects is entirely described by mathematical functions. It is not very realistic and cannot create complicated deformable clothes, but it is fast. The geometric approach is suitable for representing single pieces of the

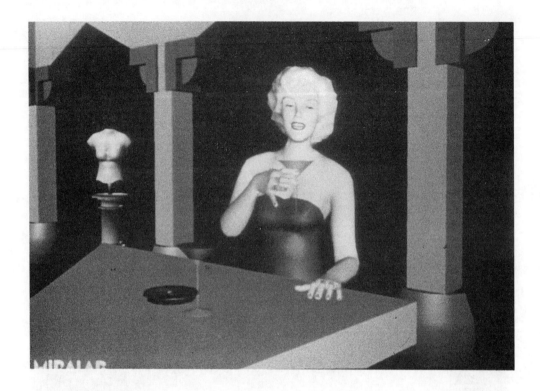

Figure 9.7. Cloth designed as a simple color (from the film "Rendez-vous à Montréal")

objects or clothes with simple shapes, which are easily computed, but geometric flexible models like Weil's model (Weil 1986) or Hinds and McCartney's model (Hinds and McCartney 1990) have not incorporated concepts of quantities varying with time, and are weak in representing physical properties of cloth such as elasticity, anisotropy, and viscoelasticity. Only physical models like Terzopoulos' model (Terzopoulos et al. 1987) and Aono's model (Aono 1990) may correctly simulate these properties. Another interesting approach by Kunii and Gotoda (1990) incorporates both the kinetic and geometric properties for generating garment wrinkles.

In our approach, we work as a tailor does, designing garments from individual two-dimensional panels seamed together. The resulting garments are worn by and attached to the synthetic actors. When the actors are moving or walking in a physical environment, cloth animation is performed with the internal elastic force and the external forces of gravity, wind, and collision response.

Our work in cloth animation (Carignan et al. 1992) is based on the fundamental equation of motion as described by Terzopoulos et al. (1987) with the damping term replaced by a more accurate one proposed by Platt and Barr (1989). When a collision is detected, we pass through the second step where we act on the vertices to actually avoid the collision. For this collision response, we have proposed the use of the law of conservation of momentum for perfectly inelastic bodies. This means that kinetic energy is dissipated, avoiding the bouncing effect. We use a dynamic inverse procedure to simulate a perfectly inelastic collision. Such collisions between two particles are characterized by the fact that their speed after they collide equals the speed of their centers of mass before they collide.

The constraints that join different panels together and attach them to other objects are very important in our case. Two kinds of dynamic constraints (Barzel and Barr 1988) are used during two different stages. When the deformable panels are separated, forces are applied to the elements in the panels to join them according to the seaming information. The same method is used to attach the elements of deformable objects to other rigid objects. When panels are seamed or attached, a second kind of constraint is applied which keeps a panel's sides together or fixed on objects. Figures 9.8, 9.9 (see Color Section) and 9.10 (see Color Section) show examples of a dressed synthetic actress. Figure 9.11 (Color Section) shows an example of walking sequence with clothes. Figure 9.12 (see Color Section) shows an example with hair, fur and skin texture.

Figure 9.8. Dressed synthetic actress

9.5. Conclusion

Modeling humans using computers is a very complex task. It will take years before we are able to represent synthetic actors who look and behave realistically. And if these actors are not to behave all in the same way, we will have to introduce interactive psychological description capabilities. New problems will arise: how to model the personality, the know-how, the common sense, the mind? We need concrete and mathematical models of domains which as yet are far from being formally described. This may be the challenge for the computer modeling of humans in the coming century.

Acknowledgments

This research has been partly sponsored by le Fonds National Suisse pour la Recherche Scientifique. The authors are grateful to Arghyro Paouri, Agnes Daldegan and Hans Martin Werner for the design of several pictures in this chapter.

References

Anjyo K, Usami Y, Kurihara T (1992) A Simple Method for Extracting the Natural Beauty of Hair, *Computer Graphics*, Vol. 26, No. 2, pp. 111-120.

Aono M (1990) A Wrinkle Propagation Model for Cloth, *Proc. Computer Graphics International '90*, Springer-Verlag, Tokyo, pp.96-115.

Armstrong B, Green M (1986) The dynamics of articulated rigid bodies for purposes of animation, *Proceedings of Graphics Interface*, Montreal, pp.407-416.

Badler NI, Webber BL, Kalita J, Esakov J (1989) Animation from Instructions, in: *Make Them Move*, Morgan Kaufman, pp.51-93.

Barzel R, Barr Alan H (1988) A Modeling System Based on Dynamic Constraints, *Proc. SIGGRAPH '88, Computer Graphics*, Vol. 22, No.4, pp.179-188.

Boulic R, Magnenat-Thalmann N, Thalmann D (1990) A Global Human Walking Model with Real Time Kinematic Personification, *The Visual Computer*, Vol.6, No.6, pp.344-358.

Boulic R, Thalmann D (1992) Combined Direct and Inverse Kinematic Control for Articulated Figures Motion Editing, *Computer Graphics Forum*, Vol. 2, No.4, pp.189-202.

Carignan M, Yang Y, Magnenat Thalmann N, Thalmann D (1992) Dressing Animated Synthetic Actors with Complex Clothes, *Proc. SIGGRAPH'92, Computer Graphics*, Vol. 26, No.2, Chicago, pp. 99-104.

Cohen MF (1992) Interactive Spacetime Control for Animation, *Proc. Siggraph'92*, pp.293-302.

Gibson JJ (1966) *The Senses Considered as Perceptual Systems*, Houghton Mifflin, Boston

Hinds BK, McCartney J (1990) Interactive garment design, *The Visual Computer* Vol. 5, pp. 53-61.

Isaacs PM, Cohen MF (1987) Controlling Dynamic Simulation with Kinematic Constraints, Bahavior Functions and Inverse Dynamics, *Proc. SIGGRAPH'87, Computer Graphics*, Vol.21, No.4, pp.215-224.

Kajiya JT, Kay TL (1989) Rendering Fur with Three Dimensional Textures, *Proc. SIGGRAPH '89, Computer Graphics*, Vol.23, No.3, pp. 271-280.

Kalra P, Magnenat-Thalmann N (1992) Simulation of Facial Skin using Texture Mapping and Coloration, *Proc. ICCG '93*, Bombay, India, pp.247-256.

Kalra P, Mangili A, Magnenat Thalmann N, Thalmann D (1992) Simulation of Facial Muscle Actions Based on Rational Free Form Deformations, *Proc. Eurographics '92*, Cambridge, pp. 59-69.

Kunii TL, Gotoda H (1990) Modeling and Animation of Garment Wrinkle Formation Processes, *Proc. Computer Animation'90*, Springer, Tokyo, pp.131-147.

Kurihara T, Anjyo K, Thalmann D (1993) Hair Animation with Collision Detection, *Proc. Computer Animation '93*, Springer, Tokyo.

LeBlanc A, Turner R, Thalmann D (1991) Rendering Naturalistic Hair using Pixel-Blending and Shadow-Buffers, *Journal of Visualization and Computer Animation*, Vol.2, No3, pp.92-97

Magnenat-Thalmann N, Thalmann D (1987) The Direction of Synthetic Actors in the Film Rendez-vous à Montréal, *IEEE Computer Graphics and Applications*, Vol. 7, No.12, pp.9-19.

Magnenat Thalmann N, Thalmann D (1990) *Computer Animation: Theory and Practice*, Springer-Verlag, Tokyo.

Magnenat-Thalmann N, Thalmann D (1991) Complex Models for Animating Synthetic Actors, *IEEE Computer Graphics and Applications*, Vol.11, No5, pp.32-44.

Miller GSP (1988) From Wire-Frame to Furry Animals, *Proc. Graphics Interface '88*, pp.138-146.

Perlin K, Hoffert E (1989) Hypertexture, *Proc. SIGGRAPH '89, Computer Graphics* Vol. 23, No.3, pp. 253-262.

Platt JC, Barr AH (1989) Constraints Methods for Flexible Models. *Proc. SIGGRAPH'89 , Computer Graphics*, Vol.23, No.3, pp.21-30.

Renault O, Magnenat Thalmann N, Thalmann D (1990) A Vision-Based Approach to Behavioral Animation, *Journal of Visualization and Computer Animation*, Vol.1, No. 1, pp.18-21.

Reynolds C (1987) Flocks, Herds, and Schools: A Distributed Behavioral Model, *Proc.SIGGRAPH '87, Computer Graphics*, Vol.21, No.4, pp.25-34.

Rosenblum RE, Carlson WE, Tripp III E (1991) Simulating the Structure and Dynamics of Human Hair: Modelling, Rendering and Animation, *The Journal of Visualization and Computer Animation* ,Vol. 2, No. 4 , pp. 141-148.

Schank RC (1980) Language and Memory, *Cognitive Science*, Vol.4, No.3, pp.243-284.

Sederberg TW, Parry SR (1986), Free Form Deformation of Solid Geometric Models, *Proc. SIGGRAPH '86, , Computer Graphics*, Vol.20, No.4, pp. 151-160.

Terzopoulos D, Platt J, Barr A, Fleischer K (1987) Elastically Deformation Models, *Proc. SIGGRAPH'87, Computer Graphics*, Vol. 21, No.4, pp.205-214.

Watanabe Y, Suenaga Y (1989) Drawing Human Hair Using Wisp Model, *Proc. Graphics International '89*, Springer, Tokyo, pp.691-700.

Weil J (1986) The Synthesis of Cloth Objects, *Proc. SIGGRAPH '86, Computer Graphics*, Vol.20, No.4, pp.49-54.

Wilhelms J (1987) Toward Automatic Motion Control, *IEEE Computer Graphics and Applications*, Vol. 7, No 4, pp.11-22.

Wilhelms J, Barsky B (1985) Using Dynamic Analysis to Animate Articulated Bodies such as Humans and Robots, in: Magnenat-Thalmann N, Thalmann D, *Computer-generated Images*, Springer, Tokyo, pp.209-229.

Williams L (1978) Casting Curved Shadows on Curved Surfaces, *Proc. SIGGRAPH '78, Computer Graphics*, Vol.12, No.3, pp.270-274.

Witkin A, Kass M (1988) Spacetime Constraints, *Proc. SIGGRAPH '88, Computer Graphics*, Vol.22, No.4 , pp.159-168.

Zeltzer D (1989) Task-level Graphical Simulation: Abstraction, Representation, and Control, in: *Make Them Move*, Morgan Kaufman, pp.3-33.

10

STV-Synthetic TV: From Laboratory Prototype to Production Tools

Armand Fellous
Laboratoire 3D, INA - France

10.1. Introduction

When first demonstrated in public at the "Virtual reality" session of IMAGINA 91, the STV-SYNTHETIC TV system was still at a laboratory, experimental, stage. During the past two years, the "Laboratoire 3D" of INA (Institut National de l'Audiovisuel-France) has focused its efforts in building a genuine film production tool from the first prototype. The making of "Racoon", a RENAULT DESIGN production, is a perfect example of our tool's possibilities.

In order to adopt the proper terminology for this session, we may say that, from the director's standpoint, making a film with 100% computer based 3D images reproduces, *virtually,* the making of a film using real images.

We use the term *virtually* since all is created within the computers. The computer is used to create virtual scenes, as, in traditional cinema, we would design a set. In this virtual scene, virtual actors evolve, actors in the largest sense of the term, meaning people or things seemingly endowed with life. We shed light, using virtual sources of light, on this virtual scene which is then filmed, virtually, using a virtual camera.

Moreover, for various reasons, whether artistic or financial, we wish to put up bridges that would allow access to and from these two worlds, real and virtual. Pragmatically, this method allows us to select which part of the final image is generated by real shots and which part from virtual shots. This array of choices has not evolved from 3D computer animation. From cinema's very beginning, the choice of natural or artificial scenery was offered underlying the same artistic and economical stakes. With this multi-technics

Virtual Worlds and Multimedia Edited by Nadia Magnenat Thalmann and Daniel Thalmann
© 1993 John Wiley and Sons Ltd

approach, 3D synthesis finds, slowly but surely, a less imperial but legitimate place in cinema.

10.2. Dynamic Coupling and Initializing

Conveniently, we can imagine that this hybrid image is obtained using two cameras each furnishing a part of the image; one pointing to a virtual world, the other to the real world. In order for this hybrid image to seem real, from a unique world, both cameras must be dynamically coupled. What does this mean?

Let us take, to simplify, two real cameras, perfectly identical, equipped with perfectly identical optical instruments. These two cameras are placed on the same kind of articulation system (allowing, for example, horizontal and vertical panning and travelling movements...).

We may say that these cameras are dynamically coupled if, for each image,

- all parameters of both lenses (zoom, focus, diaphragm...) are set to the same values, and
- the articulated systems supporting the cameras undergo exactly the same changes in movement.

As such, the hybrid image is composed of part of the camera(1) image and part of the camera(2) image, and the geometrical coherence creates the illusion that only one camera has been used.

Dynamic coupling can be obtained mechanically by using, for example, a system of rods. A cameraman manipulates one of the shooting systems and the other system follows. We say, in this particular case, that the second system is *slaved* to the first. Other systems are motorized, therefore, the cameraman works from a control panel, sending, simultaneously, the same instructions to both cameras.

The coupling system may produce an image seemingly from a unique world, filmed by only one camera, but, unfortunately, this is not always sufficient to make what we see of this unique world understandable.

Here is an example using two coupled systems, (1) and (2). The system(1) is filming someone on a blue background sitting on a blue cube and a red vase on another blue cube. System(2) is filming the set with a chair and a pedestal table. The hybrid image is obtained by inlaying the person and the vase to the set with the chair and pedestal table, a technique called chroma-key: all that is blue in the image produced by system(1) is replaced by what is found at the exact same place in the image produced by system(2).

How can we be sure that, when both cameras are joined in action, the person will be, in the resulting image, sitting in the chair and the vase placed on the pedestal table, and, that neither one of them will be travelling through the set?

The answer is obvious. If at a precise moment both systems occupy the same relative position w.r.t. their own space, due to dynamic coupling it will be so for the remaining of the application. This implies, as a first condition, that the respective positions of the two blue cubes must be exactly the same as the respective positions of the chair and pedestal table.

When system(1), for example, is *slaved* to system(2), we proceed as such: once system(2) is positioned in its world, we move system(1) through its own world while observing the composed image, until... the person is sitting in the chair and the vase is placed on the pedestal table! This could imply a lot of measuring and mathematical calculations, instead of trials and errors. When the result has been achieved, we are *relieved* and say that system(2) is *initialized* (w.r.t. system(1)). The strange use of *initialization* comes from the fact that, since there is coupling, the initial coherence existing at the beginning of the sequence implies a coherence throughout the entire sequence.

We should remember, from what has been mentioned, that, if the person slides from the chair or the vase from the pedestal table while the camera is in movement, it could be for any of the following reasons:

- both systems are not sufficiently identical,
- the dynamic coupling is not good enough,
- the chair or table's position should be reexamined,
- the initialization is not sufficiently accurate.

On the other hand, when the person remains firmly seated on the chair, and the vase on the pedestal table, we can say that:

- all has been sufficiently well realized, or that
- all which seemed unacceptable has been cut while editing.

10.3. The STV System

10.3.1. STV-Synthetic TV Procedure in a Nutshell

By replacing the couple (real world, real shooting system) used in the previous example with the couple (virtual world, virtual shooting system), you find the SYNTHETIC TV system. This system was developed by INA as part of the EUREKA 283 project in co-operation with TDI(France), TELSON(Spain) and VIDEOTIME(Italy).

More precisely, the system being offered today by INA is a dynamic coupling in which *the virtual camera is slaved to the real camera*. Coupling is obtained by placing captors on the real shooting system(1), that continuously inform the computer of the executed actions on system(1), which are then transmitted and applied to the virtual system(2). The identity of both systems symbolizes that the virtual system(2) is a sufficiently precise replica of system(1). This is the result of an extensive study done on the real system(1), during a laboratory operation called system calibration, involving a series of precise measures (parameterization) taken on the mechanical parts and on the images produced.

10.3.2. The System Offered by INA

A. Shooting system
This system is composed of a 2/3" Betacam video camera equipped with an Angenieux 14 × 8 lens. The camera is set on a pan/tilt head, which can, itself, be placed on a tripod or on an elevation column. This tripod can be attached to a rail travelling device with a range of several tens of meters.

B. Control car
A control car was specially conceived to allow the system to benefit from its full potential no matter where the sequence is to be shot, in a studio of course, but also in the field. This air conditioned car, supplied by its own power generating set, is furnished with video recording equipment, an inlayer, an editing table and graphics workstations. Let us note that, although the shooting system generally works *on-line,* meaning it is directly linked to the control car from which it can move several meters, it can also function in an independent manner, *off-line,* when circumstances make it necessary, with, however, less interactivity.

C. The technical team
Two or three technicians, depending on the complexity of the shooting, are made available to insure the proper realization of the specific operations linked to the procedure, as for example, the initialization of the camera, and for other tasks indirectly related to the procedure. Let us note, however, that the user of this mechanism remains, throughout the entire shooting, in perfect control of the general aspects of the film, nonspecific to the STV procedure, in particular artistically.

10.3.3. The Sectors Directly Concerned by STV

These are fiction programs, educational and institutional films, television programs, entertainment and talk shows. But, other sectors, which were less obvious from the start, are appearing: industrial design, which we shall look at after the Renault Design example, and the study of architectural impact.

Using the example of a vast architectural project: the decision-makers must, in general, assure, before undertaking the actual construction of the building, the pertinence of the chosen project. Of course, several methods are already available for this, other than the plans themselves: there are color perspectives, scale models of various sizes and films using synthetic images. These films would supply, without doubt, due to the achieved performance in the realism of architectural reproductions, a most reliable appreciation if ...we could visualize the project in its real future environment (meaning to create a composed image: virtual building, real scenery) and, if this project is made into an actual living area, see people evolving (meaning real people, virtual building).

This combination (real people in a synthetic scenery) was the goal of the second experimental film, shot at INA, using this procedure. "Lune de Miel" was projected at IMAGINA 92. The film was entirely shot in studio using blue backgrounds and the chroma-key technique explained above. This experience allowed us to compare and evaluate our procedure with the demands for this type of shooting. The experience generated a better evaluation regarding the importance and care brought to the adjustment of lights. This, however, did not affect the overall occupation time of the studio.

10.4. The Filming of "Racoon" with Renault Design

10.4.1. Purposes of the Project

The objective was to move a synthetic vehicle in real scenery, with a level of realism such that the special effects have, if not completely indetectible, no risk of harming the correct appreciation of the vehicle's qualities ...this was the goal declared in the accord signed with RENAULT DESIGN in February 1992. An objective which had all the signs of a technical wager: the first trials of the method were held in the parking lot at INA, fifteen days before the actual shooting of the film began.

I would like to emphasize the motives RENAULT DESIGN had to experiment with this type of film.

Over the past three years, their Computer Graphics department has perfected a purely virtual visualization technique (virtual vehicle in virtual scenery) for the designers and decision-makers of RENAULT. This system was used to create films such as "La Laguna" and "La Scenic" both known for their excellent technical quality.

Faced with the reality that their approach could never obtain a globally realistic result without considerable work on the scenery, which, in turn, would never reach the vehicle's realism, they decided to try natural backgrounds using STV.

Furthermore: without neglecting, in terms of images, its impact on RENAULT's clients, this type of film represents for RENAULT DESIGN a genuine experimental and validation tool for the designers' new concepts and participates, in a concrete effort, to improve the development of new prototypes while diminishing the costs and shortening the conception-validation cycle.

I am now given with the task of exposing, as clearly as possible, the techniques we had to develop and operate for this particular film. The realism of the sequences we have obtained depends on various factors; some are directly taken into account by STV-Synthetic TV, others not as much and some are not influenced at all. I will limit myself to the first two categories.

In this case of a real/virtual hybrid, the vehicle is virtual and the rest is real scenery. If the objective of RENAULT DESIGN was to make a film in which the vehicle would have remained immobile, the shooting would, from our standpoint, have directly carried out the STV process: the control of the virtual camera by the real camera, the first system filming the synthetic vehicle while guided by the second filming system shooting the real luminous scenery in the lac de Saint-Cassien (Var) vicinity.

But the RENAULT team, reminding us that their activities consist in manufacturing automobiles, not vases, rapidly convinced us of the need to see the car travel, naturally, on the road, and even, although somewhat uncommon, sailing on the lake, since it is amphibian. We were therefore forced to invent a technique in order to create these effects.

10.4.2. How to Film a Virtual Vehicle?

The first difficulty involved with filming a virtual vehicle *in movement* on a real background may be summarized as such: in our procedure, the real camera, handled by a cameraman, pilots the virtual camera. As such, the central part of the action, the vehicle's path, which normally determines the camera man's work, cannot be seen since it is in a virtual space. In other terms, how can the cameraman work on the composition of the image when he can only see the real part, which, in this particular case, is not the most important?

This possibility is at the core of STV-Synthetic TV. It has already been exploited, using the first prototype, in one of the first test-sequences produced by the "Laboratoire 3D" of INA in December 1990. In this particular sequence of the film "Le Labo et la Bête", a small twin-engine plane, yellow and virtual, penetrates the laboratory's aerial space and after reaching the far end returns from where it came, mission accomplished. The result could be compared to a news report, a real life situation allowing the cameraman no anticipation.

We obtain this effect by using, on location, a graphic workstation piloted by the real camera. This station is able to generate, at every moment, an image of the virtual world coherent with the image of the real world, furnished by the real camera. We then create a composed image in real time using the two different sources (real and virtual cameras), and transmit it to the viewfinder of the camera, giving the cameraman a simultaneous vision of both worlds. In fact, he receives and views all the elements that, *in fine*, will compose the image. As such, this system is sometimes described as a mixed camera having a foot in both worlds, real and virtual. In a matter-of-fact manner, this allows the cameraman to frame the scene as if a real vehicle was moving on the set.

10.4.3. How to Animate the Vehicle?

This difficulty resolved, we may ask ourselves:

- how can we create, in a virtual space, a perfect replica of the real road in order to see the virtual vehicle move on it? and
- how can we create a realistic animation of this virtual vehicle, making it act like a real car, with speed variations, suspension movements, following the road's profile?

Our solution, which solves both these problems simultaneously, uses the STV procedure with additional developments.

It seemed safer, as a first step, to trace the virtual vehicle's movements on those of a real vehicle having similar roadhandling behavior and taking the same path on the real road. It is, in fact, not at all obvious to generate, in a purely synthetic manner, such a realistic animation.

Therefore, our solution consisted in using a "rotoscopy" of a real vehicle on site. The vehicle, in this case a Jeep Cherokee, was covered with a large amount of visual bearings, targets, placed carefully by us. We filmed several shots of the Cherokee using the STVcamera; then, after the director's selection of the preferred shot, we analyzed the images in the control car, and finally could compute an identical animation for the virtual vehicle in its given space. The RENAULT team was then able to replay the virtual vehicle's animation and film it in a real background, from various angles and as many times as necessary in order to obtain a perfectly satisfying shot.

These are, for the most part, the methods used during this particular filming. One last remark: the real images shot for the "Racoon" do not include the Racoon (car), they can therefore be used to visualize several other prototypes that the conceptors of RENAULT DESIGN might already have in store. In this sense, we can imagine the importance of this type of system, with the storage of real scenery, for the visualization of future projects.

Figures 10.1 and 10.2 (see Color Section) show frames from "Racoon".

10.5. Foreseen Expansions

Outside and parallel to the utilization of the actual mechanism, we are working, at the "Laboratoire 3D" of INA, on the extension of the system capacity. This extension concerns many directions:

1) Improving the dynamic coupling.
2) Simplifying the system's operations: installation, initializing procedures, filming, post-treatments.
3) Diversifying the equipment that may, after calibration, be part of the mechanism: lens or optical instrument, camera, head,...
4) Integrating of shots taken in 35mm film.
5) Integrating motorized equipment, controlled by computers.

Also foreseen:

6) Industrialization of the product.
7) Commercialization through the sale of systems.

10.6. Conclusion

For a research laboratory, it is with great satisfaction that we observe our results rapidly transformed into operational tools and immediately employed by the concerned professionals. It also implies the accomplishment of tasks for which researchers have not been prepared. I would like to thank the team from the "Laboratoire 3D" of INA, Y. Brosse, J-H. Chenot, J-E. Noiré, P. Tomi, H. Sénaneuch[*], who have demonstrated the competence and flexibility needed for the realization of this project involving various fields such as mechanics, optics, electronics and, of course, computer programming. In contrast, few researchers in Computer Graphics have had the chance to work amidst lavender fields in summertime.

[*] also to be thanked: T. Higgins, B. Vincent, P. Maylin, M. Thomas, N. Cholet.

11

Synchronization in Virtual Worlds

**Michael Papathomas, Christian Breiteneder, Simon Gibbs,
Vicki de Mey**
Centre Universitaire d'Informatique, University of Geneva, Switzerland

11.1. Introduction

Virtual worlds can be regarded as an approximation of Sutherland's The Ultimate Display (Sutherland 1965). This vision was outlined more than twenty years ago, but it has taken considerable time and effort in computer graphics, display, and rendering technology to "materialize" this vision. It was not until recently that progress in hardware development made the special hardware required for virtual worlds available and affordable on a larger basis.

As virtual worlds become more sophisticated they are incorporating sound, video and other media. The combination of multimedia and virtual worlds is undertaken for several reasons. First, and most important, multimedia sources can be used to enrich the appearance of virtual worlds, either in terms of making virtual worlds more real or more interesting and appealing. Second, in some cases the use of multimedia techniques simplifies the development of virtual worlds since parts of relatively complex worlds can be replaced by video. Third, since both fields have much in common – especially the eminent role of computer graphics and the dependency upon hardware – a unified perspective for application development environments and application frameworks is advantageous.

Unfortunately, building virtual worlds is a time consuming task due to obstacles on different levels. What is needed are environments that make the development of these applications easier and provide prototyping support. The wide choice of hardware, design and application possibilities demands flexible and open environments that enable substitution of software and hardware components as well as support for implementing

Virtual Worlds and Multimedia Edited by Nadia Magnenat Thalmann and Daniel Thalmann
© 1993 John Wiley and Sons Ltd

alternatives. This is especially true for distributed virtual worlds where a wide range of interfaces and platforms must be supported since different locations cannot be expected to have the same hardware. In addition, high-level tools may allow building applications by reusing existing components rather than by programming new code.

Our approach to prototyping virtual worlds is to develop a collection of flexible components that can be connected in a variety of configurations. These components process media streams, e.g., audio data, animation events, or data coming from input devices. For this approach to succeed, a key concern is that components be capable of operating under a variety of synchronization requirements. This chapter explores synchronization in virtual worlds and gives examples of the synchronization requirements imposed on system components.

The remainder of the chapter is organized as follows: in the following section we describe some of the software and hardware possibilities in order to justify the requirements for open and flexible systems. Section 11.3 explains our component-based approach for prototyping virtual worlds and sketches an environment that supports the approach. We describe a test application that has been implemented called a Virtual Museum. In section 11.4 we discuss synchronization issues in virtual worlds and the problems that have to be solved. We give several examples of virtual worlds with synchronization requirements and consider the impact on component design.

11.2. Choices in Designing Virtual Worlds

The wide range of options for designing virtual worlds leads to many issues such as coordinating input and output devices, synchronization of system activities, combining different data types, etc. An approach to addressing these topics will be described later in this chapter. This section will highlight some of the areas where a developer faces choices when designing virtual worlds.

11.2.1. Different Tracking and Interaction Devices

Tracking systems monitor the location and orientation of various body parts, e.g., the hands or the head. Many interaction devices also include a tracking system. There are five types of tracking systems (Bishop et al. 1992, Pimentel and Teixera 1993): magnetic, acoustic, inertial, mechanical, and optical. Magnetic systems, such as the Polhemus and Ascension trackers, emit magnetic fields which are detected by one or more antennas. Because of their small size and the freedom of movement, magnetic systems represent the most popular type of trackers. Acoustic systems, typified by the Logitech Mouse, use ultrasonic pulses. Inertial systems use gyroscopes to measure yaw, pitch, and roll. The BOOM viewer, which is an example of a mechanical system, uses a rigid framework to measure position and orientation. Optical systems use triangulation techniques to determine positions from cameras at known locations. All these technologies have their advantages and disadvantages in terms of delay between sensor movement and the resulting signal being processed, update rate, accuracy, range (distance between signal source and receiver) and interference with objects in the "real" world.

Wands are simple and robust interaction devices and are, therefore, often used in presentations. A wand consists simply of a tracker, some switches and sometimes a thumbwheel for entering scalable data.

6 DOF (degrees of freedom) devices, come in two categories: force balls and 6 DOF mice. Force balls, typified by the Geometry Ball and Spaceball, cannot be moved. Position and orientation are defined by pulling, pushing, or rotating a sphere (the ball). Some of these devices also have programmable buttons. Force balls are good for navigation and positioning, but require some training. 6 DOF mice are basically conventional mice equipped with some tracking sensors.

Hand measurement devices, such as the DataGlove, basically measure the flexion angles of fingers and the position and orientation of the wrist. These kinds of devices have been extended to allow for the simulation of tactile feedback.

Another interesting and new device is a "one-hand keyboard" in the form of a handgrip that allows the generation of all keyboard sequences by using five buttons each with seven positions. The handgrip can also be equipped with a tracking sensor.

11.2.2. Different Media Devices

Computer-controlled audio/video equipment adds another dimension to a virtual world system. Media input devices include, for example, video cameras, videodisc players, MIDI (Musical Instrument Digital Interface)-devices (these devices are also often used for interaction), microphones, CD-players, etc. Media output devices include recorders or display devices. Other media devices control or process media streams. They range from video and audio switches, as simple examples, through audio tuners and video overlay devices, to very sophisticated video mixers that offer complex video transitions and effects. In addition, several audio and video formats contribute to an even greater variety.

11.2.3. Different Types of Data

Many types of data contribute to the user's impression of a virtual world. The essential type is 3D model data that defines the virtual universe, the scene and its objects. Objects and their positions may be changed by a user, some objects may be animated by an associated process. Images should be available to be used as, for example, textures to improve the impression of reality. Media data, such as sound and video (analog or digital), have to be stored and played back when appropriate. In addition, users might query text information about objects that has to be stored and indexed.

The existence of several data and compression formats for images, model, audio and video data introduces various specializations of these types. The nature of these data types is heterogeneous. While images, for example, can be regarded as large binary objects, media data can be highly structured and is represented as sequences that require processes that control their presentation.

11.2.4. Different Degrees of Reality

Hardware choices and application requirements permit different "degrees" of reality. There are a number of possibilities for the representation of the virtual world, its objects and especially the participants. Of course, the degree of reality depends on the richness of the model specified. The world and its objects can be represented by (colored) 3D wire frame objects if the hardware does not have sufficient speed for complex rendering. The next step up in quality could be the use of shaded models using, for example, flat shading, Gouraud or Phong shading. Surfaces of 3D models can be enhanced by the use of textures that, in special cases, may be animated as well. Lighting can vary from simple point lights to sophisticated light sources and dynamic lighting. The use of ray tracing and radiosity contributes considerably to the impression of reality.

Different degrees of reality are also important for the geometric representation of participants. As with other objects in the virtual world, this representation can range from simple colored wire frames, through shaded models, to sophisticated texturing. For example, participants could be represented by deformable 3D models onto which videos of the participants' faces are mapped. Even simple models can cause a very realistic impression as the TalkingHeads project at the MIT Media Lab has shown (Brand 1987). Modern equipment can map video signals on complex objects in real-time.

For a high degree of reality, consistency and coherency in the information received via different channels are likely to be the most critical factor. If this coherence cannot be established, the best modelling and rendering techniques, and the best resolution will not be able to reestablish the lost sense of reality.

Besides visual information, there are other factors that contribute to the perception of a higher degree of reality. Sound, for example, is another means to enlarge the feeling of reality, especially when 3D sound is supported.

11.2.5. Different Styles of Interaction

Different styles of interaction with virtual worlds are another design dimension. Pull down menus, as in desktop environments, are frequently used but often augmented by other techniques. Very popular is the use of wands since they can also be represented easily in the virtual world. For selecting a particular item, the user points at it and presses a button which selects the nearest object in the specified direction. In some systems, a "beam" originating at the wand and pointing at the object helps the user make selections. For navigation, the wand is positioned in the desired direction and a button is pressed for movement. The thumbwheel can be used for regulating speed. Another common interaction technique is to use a DataGlove and specify commands via hand gestures. Again, a "virtual" hand helps the user in orientation and selection. These approaches might be supplemented by voice input. Even subsystems with small vocabularies, discrete (versus connected) utterances, and user-dependent recognition features can offer substantial user support.

Instead of menus, interaction may rely on 3D toolboxes from which simple 3D icons representing some functionality can be grabbed and used. In addition, agents or guides might be exploited to perform certain tasks for the user (an agent) or to help a user, for example, to navigate through a virtual world (a guide).

Given all the choices, as detailed above, in designing virtual worlds, some type of strategy is needed to allow a designer the flexibility to experiment. The next section describes such a strategy by presenting the foundation for a rapid prototyping environment for virtual worlds.

11.3. Constructing Virtual Worlds

Virtual world construction has two distinct aspects — world infrastructure and world modelling. By world infrastructure we mean the underlying software and hardware used for simulating virtual worlds in general. This infrastructure must provide for audio and visual rendering, management of input and output devices, and synchronization of system activities. World modelling, on the other hand, deals with the design of particular worlds, i.e., specifying their visual appearance and behavior. The preceding section described some of the factors that differ among virtual worlds. The differences are not only in content, as when world models contain different objects, but also in the infrastructure used when simulating models. These possible infrastructures need to be explored and evaluated. In other words, we seek a development environment that allows us to prototype and experiment with virtual world infrastructures.

There has been earlier work on "toolkits" for virtual world construction. Examples include the MR toolkit (Shaw et al. 1992) and commercial products such as Sense8's WorldToolKit. The difference with our approach is that we view the design of virtual world infrastructures as having many similarities to the design of interactive multimedia applications. Thus, we do not use a toolkit specific to virtual world construction, but rather a set of components intended for multimedia applications in general.

11.3.1. Virtual World Components – Media Objects

The components used by our development environment are called media objects (Gibbs 1991). A media object is a software handle on an entity, such as a software component or a piece of hardware, which processes media streams. Loosely speaking, a media stream is a flow of information. The term derives from viewing time-based media as streams of some form, for example video can be viewed as a stream of frames and digital audio as a stream of samples.

Media objects are divided into three categories: sources, sinks and filters. Sources produce media streams, sinks consume streams, while filters transform streams. Streams enter and leave media objects via ports. For example, we view a renderer as a media object which consumes animation events (such as moving a graphical object within a 2D or 3D space, defining a light source, changing the viewpoint etc.) and produces a sequence of images. In other words, a renderer is a filter with an "animation event" input port and an "image sequence" output port. The appendix lists many of the components we have developed or are now developing. In addition to animation events and image sequences these components work with streams of PCM(Pulse Code Modulation) audio (digital audio samples), MIDI events, music events (high-level commands such as to play a particular track or to change the tempo), sound events, various analog video formats, and what we call geometry events (position and orientation data).

11.3.2. Connecting Components

To develop applications that run on a particular platform, components accounting for the functionality of the platform must first be implemented. For example, if the platform contains an audio capture board, then a media object for the board and streams of the audio data format used by the board, would be needed.

Figure 11.1a shows our hardware platform and the various digital communications paths available. Connections between the media objects that correspond to this platform involve several mechanisms. Some connections are based on interprocess communication or shared memory, others rely on a computer- controllable composite video routing switch (see Figure 11.1b) or a manually-configured patch-panel (see Figure 11.1c).

Applications are built by connecting components. A group of connected components is called a component network. When components are connected, their ports must be compatible, that is one must be for input, the other for output, and they must both handle similar media streams — one cannot connect an audio output port to a video input port. The application developer specifies connections either by explicit calls in the application code or by using a configuration tool allowing direct manipulation of icons representing components through a graphical editor (de Mey et al. 1992).

11.3.3. The Virtual Museum

We have used media objects to construct a virtual world called the Virtual Museum (de Mey and Gibbs 1993). The Virtual Museum is a 3D building in which 2D and 3D artifacts are presented to visitors by using recorded video frames, moving video or raster images (see Figure 11.2, Color Section). Features of this virtual world include:

different views   The museum can be simultaneously viewed in 3D and 2D. As a museum visitor moves through the 3D model, a marker tracks his/her position on a 2D floorplan.
different forms of interaction   As the visitor moves around the museum, he/she enters and exits "sensitive" regions which trigger the presentation of artifacts. The position of the sensitive regions is indicated on the 2D floorplan and through 3D visual cues. Navigation in the museum is principally done in 3D via an input device that allows six degrees of freedom in movement; it is also possible to "teleport" by pointing within the 2D floorplan.

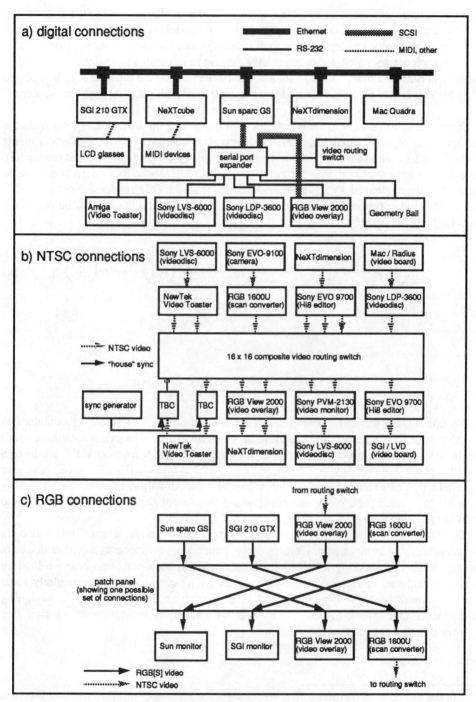

Figure 11.1. Hardware components and their connections

different media   Museum artifacts incorporate various media including still and moving video, raster images, 3D scanned objects (3D models of real-world objects whose shape and color are captured through scanning), and simple geometric models. Some artifacts are animated, for example they may move or change their size.

guides and recorded tours   Video "guides" can be overlaid on the museum and then played back. It is also possible to record and playback particular paths through the museum.

Figure 11.2 shows a component network which provides the infrastructure for a simple configuration of the Virtual Museum. The network is composed of six individual media objects[1]. These components produce a stream of geometry events from an input device (G), translate this stream into requests for movement within a 3D space (N), interpret movement requests in the context of a geometric model of the museum (M), render geometric models and overlay video frames (R3), provide video frames (VD), and display the output of the rendering process (F).

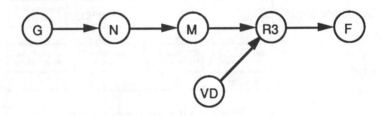

Figure 11.2. Virtual Museum component network

An extension of this basic configuration is shown in Figure 11.3 where an animator (A) transforms or displaces parts of the museum (e.g., rotates an artifact), a model tee (MT) duplicates its input to produce two output streams, and a model recorder (MR) produces a timestamped log of requests. A 2D renderer and a second framebuffer (R2 and F) have also been added. The extended configuration has new functionality, in particular it is now possible to animate parts of the museum, record "walkthroughs" for future playback, and view the museum floorplan.

To summarize, our approach is to construct virtual world "infrastructures" by connecting media processing components. Unfortunately, connecting components together does not always result in a working application; the components may place too heavy a load on available hardware or simply fail to work together. The last problem is particularly acute since it cannot be solved by more and faster hardware. Several issues in designing components that "work together," or what we call component synchronization, are examined in the remainder of the chapter.

---

[1] In this and other infrastructure diagrams, nodes represent components, i.e., media objects, and edges represent component connections. A short description of the various components is given in the Appendix.

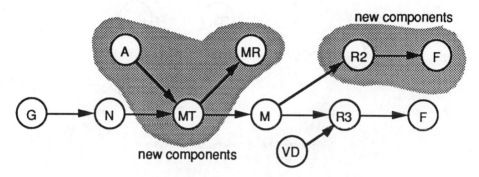

Figure 11.3. Extended Virtual Museum component network

11.4. Synchronization in Virtual Worlds

There are different synchronization issues pertaining to virtual world applications. These range from the network and operating system level to user coordination at the application level. In the Virtual Museum, discussed in the previous section, limited attention was given to synchronization, mainly due to the loose synchronization requirements of this example application. In this section we will present examples that illustrate synchronization issues in virtual world applications structured as component networks. We identify some synchronization requirements of these applications and, briefly, discuss a promising approach for supporting synchronization, based on the ability to control the activity of components in time. Our current work in this direction is also discussed.

11.4.1. Synchronization in Component Networks

11.4.1.1. Synchronized Display

A simple example, illustrating the need for synchronization of components, is the synchronized display of 3D graphics on two separate displays. Such a situation occurs, for example, with the presentation of image pairs on a stereo head-mounted display.

Figure 11.4 shows a component network for this application. The functionality of these components was described in the previous section. Indexes are used to distinguish between several instances of the same kind of component.

The main synchronization issue in this application is that the $R3_1$ and $R3_2$ components operate asynchronously. They may in fact run on different processors and, depending on the load, generate their output at varying speeds. Consequently, it would not be possible to achieve or maintain the synchronized display unless some provision is taken for synchronization. The components could be aware of the synchronization requirements of the application and could take some action for synchronization. However, we would like such components to be generally usable so that including the synchronization within the components in an *ad hoc* way would not be appropriate.

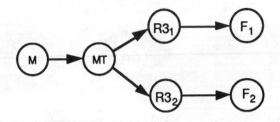

Figure 11.4. Synchronized display

Another problem resulting from the asynchronous operation of components concerns the relative operation speeds of the M component and R3 components. If the scene descriptions are produced at a rate much higher than that at which a R3 component can consume them, some provision should be made, assuming it would be acceptable for the application, to slow down the M component.

11.4.1.2. A Virtual Museum with Multiple Participants

This application is an extension to the Virtual Museum, discussed in section 11.3, in order to allow two, or more, remotely located users to "walk around" in the museum together, make comments and exchange information about the artifacts. Although such an application could have multiple users, to simplify the discussion, we assume only two users.

In addition to the functionality of the original Virtual Museum, this application provides the following:

- *Audio communication:* The two participants are linked by a duplex audio channel for voice communication.
- *Telepointing:* A pointing device allows a user to point and select items exposed in the museum. The pointer is visible to the remote user provided he is looking in the right direction.

The participants are not forced to look in the same direction; they are aware of the position of the other participant by an object representing the other participant displayed within their field of view. Figure 11.5 shows the main components of the multiple participant version of the Virtual Museum.

As we now have two users, a number of components present in the Virtual Museum have been duplicated and their names are indexed by a number indicating the associated user. There are also some additional components for audio communication, and the behavior of some components has been adapted to the shared environment as described below:

ADC, DAC: Used for producing and playing digital audio in each user's environment.

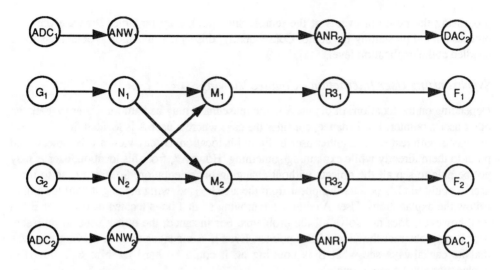

Figure 11.5. Virtual Museum with two participants

ANR, ANW: Used for transmitting digital audio over the network.

N_1, N_2: Navigator components that support some additional functionality with respect to the navigator component in the single-user version of the Virtual Museum. They are used for generating pointing events as well as events to change the user's position and orientation in the museum. The pointing and orientation events are also directed to the model component of the remote user so that the pointing and position of one user are also visible to the other user.

This example application illustrates two synchronization issues: the synchronized presentation of data streams and the synchronization of user actions to facilitate their interaction.

Data Stream Synchronization
An interstream synchronization issue in this application is to keep time shifts in the presentation of the pointing and audio data streams within some interval in order to preserve the consistency of the information conveyed by these data streams.

Consider, for example, the case where a user points to an object, says something about it, then points to another object and says something else. If the time lag between the presentation of the audio stream and the pointing exceeds some limit, it would be possible that the user hears the explanation concerning the second object while the pointer is still pointing at the first one.

One could rely on the network and operating system for providing a link that adequately supports the synchronized transmission of the audio and pointing streams. This would be the most general solution to this problem and would ensure that the two streams arrive synchronized at the remote user's environment. However, the main problem in the synchronized presentation of the audio and pointer streams comes from the time needed for processing the pointing events at the remote site which may be larger than the time for processing and presenting the audio. Consequently, this synchronization problem has to be handled at the application level.

Synchronizing User Interaction - Coupled Viewing

Depending on the locations of the users in the museum, it may be hard for a user to track the other user's pointer. For instance, consider the case where a user A is located far from a set of objects with respect to another user B. From his location, B may view all the objects and point to them directly while explaining something. However, from his location, user A may not be able to see all the objects without changing his orientation. So, from time to time, user A could see B's pointer disappear from the area he is viewing making it hard for him to follow the explanations. User A could keep moving so that he is located next to user B but this, however, does not solve all the problems. For instance, the object used to represent user B may obstruct the view of B's pointer. Even if A manages to keep moving in a way that he can always see what B is pointing at, it could be hard for him to follow B's explanations at the same time.

The users could deal with this synchronization issue by following some social protocol. For instance, user A could request user B to slow down or repeat his pointing. Alternatively, the application could provide support for synchronizing their interaction by coupling, on user demand, user A's location and orientation to those of B for some time period. Following this scenario, user A, who now sees exactly what B sees, may lay back and follow B's explanations as he moves around in the museum and points to artifacts. During coupled viewing, A could still use his pointer to communicate with B. Coupled viewing ends as soon as any of the users requests it. The approach of temporarily coupling some users' "senses" could be more generally applied to facilitate information sharing and communication in virtual worlds.

11.4.1.3. Synchronization to User Motion

This example, taken from (Friedman et al. 1992), concerns the synchronization of user motion with rendered graphics and sound output. The application tracks, through position sensors, the motion of two drum-sticks, renders a 3D model of the sticks and drums, and generates the appropriate drum sound when the rendered drum-sticks hit a drum's surface. The main issue in this application is the synchronization of user motion with the rendered graphics and sound output to give an impression of reality. For this, time lags in displaying changes to the 3D drum-sticks model in response to user motion should be kept under 100 ms.

A component network for this application is shown in Figure 11.6. The components serve the following purposes:

> N: tracks the position of the drum-sticks and outputs a sequence of positions for the drum-sticks.
> M: takes as input a sequence of positions and outputs rendering commands and commands for generating sound.
> SND: generates sound output.

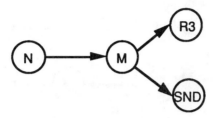

Figure 11.6. User motion

Three main problems in maintaining synchronization in this application, further discussed in (Friedman et al. 1992), are:

• Latency and noise in tracking the drum-stick positions.
• The delay introduced by the processing pipeline (in particular M and R3).
• Delays caused by the network contention and operating system activity.

The approach proposed for solving these problems is to predict future user positions using a Kalman filter. This gives a fixed amount of lead time for the computations and the application can cope with unexpected delays shorter than the lead time. Apart from an accurate technique for user motion prediction, an approach for recovering from prediction errors is proposed. This approach is based on identifying sensitive points and precomputing the possible alternatives.

11.4.1.4. The Virtual Orchestra Application

In this application we are interested in maintaining the synchronized playback of music with animation while allowing a user, acting as a conductor, to change the music tempo interactively. Synchronization is specified by stating that certain musical events should occur at the same time as a visual event in the animation. For example, we would like a MIDI event, such as playing a note, to occur at the same time as a frame showing an instrument playing is displayed. Figure 11.7 shows the component network for this application. The components in the network are:

C: receives input from an input device, such as the mouse, used by the user who acts as a conductor, and outputs changes to the tempo.
MSQ: reads MIDI events from a file and sends them to a MIDI instrument at the appropriate times. It receives, as input, changes to the tempo and modifies accordingly the pace at which MIDI events are output.
MSY: receives and plays MIDI events.
A: receives changes to the music tempo and outputs changes to scene descriptions. It continuously adapts its computation according to the tempo changes so that the specified frames are displayed at the same time that the associated musical events occur.

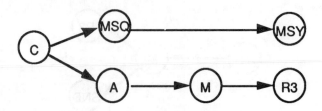

Figure 11.7. Virtual orchestra

This application illustrates the possibility of achieving synchronization by modifying the activity of a component, the Animator (A), so that some events, such as the display of a frame, occur at specific instants in real-time. This is possible because the Animator has the ability to generate a scene for any specified instant in animation time, including future times, i.e., scenes are represented as a function of animation time.

The animator knows the time it takes for rendering a scene and the current position both in real time and animation time (the mapping between animation time and real time depends on the tempo). It determines the number of frames that can be displayed before reaching the real-time instant when the next musical event occurs. This allows it to send scenes to the renderer that "hit" musical events.

Whenever the tempo is changed, the real time of musical events and, consequently, the time at which an animation event should occur change. The Animator changes the animation rate accordingly following the approach described above.

This approach for synchronization relies on the ability to change the rate of a component's activity in time. It would not be possible to apply the same technique if the animation took place by displaying a number of precomputed frames at a fixed rate.

11.4.2. Synchronization Issues in Virtual Worlds

Without trying to be exhaustive, we may distinguish the following synchronization issues in virtual world applications:

- *Time-based media synchronization:* This has to do with the rate at which one or more streams of data are presented. Intrastream synchronization imposes requirements on the presentation of a single data stream whereas interstream synchronization concerns the joint presentation of several streams. The synchronization requirements vary depending on the media type and application. For instance, the synchronization tolerance of an audio stream is lower than that for animation. The need to synchronize the presentation of data streams was illustrated in the multi-participant Virtual Museum example discussed in section 11.4.1.2.

- *User-level synchronization:* These issues have to do with the synchronization requirements imposed by the user-interaction mode of a single or multi-user application. The example application, discussed in section 11.4.1.3, illustrated the difficulties of tightly synchronizing system response to user motion in order to provide an illusion of reality. The example of the multiple-participant museum illustrated the need to synchronize user activity to facilitate user interaction. This raises questions, discussed extensively in (Ellis et al. 1991), about the degree to which a system should enforce or support some user-interaction/synchronization policy. The choice and adequacy of a synchronization policy are highly dependent on the application.
- *Asynchronous operation of system components:* Different components of a virtual world application have different execution speeds and response time requirements. If the operation of components is tightly synchronized, then the application response time would be dominated by the slower components and would vary depending on the number of components and their execution speeds. This would be very annoying for the component that provides feedback to user input actions, especially for sophisticated interface devices supported in virtual environments. This suggests structuring applications as a set of components operating asynchronously. Managing the execution and interaction of asynchronous components involves concurrent programming problems at various application levels. The component networks approach, used in the previous sections, supports the asynchronous operation of components. The examples in 11.4.1.1 and 11.4.1.4 illustrated the need to synchronize component execution.
- *Distributed processing:* There are a number of reasons for supporting distribution in virtual world applications. One reason is to distribute processing to a set of independent processors because of the processing power requirements of an application, as illustrated by the synchronized display example in section 11.4.1.1, where the generation of images for each eye can take place on separate processors. Other reasons are to avoid the bottlenecks of centralized approaches, and the inherently distributed nature of the application such as the use of independent user workstations in the shared Virtual Museum. The component-based approach, discussed in section 11.3, incorporates support for distribution; components in a component network may reside on separate workstations.

There is much ongoing research addressing the above issues. In order to support time-critical applications, research is taking place on the organization and instrumentation of general purpose workstations from both the hardware and software perspectives (Hanko et al. 1991). The quality of service requirements for real-time, synchronized transmission of multimedia data across networks (Little and Ghafoor 1991) is also being investigated. Servers and toolkits are being developed for the synchronized presentation of time-based data streams on a single workstation in the presence of unexpected network and operating system delays (Anderson and Homsy 1991, Dannenberg et al. 1992).

Our approach, which is more concerned with the design and reuse of application-level components, can benefit from these developments. However, we still need to specify synchronization between components at the application level. The next section briefly discusses support for synchronization in component networks and briefly presents our work in this direction.

11.4.3. Component Synchronization

The component-based approach discussed in section 11.3 provides support for asynchronous and distributed execution; no support, however, is provided for synchronization. The components in applications, such as the examples in section 11.4.1, could be implemented in a way that satisfies the synchronization requirements of the application. However, this does not fit well with our approach for constructing virtual worlds. If the synchronization needed for a particular application is hardcoded within the components, such components would not be easily reusable across applications with varying synchronization requirements. We are aiming at an approach along the following lines:

- Support the reuse of components across applications.
- Make it easy to synchronize components with other components in an application without having to rewrite them.
- Provide general solutions to the synchronization problems that can be reused by applications with similar requirements.
- Use interactive, high-level tools, such as a component configuration tool, for applications where there is a need for synchronization.

Without totally excluding the approach of developing and using application-specific components when necessary, we have been working towards a more general approach for component synchronization that adequately addresses the above points.

This approach, discussed in (Gibbs 1991) and (Gibbs et al. 1991), is based on the idea that components provide operations for controlling their activity in time. These operations include starting and stopping a component's activity in time, cueing, changing the direction of time or changing the speed of its clock.

The temporal operations may be used by applications or internally within components for synchronizing component networks. The problem lies, however, in finding general patterns, or "synchronization protocols", by which components invoke these operations. Identifying these synchronization protocols would simplify designing components that can satisfy different synchronization requirements when placed in different component networks.

11.5. Conclusion

We have argued that developing virtual world applications is hampered by a wide variety of design choices and that tools for prototyping and experimenting with virtual worlds are needed. Our approach to prototyping virtual worlds uses a collection of "plug-compatible" components. Generally these components process data streams, such as audio samples, sensor events, and animation events. They encapsulate asynchronous execution, distribution and hardware dependencies. Components, when connected, form the infrastructure needed for running a virtual world. By altering connections and adding components, different infrastructures, supporting virtual worlds with different capabilities, can be created. By designing new components, additional hardware devices and software services can be incorporated. A consequence of this approach is that components are subject to synchronization requirements that vary from configuration to configuration. We have shown several examples of different synchronization requirements and discussed their impact on component design.It is our contention that synchronization is one of the key issues in virtual world construction – it appears in many guises through all levels of system design. A flexible set of synchronized components will allow us to build distributed, multi-user, multimedia virtual worlds. By studying the examples shown in this chapter and other virtual world applications, we hope to develop such a set.

Acknowledgments

We would like to acknowledge the support of the Swiss National Research Foundation (Fonds National de la Recherche Scientifique) under project number 20-29053.90 and the Austrian National Science Foundation (Fonds zur Förderung der wissenschaftlichen Forschung) under contract number J0770-PHY. We would also like to thank Dan Baum, Efi Fogel, Dave Ligon, Jim Winget, Ben Garlick, and Rolf Van Widenfelt, all of Silicon Graphics Inc., for use of the Barcelona Pavilion model.

References

Anderson DP, Homsy G (1991) A Continuous Media I/O Server and Its Synchronization Mechanism, *IEEE Computer*, pp.51-57.

Bishop G et al. (1992) Research Directions in Virtual Environments, *Computer Graphics*, Vol.26, No3, pp.153-175.

Brand S (1987) *The Media Lab - Inventing the Future at MIT*, Donnelley & Sons Company, Harrisonburg, Virginia.

Dannenberg RB et al. (1992) Tactus: Toolkit-Level Support for Synchronized Interactive Multimedia, *Proc. Third International Workshop on Network and Operating System Support for Digital Audio and Video*, pp.264-275.

de Mey V, Breiteneder C, Dami L, Gibbs S, Tsichritzis D (1992) Visual Composition and Multimedia, *Proc. Eurographics '92*, pp.9-22.

de Mey V, Gibbs S (1993) *A Multimedia Component Kit: Experiences with Visual Composition of Applications* to appear ACM Multimedia '93

Ellis CA, Gibbs SJ, Rein GL (1991) Groupware: some Issues and Experiences, *Comm. ACM*, Vol.34, No.1, pp.38-58.

Friedman M, Starner T, Pentland A (1992) Device Synchronization Using an Optimal Linear Filter, *Computer Graphics, Special Issue, Symposium on Interactive 3D Graphics*.

Gibbs S, (1991) Composite Multimedia and Active Objects, *Proc. OOPSLA'91, ACM SIGPLAN Notices*, Vol. 26, No .11, pp.97-112.

Gibbs S, Dami L, Tsichritzis D (1992) An Object-Oriented Framework for Multimedia Composition and Synchronization, in *Multimedia Systems, Interaction and Applications* (Ed. L Kjelldahl), Springer-Verlag, pp. 101-111.

Hanko JG et al. (1991) Workstation Support for Time-Critical Applications, *Proc. Second International Workshop on Network and Operating System Support for Digital Audio and Video*, Springer-Verlag, LNCS 614, pp.4-9.

Little TDC, Ghafoor A, (1991) Spatio-Temporal Composition of Distributed Multimedia for Value-Added Networks, *IEEE Computer*, October 1991, pp.42-50.

Pimentel K and Teixera K (1993) *Virtual Reality*, Intel/Windcrest/McGraw-Hill Inc.

Shaw C, Liang J, Green M, Yunqi S (1992) The Decoupled Simulation Model for Virtual
    Reality Systems, *Proc. CHI'92*, pp.321-328.
Sutherland IE (1965) The Ultimate Display, *Proc. 1965 IFIP Congress* , pp. 506-508.

Appendix: Example Components

The following lists many of the components we are developing for our particular hardware
platform. For each component we give a short name (used in configuration diagrams such as
Figure 11.2) and indicate the media streams that enter and leave the component. Some
components can operate even though not all of their input ports are connected; we use
square brackets to indicate such nonessential input ports. Generally, there may be several
versions of a component, each will have the same input ports but output ports may differ
from version to version. In the table below, square brackets also indicate output ports which
are not present in all versions of the component.

component description	name	input port(s)	output port(s)
audio digital-to-analog converter	DAC	PCM audio	analog audio
audio analog-to-digital converter	ADC	analog audio	PCM audio
audio net reader	ANR	PCM audio	PCM audio
audio net writer	ANW	PCM audio	PCM audio
audio file reader	AFR		PCM audio
audio file writer	AFW	PCM audio	
audio renderer	SND	sound events	analog audio
MIDI synthesizer	MSY	MIDI events	analog audio
MIDI sequencer	MSQ	music events	MIDI events
6D input device ("GeoBall")	G		geometry events
navigator	N	geometry events	animation events
conductor	C	geometry events	music events
animator	A		animation events [sound events] [music events]
modeller	M	animation events	animation events [sound events] [music events]
model tee	MT	animation events	animation events animation events
model recorder	MR	animation events	
model player	MP		animation events
model record/play/edit	MRPE	animation events	animation events
2D and 3D renderers	R2 R3	animation events [NTSC video]	RGB images
framebuffer	F	RGB images	RGB video
workstation monitor	MW	RGB video	
video monitor	MV	NTSC video	
read-only videodisc player	VD		NTSC video
write-once videodisc player	VDRW	NTSC video	NTSC video
video overlay	VO	RGB video NTSC video	RGB video
scan converter	SC	RGB video	NTSC video
video mixer and effects processor	VMIX	NTSC video	NTSC video

Figure 11.2. Virtual museum

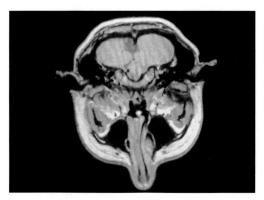

Figure 13.1(a)

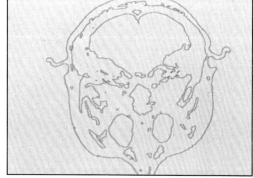

Figure 13.1(b)

Figure 13.1. MRI-slice image (a) and its corresponding binary contour representation obtained with the MTC procedure (b)

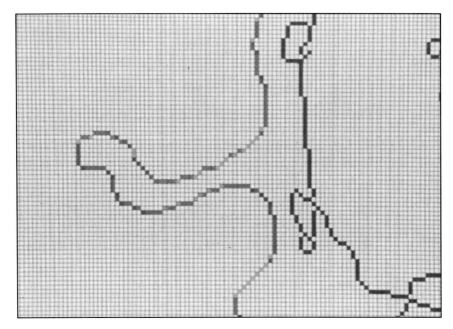

Figure 13.2. Portion of a thinned MRI-slice contour

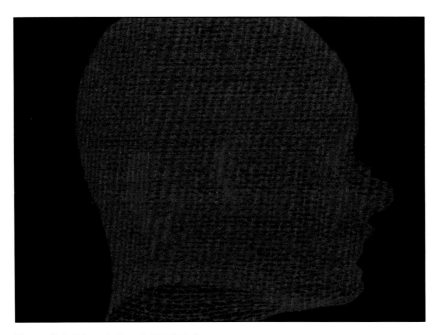

Figure 13.4. Triangulation of 64 MRI slice contours

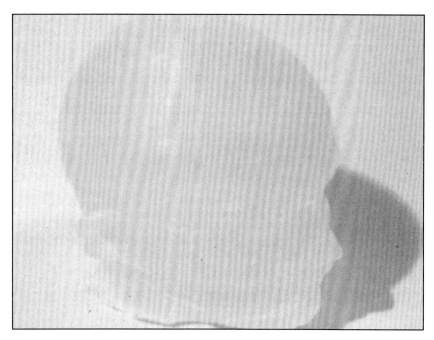

Figure 13.5. Stereolithographic hardcopy of a human head

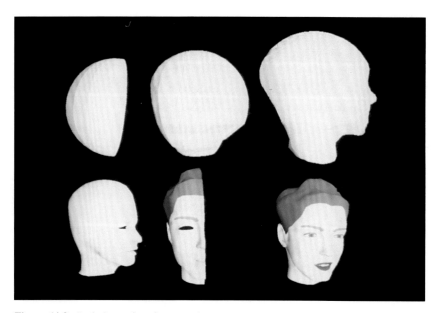

Figure 14.2. Sculpting a face from a sphere

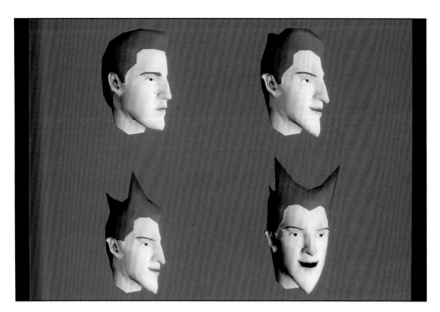

Figure 14.3. Making a devil

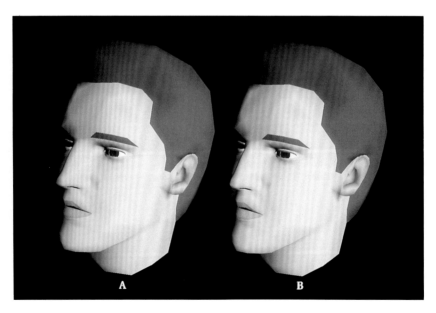

Figure 14.6. Interactive decimation of a head

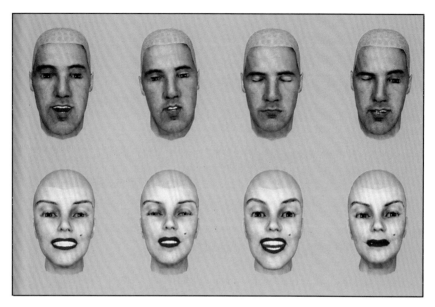

Figure 14.9. An example of a facial animation sequence

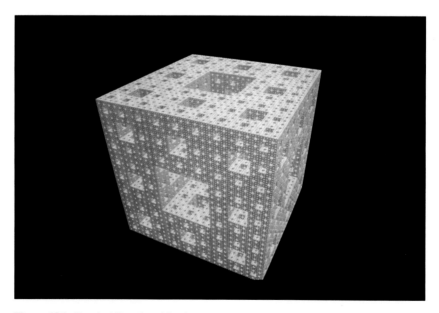

Figure 15.1. Sierpinski's cube of levels

Figure 15.3. A ray-traced scene: classical algorithm

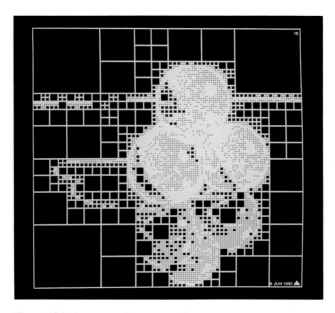

Figure 15.4. A ray-traced scene: quadtree

Figure 15.5. A ray-traced scene: difference image

Figure 15.7. Image rendered using progressive ray tracing

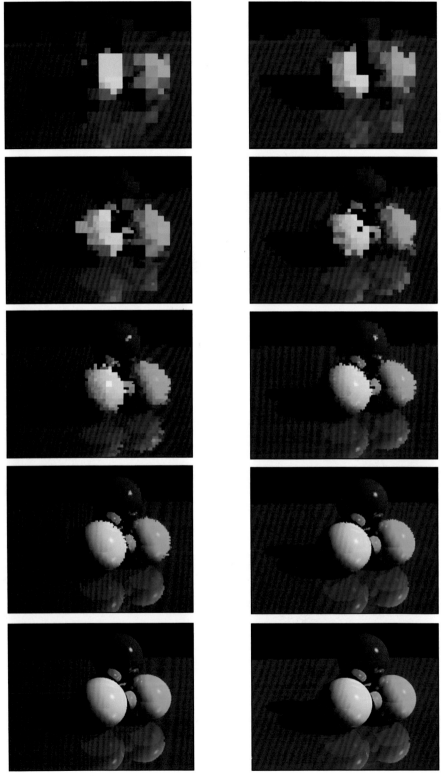

Figure 15.6. 10 progressive steps

12

Software for Geometric Computation: The XYZ GeoBench and Program Library

Jurg Nievergelt
Informatik, ETH, Zurich, Switzerland

12.1. Software for Geometric Computation and the Project XYZ

Geometry merged with automatic computation during the early days of computer graphics in the late fifties (e.g. Sutherland's Sketchpad) to create the discipline of geometric computation. The appearance of computer-aided design (CAD) systems in the sixties greatly widened its range of applications, and gave increased importance to the nagging problem of correctly treating degenerate configurations; whereas a picture can tolerate an occasional error, an engineering design cannot. Computer scientists with a practical orientation working on graphics and CAD pushed the field forward. They developed many interesting algorithms, such as for visibility, and entire classes of related algorithms, such as scan-line algorithms. They collected experimental evidence for comparing the efficiency of different algorithms, and discovered the tantalizing and tough problems of how to compute reliably with degenerate configurations in the presence of roundoff errors. Practitioners laid the foundation for a discipline of geometric computation.

In the seventies, led by Shamos' pioneering Ph.D. thesis, theoretically oriented researchers took over. They brought the finely honed tools of algorithm design and analysis to bear on geometric algorithms and created a new theoretical discipline of computational geometry.

Virtual Worlds and Multimedia Edited by Nadia Magnenat Thalmann and Daniel Thalmann
© 1993 John Wiley and Sons Ltd

The well-defined, conceptually simple algorithmic problems of geometry, and the highly developed techniques of algorithm analysis, proved to be a perfect match. Computational geometry has now enjoyed two decades of rapid progress. It turned a field characterized by trial-and-error into a discipline where no programmer can work competently in ignorance of theory.

Today's research community in computational geometry still focuses primarily on theoretical problems. Research often stops short of investigating practical issues of implementation, so readers are left wondering whether a proposed optimal algorithm is useful in practice – a question not easily answered, but one that must be answered by the researchers, and not left to the applications programmer. It has become abundantly clear that the development of robust and efficient software for geometric computation calls for specialists with a broad range of experience that ranges from algorithm design and analysis to numerics and program optimization.

Even a prototype implementation of just one sophisticated geometric algorithm is an arduous endeavor if attempted without the right tools, such as: a library of abstract data types (e.g. dictionary, priority queue) and corresponding data structures (e.g. balanced tree, heap), reliable geometric primitives (e.g. intersection of 2 line segments), and visualization aids. What the applications programmer needs, but cannot find today, are reliable and efficient reusable software building blocks that perform the most common geometric operations. Geometric modelers, the core of CAD systems, do not address his problems – they are typically monoliths from which an applications programmer cannot extract any useful part for his own program.

The project XYZ (eXperimental geometrY Zurich) aims at a broad range of goals all of which are essential for turning geometric computation from a specialty into a widely practiced discipline:

1. Technology transfer: Exploit recent progress in computational geometry through a systematic study to determine algorithms that lend themselves to robust and practically efficient programs.
2. Verify and evaluate algorithms experimentally: Study the problem of consistency in the presence of roundoff errors, build robust programs to handle all degenerate cases, and implement and compare different algorithms for the same problem, executing them using different number systems.
3. Use state-of-the-art software engineering techniques in a workbench that supports the development of a library of production-quality programs: The XYZ GeoBench (written in Object Pascal for the Macintosh) is a loosely coupled collection of modules held together by a class hierarchy of geometric objects and common abstract data types.
4. Test the software developed by exposing it to the rigors of applications. The GeoBench is being used in education as a programming environment for rapid prototyping and visualization of geometric algorithms. Other application projects underway include: software for terrain modeling, and interfacing the GeoBench as a 'geometry engine' to a spatial data base system.

12.2. The Program Library: Criteria for Selection, Types of Algorithms, Performance

There is no shortage of algorithms for inclusion in a program library for geometric computation. The problem is one of selection, whereby we emphasize the following criteria.

Robustness. A library routine must yield meaningful results for any geometric configuration, including highly degenerate ones. Unlike random data where degenerate configurations are rare, many practical applications generate a lot of highly degenerate configurations – degeneracy comes from the regularity that is inherent in man-made artifacts. The effort to guarantee correct results under all circumstances accounts for the lion's share of programmer time.

Practical efficiency. We strive for programs that are efficient in practice, that is, outperform competing programs on realistic input data. Example: An optimal algorithm can often be modified to run faster on a battery of realistic test data, even though worst-case optimality is no longer guaranteed. This may occur, for example, by replacing a balanced tree implementation of a dictionary by an array implementation. The XYZ library leaves such choices of data structure to the user.

Standard problems of geometric computation. A program library is never comprehensive enough to solve most users' problems directly. We limit ourselves to basic problems that serve as building blocks for advanced geometric programs.

Well understood, elegant algorithms. Algorithms that stand out by virtue of elegant simplicity can be implemented in a straightforward manner. Even when not asymptotically optimal, these tend to do better than their complicated counterparts with respect to robustness and practical efficiency. Some 'optimal' algorithms are just too complicated for a reliable, robust implementation.

12.2.1. Performance and Optimization

As an example of our approach to selecting algorithms for inclusion in the XYZ library, consider the well-known problems of finding the closest pair and all-nearest-neighbors in a set of n points given in the plane. These problems date from the early days of computational geometry (Shamos and Hoey 1975) and admit several optimal algorithms (Preparata and Shamos 1985). Convinced that plane-sweep yields the practically best algorithms for many simple 2-d problems, we developed new algorithms for these well-known problems (Hinrichs et al. 1988, 1992) and compared them to other algorithms implemented on the GeoBench, using comparable coding techniques. Additional experimental results can be found in (Schorn 1992).

As is the case for many proximity problems, closest pair and all-nearest-neighbors can be solved easily in linear time after the powerful $O(n \log n)$ preprocessing step of computing the Voronoi diagram. But the diagram contains much more information than required, and this costs time, as reflected in the run times in Figure 12.1 below. Vaidya's box-shrinking algorithm (Vaidya 1989) is another general approach that works in any number of dimensions. In contrast, plane-sweep yields direct solutions tailored to 2-d point proximity problems whose code complexity, memory requirements, and run times compare favorably with its competitors, as figure 12.1 below shows. All algorithms are implemented as part of the XYZ library. The box-shrinking algorithm is optimized for $d = 2$; the Voronoi-based algorithm uses the efficient Fortune's sweep (Fortune 1987). The graph with logarithmic scales in Figure 12.1 shows run times in seconds for these three algorithms on a Macintosh IIfx, implemented using the same floating point arithmetic. The test data are random point sets uniformly distributed in a square. Assuming a formula of the form $c \cdot n \cdot \log_2 n$ for the run times, the table shows the experimentally determined constants for all three algorithms, and the maximum size of a configuration that can be handled in a 4 MB partition.

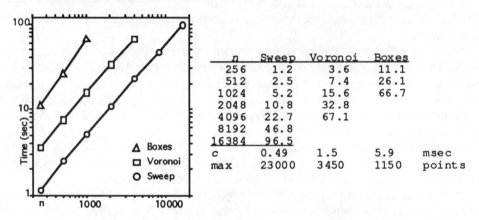

n	Sweep	Voronoi	Boxes	
256	1.2	3.6	11.1	
512	2.5	7.4	26.1	
1024	5.2	15.6	66.7	
2048	10.8	32.8		
4096	22.7	67.1		
8192	46.8			
16384	96.5			
c	0.49	1.5	5.9	msec
max	23000	3450	1150	points

Figure 12.1. Performance measurements for three all-nearest-neighbors algorithms

2-d algorithms currently in the library include:

- Convex hull (Graham's scan, divide and conquer)
- Diameter, distance and intersection of convex polygons
- Tangents common to two convex polygons
- Boolean operations (union, intersection, difference) on polygons
- Contour of a set of rectangles
- Winding number
- Point(s) in polygon test
- Intersection of line segments (sweep line for the first intersection and for reporting all intersections, sweep line for the special case of horizontal and vertical line segments)
- Closest pair of points (sweep line [with heuristic], projection method, divide and conquer, probabilistic)
- Closest pair of line segments
- Closest pair of convex polygons
- All-nearest-neighbors (sweep line, simplified sweep line, extraction from Voronoi diagram, Vaidya's box-shrinking algorithm, projection method)
- All-nearest-neighbors in a sector
- Voronoi diagram (sweep line)
- Euclidean minimum spanning tree (EMST)

- Traveling salesman heuristics (nearest neighbor, EMST, convex hull, tour optimizer)
- 2-*d* tree operations (insert, range query, show partition)
- quad-tree operations (creation, boolean operations)
- Lower envelope of a set of line segments
- Triangulation of a (monotone) polygon [with holes]
- Smallest area disk enclosing a set of points (randomized incremental, also in *d*-dimensions)
- Guard File algorithms (retrieval of geometric objects in response to intersection queries)

The presence of distinct algorithms for solving the same problem reflects our concern for experimental assessment and comparison.

12.3. The XYZ Software Packages

The main goal of the project XYZ is to make available to the practitioner a loosely coupled collection of carefully crafted software packages, in particular:

- The XYZ GeoBench, a programmer's workbench
- The XYZ Program Library, an open-ended collection of geometric algorithms
- The XYZ Grid File, a package for managing spatial data on disk

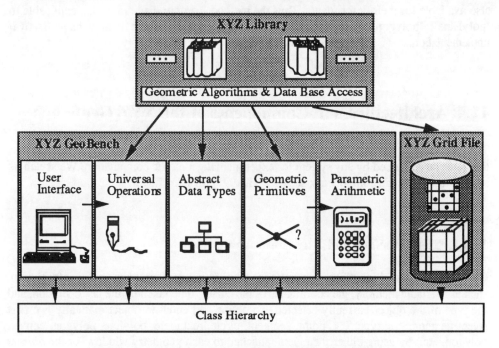

Figure 12.2. The relationship among the XYZ software packages

The relationship among these three packages and the class hierarchy that defines all common object types are shown in Figures 12.2 and 12.3, where an arrow indicates the relationship 'is_based_on'.

The GeoBench is the programmer's workbench and run-time environment that holds all the library programs and the disk storage grid file package together, keeping them data-compatible. Its components serve the following functions. The user interface manages windows for interactive data generation and algorithm animation, as illustrated in Figure 12.4. A collection of the most important geometric primitives and abstract data types, and various implementations thereof, saves the programmer a lot of time-consuming detail work. A parameterized arithmetic package supports experimental program validation by providing floating point arithmetic of varying precision and base.

The library is an open-ended collection of geometric algorithms that work in central memory, and of disk access procedures that pack geometric objects into grid files and perform queries on them. The grid file disk management package provides multidimensional data access for an arbitrary number of dimensions, each of which is individually measured by one of the types integer, long-integer, or real.

Figure 12.3 shows the backbone of this software: the class hierarchy that defines the common data types and serves as interface between all software components. This tree describes the 'is_a' relationships among the classes currently in the GeoBench. Algorithms are methods associated with the class on which they operate. For example, the Voronoi algorithm is a method in the class 'pointVector' that yields an object of type 'voronoiDiagram'. The principle of inheritance insures that all methods for a given class are also available for their descendants. Thus the method Voronoi diagram is also applicable to 'polyLine', 'polygon', and 'convexPolygon', for each of which it may have its own implementation.

12.4. Architecture and Components of the XYZ GeoBench

The GeoBench, a workbench for algorithm development, embodies solutions to many issues that must be addressed by any system for experimental geometric computation. We sketch its architecture and main components; see (Schorn 1991) for more detail.

12.4.1. User Interface and Algorithm Animation

GeoBench follows Macintosh conventions. An *info window* contains useful information, such as available memory, the coordinates of the cursor, time taken by the last operation, and the type of the object currently selected. To define and enter an object manually, we first select its geometric type (e.g. point, segment, circle, rectangle, polyline, polygon, convex polygon, etc.) by using either the palette attached to each geometry window, or the *objects menu*.The latter can also create random data.

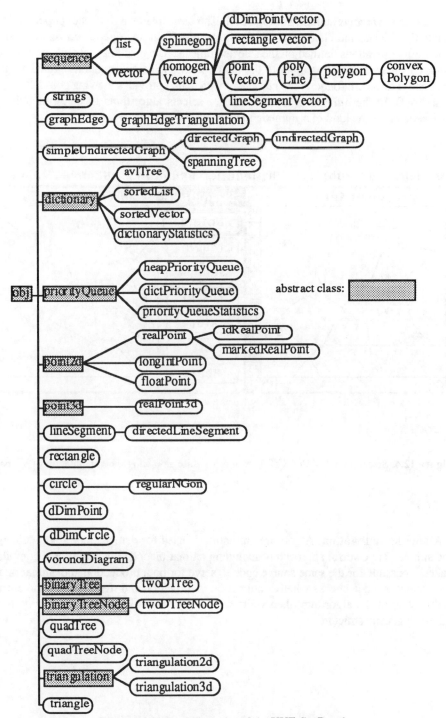

Figure 12.3. Class hierarchy of the XYZ GeoBench

Geometry windows support computation. The user creates a new one, populates it with geometric objects, and chooses the desired operation from the *operations menu*. The latter shows only operations defined on the selected objects. The result appears in a newly created window, where it serves as input to the next operation. Transformations (translate, rotate, scale and reflect) are found in the *edit menu* which also provides viewing commands (zoom in and out). In the *animation menu* the user selects algorithms to be animated, in the *arithmetic menu* the kind of arithmetic to be used.

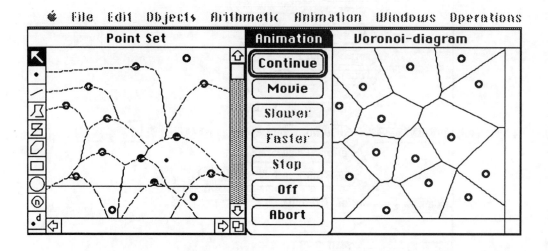

Figure 12.4. Screen dump of the XYZ GeoBench while animating the computation of a Voronoi diagram using Fortune's sweep

Algorithm animation. Algorithm animation is used for demonstrating and debugging. The simple yet powerful approach of including animation code via conditional compilation makes it possible for the same source code to serve for both production and animation runs. The animation code checks whether animation is turned on and if so, updates the currently visible state of the algorithm, then waits for the user to let it proceed. This code has the following general structure.

```
...
{ Geometric algorithm changing internal state. }
{$IFC myAlgAnim }
        if animationFlag[myAlgAnim] then
                { Update graphical state information, usually draw some objects. }
                waitForClick(animationFlag[myAlgAnim]);
                { Update graphical state information, usually erase some objects. }
        end;
{$ENDC }
...
```

The procedure 'waitForClick' lets the user control the algorithm being animated. It supports single step mode and a movie mode with user-selectable speed (see the 'Animation' dialog box in the previous screen dump). All drawing on the screen uses XOR graphics, with the benefit that erasing is the same as drawing. Animating an algorithm consists of choosing a representation of the internal state (e.g. position of the sweep line, objects in the *y*-table, deactivated objects, etc.) and determining appropriate locations in the program where this information needs updating.

12.4.2. Primitive Objects and Operations

The type 'point2d' is the basic building block for all geometric objects: all primitive operations (a surprisingly small set of about a dozen geometric operations) are methods in this class and are usually implemented in three different ways taking advantage of the respective arithmetic. A dozen geometric primitives take care of most operations that occur in all library programs. 'whichSide' is the most frequently used primitive: it determines on which side of a directed line segment a given point lies.

12.4.3. Interchangeable Arithmetic and Parameterized Floating Point Arithmetic

The choice of arithmetic has a significant impact on the behavior of an implemented algorithm, in particular for degenerate or nearly degenerate configurations, and we wish to experiment with different arithmetics. In the best case, no line of code of an implementation must be modified in order to try out a different model of arithmetic. Since points are the basic building block of all geometric objects, we achieve this goal by defining an abstract class 'point2d' (Figure 12.5); it has no instance variables for the coordinates, but it specifies an interface that includes access procedures to the coordinates, and various geometric primitives.

From this abstract 'point2d' we derive concrete point objects having instance variables and implementing geometric primitives in their respective arithmetic systems. Algorithms that use only the functions and procedures specified by the abstract type 'point2d' can run in any of the three kinds of arithmetics currently supported.

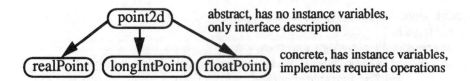

Figure 12.5. The abstract class 'point2d' and its descendants

In order to study not only the built-in floating point arithmetic (as used in 'realPoint' whose *x*- and *y*-coordinates are of type *real*), the GeoBench contains a software floating point package with arbitrary base and precision (used for the coordinates of the object 'floatPoint'). Although it can be used to simulate high precision arithmetic, its main purpose is low precision to accentuate rounding errors and other problems of floating point arithmetic and thus facilitates testing.

12.4.4. Abstract Data Types

The abstract data types most often used by geometric algorithms are sequence, dictionary, and queue. The GeoBench has several implementations for each of these, e.g:

Sequence: linked list and (dynamic) array
Dictionary: balanced and unbalanced tree, sorted list, sorted vector
Priority queue: heap, or based on any dictionary implementation.

Different implementations have a great impact on efficiency, favoring different data configurations and a priori knowledge about them. List structures are useful when no a priori bound on the number of elements is known, array implementations are faster when they are feasible, and support more functions (based on address computation).

12.4.5. Universal Operations

Object oriented programming lets us specify a common interface understood by all objects in the system by placing this interface at the root of the object hierarchy. All objects in the GeoBench are descendants of the root object 'obj' and thus share many common methods that we call 'universal operations'. A typical example is the ability for an object to display itself on the screen. Other universal operations include:

Memory management: Create, initialize, duplicate, destroy objects.
Interactive input/output: Display, highlight, flash an object.
File input/output: Save objects permanently on secondary storage.
Geometric transformations: Translate, rotate, scale, mirror image with respect to a given line.
Generate random instances.

Class description and method execution: Given a list of arbitrary objects, each class delivers all the methods it can execute on these objects in human readable form. Given three points, e.g., the class 'point2d' offers a method for creating a circle, the class 'pointVector' offers a method for computing a closest pair and a Voronoi diagram.

12.5. Uses and Applications

During its entire period of development, the XYZ GeoBench and program library have served as a useful demonstration package and tool for algorithm animation in courses on algorithms and data structures. Now that the GeoBench is essentially complete, we are also using it as a programming environment for term projects and in a course on computational geometry. Work on realistic applications started only recently; we briefly describe two ongoing projects.

12.5.1. Layered Objects and Triangulated Surfaces for Terrain Modeling

Layered objects are an attempt to reconcile two conflicting facts of geometric computation: on the one hand, it is well known that 2-dimensional geometric algorithms are usually a lot simpler and more efficient (often $O(n \log n)$) than their 3-d counterparts (usually $O(n^2)$ or higher); on the other hand, most applications call for 3-d geometry. Fortunately, the objects to be processed in any one application are often subject to restrictions that make it profitable to define various restricted classes of 3-d objects with special properties that yield to simpler algorithms than unrestricted 3-d objects.

Layered objects are a striking example of the benefits and limitations of this approach: a 3-d object is represented or approximated as a vector of layers (parallel slices orthogonal to the z-axis), where each layer is defined by its thickness and a 2-d contour. Important classes of real-world objects are naturally modeled as layered objects, such as terrain (using contour lines), certain semiconductor devices (perhaps using projections and cross-sections), and, in general, objects whose shape is defined by one or more functions of the type $z = f(x, y)$. Layered models are particularly appropriate in CAD systems for stereolithography, a new manufacturing technology that 'grows' 3-d objects one layer at a time. Each layer is defined by tracing its outline with a laser and marking the part that is to remain; the latter hardens on top of the preceding layer when exposed to light.

Layered objects are particularly effective, as is the case with maps, when the number L of layers needed to achieve a desired accuracy is small compared to the complexity n of the 2-d figures in each layer. Operations on layered objects typically trigger a sequence of calls to 2-d algorithms, one for each of L layers, and thus work in time $O(L\, n \log n)$. This often compares favorably to the complexity $O(N^2)$ of a quadratic algorithm on a comparable unrestricted 3-d object of complexity N, where a fair comparison suggests $n < N < L\, n$.

Layered objects simplify the problems of 3-d processing, but they do not eliminate the necessity to consider the third dimension explicitly. When computing the visible surface, for example, we wish to look at a layered object from an arbitrarily chosen point of view (not necessarily at infinity). This results in clipping a stack of layers against a pyramid in arbitrary position, a true 3-*d* problem. A second example is the problem of correct treatment of all degenerate configurations: layered objects exhibit new types of degeneracies beyond those that occur in 2-*d*. In addition to visibility, we have implemented boolean or set-theoretic operations, as shown in Figure 12.6 below.

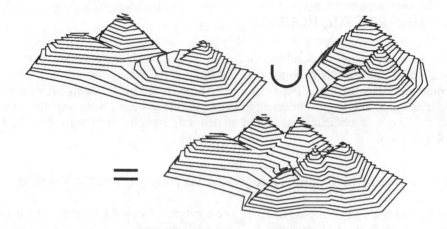

Figure 12.6. Union of two layered objects

But the staircase shape of layered objects makes them unsuitable models for the graphic representation of smooth objects, so we are also introducing triangulated surfaces as an alternative 3-*d* model. As terrain modeling requires seemingly realistic images, we experiment with the automatic generation of synthetic images, with gray-levels or color-shading (a graphics problem rather than a geometric problem). As an example, the terrain image in Figure 12.7 is generated automatically from geographic (x, y, z)-data that represents Switzerland on a 250m × 250m grid.

12.5.2. A Geometry Engine as Front End to a Spatial Data Base

The interplay between geometric algorithms and spatial data bases. The growing importance of spatial data bases, for which efficient data access is perhaps the major technical issue, has created a fertile interaction between computational geometry and spatial data structures suited for processing large volumes of data stored on disks. Traditionally, algorithms of computational geometry and their complexity results are based on the 'random-access-machine model of computation'. This model provides realistic performance predictions as long as all the data fits in central memory, where access time to any data element is constant. When large data configurations must be processed off disk, on the other hand, disk access usually becomes the bottleneck. The efficiency of computation is then determined primarily by the interplay between two issues: 1) How data is stored on disk, and 2) in what order algorithms access data.

Figure 12.7. Gray level map of the southern slope of the Alps (Ticino and Lombardia) automatically generated from geometric data

1) **How spatial data is stored on disk.** We have studied the major design choices and their consequences in two surveys of spatial data structures (Nievergelt 1989; Widmayer 1991). For the XYZ GeoBench we have chosen a Grid File (Nievergelt et al. 1984) as a general-purpose multidimensional data structure for storing geometric objects on disk. (Nievergelt and Hinrichs 1987) describes how a broad range of proximity queries are answered efficiently on large collections of objects stored as points in parameter space.

2) **In what order algorithms access data.** Geometric algorithms can be classified according to their data access pattern as follows:

- Sweeps: data is accessed in an order (e.g. of increasing x) known a priori.
- Boundary traversal: data access obeys a spatial locality principle, but is only known at run time.
- Recursive partitioning: data access is usually random.

The advantages of a predictable data access pattern, and the disadvantages of random access, are even more pronounced when the data is processed off disk. Thus the preponderance of sweep algorithms in the XYZ library, and the choice of layered objects for 3-d modeling, are a consequence of our aim at applications such as terrain modeling that require efficient processing of very large data volumes.

In an effort to provide rapid retrieval of the most frequently occurring proximity queries on spatial data bases, namely, stabbing and intersection queries, we have developed the Guard File (Nievergelt and Widmayer 1993) access and update algorithms for geometric objects that meet certain shape constraints.

The tight coupling between the XYZ GeoBench and its Grid File allows us to focus on algorithms that interact in a particularly efficient way with the grid file data structure. The typical situation in applications that process large volumes of spatial data, however, is different. Usually, the user's data is organized and stored in some commercial spatial data management system that provides a few types of spatial queries only – clearly a spatial data base system cannot anticipate the access patterns of all algorithms its users might run on its data. Thus it is an open question in spatial data base research as to how efficiently geometric algorithms interface with typical built-in queries. In order to explore this issue, we started a joint project with the database research group at ETH (H.-J. Schek) where the GeoBench is used as a front end to a spatial data base system built on DASDBS (Dröge et al. 1990). The first experiments aim to use the GeoBench as a powerful user interface for retrieving data from the data base, perform geometric operations on it, and finally store (modified) objects back in the data base. In a second phase we aim at a tighter coupling based on the extension capabilities of DASDBS, i.e. the ability to manage arbitrary geometric objects provided a certain set of (geometric) operations is supplied.

12.6. Conclusion

We have presented an overview of a research project that attacks the practical problems of software development for geometric computation on a broad front. The XYZ GeoBench in particular has proven its usefulness in numerous implementations of geometric algorithms. Its animation capability is regularly used for demonstrating algorithms in courses at ETH. Experiments have led to some surprising insights about efficiency and robustness of well-known algorithms. Several application projects are underway, in particular the interaction between a 'geometry engine' and spatial data bases. Current efforts focus on making the GeoBench run on a parallel computer and exploit the parallelism inherent in many geometric algorithms.

Acknowledgments

Peter Schorn is the main architect of the GeoBench; Christoph Ammann, Michele De Lorenzi, Adrian Brüngger and many students have made valuable contributions. Hans Hinterberger and Björn Beeli implemented the XYZ Grid File. This chapter is a compressed and updated version of two papers (Nievergelt et al. 1991) and (Schorn 1991).

References

Bieri H, Noltemeier H (eds.) (1991) Computational Geometry: Methods, Algorithms and Applications. *Proc. CG'91, International Workshop on Comp. Geometry*, Bern, Springer LNCS, 553.

Dröge G, Schek HJ, Wolf A (1990) Erweiterbarkeit in DASDBS, *Informatik Forschung und Entwicklung* 5,4 (special issue on Non-Standard-Data-Systems), pp. 162-176.

Fortune S (1987) A Sweepline Algorithm for Voronoi Diagrams, *Algorithmica* 2, pp. 153-174.

Hinrichs K, Nievergelt J, Schorn P (1988) Plane-Sweep Solves the Closest Pair Problem Elegantly, *Information Processing Letters* 26, pp. 255-261.

Hinrichs K, Nievergelt J, Schorn P (1992) An all-round sweep algorithm for 2-dimensional nearest-neighbor problems, *Acta Informatica*, Vol.29, pp. 383-394.

Nievergelt J, Hinterberger H, Sevcik K (1984) The Grid File: An adaptable, symmetric multikey file structure. *ACM Trans. Database Systems*, Vol. 9, No. 1, pp. 35-45.

Nievergelt J, Hinrichs K (1987) Storage and access structures for geometric data bases. *Proc. Kyoto 85 Intern. Conf. on Foundations of Data Structures* (eds. Ghosh et al.), Plenum Press, pp. 441-455, NY.

Nievergelt J (1989) 7 ± 2 criteria for assessing and comparing spatial data structures, in A. Buchman et al. eds.: Design and Implementation of Large Spatial Databases, invited paper, *1st Symp. SSD'89*, UC Santa Barbara, Lecture Notes CS 409, Springer, pp. 3-27.

Nievergelt J , Schorn P, Ammann C, Brüngger A, De Lorenzi M (1991) XYZ: A project in experimental geometric computation, in (Bieri and Noltemeier 1991), pp. 171-186.

Nievergelt J, Widmayer P (1993) Guard File algorithms for efficient retrieval of geometric objects in response to intersection queries, submitted.

Preparata F, Shamos MI (1985) *Computational Geometry: An Introduction*, Springer.

Schorn P (1991) Implementing the XYZ GeoBench: A programming environment for geometric algorithms, in (Bieri and Noltemeier 1991).

Schorn P (1992) The XYZ GeoBench for the experimental evaluation of geometric algorithms, *DIMACS Workshop on Computational Support for Discrete Mathematics*.

Shamos, M, Hoey D (1975) Closest-Point Problems, *16th Annual IEEE Symposium on Foundations of Computer Science*, pp.151-162.

Vaidya P (1989) An $O(n \log n)$ Algorithm for the All-Nearest-Neighbors Problem, *Discrete & Computational Geometry*, Vol.4 , pp.101-115.

Widmayer P (1991) *Datenstrukturen für Geodatenbanken*, Tech. Report, Univ. Freiburg.

13

3D-Copying Using Surface Reconstruction from Tomography Slices

Peter Stucki, Abdelhakim Ghezal
University of Zurich, Department of Computer Science
Multimedia Laboratory, Zurich, Switzerland

13.1. Introduction

There exist several approaches to the computerized reconstruction of 3D-objects from tomography slices and it is common practice to classify them into volume-oriented and surface-oriented categories (Höhne et al. 1988; Fuchs et al. 1989).

The volume-oriented 3D-reconstruction is used whenever views representing inhomogenous volume structures are required. This is the case for complex three dimensional, microscopic structures such as anatomic arterial systems and small tumors for example. The exact diagnosis of these structures is essential for planning clinical surgery, radiation therapy or invasive procedures in medicine. The underlying processing principles in volume-oriented 3D-reconstruction are based on volume elements (voxel) that are handled according to procedures commonly used in digital image processing.

The surface-oriented 3D-reconstruction is used whenever views of homogeneous volume structures are required. In this case, the end-user community is not restricted to the medical professional but it may include scientists and engineers interested in a variety of different scientific visualization tasks. Hull-based 3D-representations find their use in many applications such as computer-aided instruction, scientific visualization, model-based recognition and super data-compression. The underlying principles in surface-oriented 3D-

Virtual Worlds and Multimedia Edited by Nadia Magnenat Thalmann and Daniel Thalmann
© 1993 John Wiley and Sons Ltd

reconstruction are based on procedures commonly used in both image analysis and image synthesis.

The potential of surface-oriented 3D-object reconstruction is based on the following characteristics: 1) The underlying polygon meshes represent a compact data structure that can be interactively manipulated and visualized as wire-frame or photorealistic representation (Ghezal and Stucki 1990), 2) the compact data structures can be stored and transmitted at minimum cost (Huang 1990), and 3) homogeneous physical 3D-objects can be built using the technique of stereolithography (Wohlers 1990).

Although many of the general principles used to process MRI-slices and to derive surface-oriented 3D-reconstructions from it are known in theory, present implementations still have some serious shortcomings. Most of them can be traced back to the fact that the implemented procedures and algorithms lack in sophistication to cope with elaborate structures and shapes. The purpose of this chapter is to describe the design and the implementation of new and robust signal processing and triangulation mechanisms that will overcome the shortcomings mentioned.

13.2. Acquisition of Magnetic Resonance Image (MRI) Data

The development and implementation of surface-oriented 3D-reconstruction procedures can be applied to any set of cross-sectional images or slices $f(x,y)$ from a 3D-object. For the experiments reported in this chapter, N = 64 slices obtained from an MRI scan of a human head are being used. For a total scanning displacement of L=8 inches, this corresponds to a transversal resolution Ts = N/L of approximately 8 MRI-slices/inch. Each of these N = 64 slices is digitized in surface and amplitude with x = y = 512 pixel, corresponding to a physical sampling resolution of 25 lines/inch in x and y and a signal range of Q = 256 amplitude levels.

13.3. Processing MRI-Slices

13.3.1 The Contour Detection Process

The detection of edges is possible under the assumption that at a given pixel position x, y, the derivative of the image function $f(x,y)$ is nonzero. An edge in an image can be characterized by its direction D and its magnitude M. The intensity profile is assumed to be more or less uniform along the edge. The simplest method to detect edges is to determine the gradient

$$G = \left[\frac{\partial f(x,y)}{\partial x} \cdot \frac{\partial f(x,y)}{\partial y} \right]^T$$

(13.1)

of the image function $f(x,y)$; an edge is said to be present when the magnitude of the gradient

$$|G| = \sqrt{\left(\frac{\partial f^2(x,y)}{\partial x^2} + \frac{\partial f^2(x,y)}{\partial y^2} \right)}$$ (13.2)

exceeds a certain threshold T. There exists a large number of publications in the open literature that are concerned with manifold aspects of edge detection. In particular many approaches have been developed that approximate the gradient in a digital domain. They can be generally classified into linear and nonlinear filtering techniques. The most commonly procedures used today are based on the Sobel-, the Laplace- and the compass-gradient algorithms (Gonzales and Wintz 1987; Pratt 1978; Pavlidis 1982).

In a first step, each pixel value of the image function $f(x,y)$ is compared to a threshold value T1 and the resulting outcome is a picture element of a binary image function $g(x,y)$. To determine the optimum value of T1, an extended amplitude distribution analysis of the raw data is necessary. For this purpose, histograms of all 64 digital continuous-tone MRI-slice representations have been analyzed. The results obtained can be described as follows: there exists a pronouncedly flat Gaussian amplitude distribution from 'white to dark gray', e.g. amplitude level 0 to 215 in the MRI-slice images and a steep but truncated Gauss-shaped amplitude distribution from 'dark gray to black', e.g. amplitude level 216 to 255 in the MRI-slice image. This observation proves to be very consistent for all digital continuous-tone MRI-slice images. Furthermore, it is strongly related to the 3D-object under consideration, e.g. the human head as object as well as the parameter settings of the Gyroscan MR-scanner used. Approximating the average amplitude quantization function with a piecewise linear envelope representation shows a major and narrow envelope intersection bandwidth that ranges from amplitude level 205 to amplitude level 215 approximately. Therefore the fixing of the threshold value T1 to an amplitude level of T=210 yields optimum results.

In a second step, a linear filtering process defined as

$$f'(x,y) = \sum_{k=-K}^{+K} \sum_{l=-L}^{+L} H(k,l)g(x-k,y-l)$$ (13.3)

is performed in which the binary image function $g(x,y)$ is convolved with a Laplacian mask $H(k,l)$ consisting of a $(2K+1)$ by $(2L+1)$ window. In the case where $K = L = 1$, the Laplacian mask $H(k,l)$ amounts to

$$H(3,3) = \begin{matrix} -1 & -1 & -1 \\ -1 & 8 & -1 \\ -1 & -1 & -1 \end{matrix}$$

(13.4)

The following thinning process requires as input a binary image function. Therefore, each pixel of the intermediate image function f'(x,y) has to be compared to a second threshold value T2 and the resulting outcome is a picture element of an inverted binary image function g'(x,y). Statistical investigations show that the selection of a value for T2 is not critical. An example of a raw-data MRI-slice image and its corresponding contour representation obtained with the above described Multiple Thresholding and Convolution (MTC) procedure is shown in Figure 13.1 (see Color Section).

If the parameters of the MTC procedure are properly matched to the characteristics of the MRI-scanner used, the fully automatically obtained contour-plots are interrupt-free and no further computationally intensive connectivity procedures are needed.

13.3.2 Thinning of MTC Processed Data

Thinning, also called skeletonization, is an important procedure used in computer vision for feature extraction. There exists a mathematical definition of a skeleton S of a region R using the Medial Axis Transformation (MAT). The definition of the MAT of a region R with border B can be given as follows: for every point p in R, The nearest neighbor n in B such that there is no other point in B whose Euclidean distance from p is less than the distance |pn|, must be first computed. The point p is said to be a skeletal point of R or it belongs to the medial axis if p has more than one such nearest neighbor. The union of all skeletal points is called the skeleton of R. Unfortunately, a direct implementation of the above definition is very time consuming due to the lengthy computation of the distance of every interior point in the given region to every point on the region boundary. This general procedure is therefore not practical.

In the open literature, a large number of methods for obtaining the skeleton of binary images can be found (Pavlidis 1982; Naccache and Shinghal 1984; Chin et al. 1987; Wang and Zhang 1989) and a few publications of algorithms for gray-scale images (Dyer and Rosenfeld 1979; Salari and Siy 1984). The latter group of algorithms still represents problems that have not yet been solved satisfactorily for application in pattern recognition. The methods known today are complicated and do not guarantee the global connectivity and the single pixel thickness of the extracted skeletons. These conditions, however, are of paramount importance for the execution of the remaining processes needed for the automatic surface reconstruction of 3D-objects.

When processing binary images, thinning consists of an iterative deletion of black picture elements, i.e., changing them to white, along a pattern until the latter is narrowed down to a skeleton consisting of open or closed curves of single picture element width. In practice, an algorithm that performs the process of pattern-thinning must fulfil the following performance conditions: 1)The deletion of a point does not remove endpoints, 2) The thickness of the skeleton is reduced to a single pixel, 3) The deletion of a point does not break connectedness, 4) The shape of the skeleton must be similar to the shape of the original object, 5) Distortion of the object topology must be kept as small as possible, 6) The deletion of a point should not cause any erosion of the region, 7) The skeleton must have a certain medial position in that region. After an extended evaluation of the performance characteristics of the many skeletonizing algorithms enumerated above, it was decided to use the fast thinning algorithm developed by T. Y. Zhang and C. Y. Suen (1984). This algorithm performs in a very efficient manner and yields good results without violating the performance conditions outlined. In order to describe the Zhang/Suen algorithm, the following definitions shall be introduced:

Definition 1:   The 8-neighbors of a pixel p1 = p1(i,j), are p2 = p(i,j+1), p3 = p(i+1,j+1), p4 = p(i+1,j), p5 = p(i+1,j-1), p6 = p(i,j-1), p7 = p(i-1,j-1), p8 = p(i-1,j), and p9 = p(i-1,j+1).

Definition 2:   The contour point of a digital pattern is defined as a pixel valued 1 (black) and having at least one of its 8-neighbors valued 0 (white).

The execution of the Zhang/Suen algorithm consists of successive passes of two basic steps applied to the contour points of the given pattern region. The first step marks a contour point p1 as a candidate for deletion if the following conditions are satisfied:

a) $2 \leq N(p1) \leq 6$,   b) $S(p1) = 1$ c) $p2.p4.p6 = 0$,   d) $p4.p6.p8 = 0$,

where $N(p1)$ is the number of nonzero neighbors of p1; that is,

$$N(p1) = p2+p3+p4+p5+p6+p7+p8+p9$$

and $S(p1)$ is the number of 0/1 transitions in the ordered sequence of

$$p2, p3,..., p8, p9.$$

In the second step, conditions a) and b) remain the same, but conditions c) and d) are changed to

c') $p2.p4.p8 = 0$,   d') $p2.p6.p8 = 0$.

Condition a) is violated when p1 has only one or seven of the 8-neighbors valued 1. In the first case this implies that p1 is the endpoint of the skeleton and obviously should not be deleted. In the second case, if p1 has seven neighbors, it should not be deleted because this would cause erosion into that region. Condition b) prevents the deletion of those points that lie between the endpoints of the skeleton which leads to disconnections of segments of the skeleton during the thinning operation. Conditions c) and d) of the first subiteration are satisfied simultaneously when p4 = 0, or p6 = 0, or p2 = 0 and p8 = 0. A point that satisfies conditions a), b), c), and d) is an East- or South-boundary point, or a Northwest-corner point in the boundary. In either case p1 is not part of the ideal skeleton and should be removed. Similarly, conditions c)' and d)' are satisfied simultaneously if p2 = 0, or p8 = 0, or p4 = 0 and p6 = 0 corresponding to north- or west-boundary points, or to a Southeast-corner point. An portion of a thinned MRI-slice contour obtained with the procedure described above is shown in Figure 13.2 (see Color Section).

13.3.3. Freeman Chain-Encoding Technique

Finally, the thinned boundary contour of each slice is encoded using the well-known Freeman chain-encoding technique for binary images as described below (Freeman 1977).

A system of integer x-y coordinates is called a grid, and a point of integer is called a digital point or pel. Let $A(i,j)$ be a pel and $A(i+1,j)$, $A(i+1,j+1)$, $A(i,j+1)$, $A(i-1,j+1)$, $A(i-1,j)$, $A(i-1,j-1)$, $A(i,j-1)$, $A(i-1, j+1)$ the 8-neighbors of $A(i,j)$. They are labelled numerically, $0\equiv$East, $1\equiv$Northeast, $2\equiv$North, $3\equiv$Northwest, $4\equiv$West, $5\equiv$Southwest, $6\equiv$South and $7\equiv$Southeast respectively. The numbers are noted counter-clockwise with respect to the relative positions of neighbors of $A(i,j)$. A set of pels is called a chain-code or digital arc if every pel except two (the first and the last) in the set has exactly two neighbors, where the neighbors are elements of the set. The first and the last ones have only one neighbor. The Freeman chain-encoding technique is based on the following algorithm: select the starting pel as one of the two pels of having only one neighbor. Identify the neighbor of the starting pel and record the relative position number ranging from 0 to 7. From this neighboring pel, identify its nonselected neighbor and record the position number. From this new neighbor, identify its nonselected neighbor and so on until the ending pel is found. Hence, the process is similar to tracing a chained link until it reaches the last link. Therefore, a curve can be reconstructed from a starting pel followed by a sequence of neighboring numbers. This sequence is called chain-code of directions. In the present application, the extracted curves are closed and the result of the Freeman chain-encoding step is a polygon representation of the outline scans which is equivalent to a finite set of collinear control points at any adjacent slices.

13.4. Generation of Synthetic 3D-Surfaces

13.4.1. Triangulation

Definition 1: A domain D in the n-dimensional Euclidean space E^n is convex if, for any two points q1 and q2 in D, the segment q1q2 is entirely contained in D.

Definition 2: A convex hull of a set of a finite set of points S in E^n is the boundary of the smallest convex domain in E^n containing S.

A triangulation of a finite set S of points is a partition of the plane called planar sub-division whenever its bounded regions are triangles. It is a planar graph on S with the maximum number of edges. This is equivalent to saying that the triangulation of S is obtained by joining the points of S by nonintersecting straight-line segments so that every region internal to the convex hull is a triangle (Preparata and Shamos 1985).

The general problem of triangulation can be stated as follows: let n be a given number of points in the plane. The question then arises of how to join these points by nonintersecting straight-line segments so that every region internal to the convex hull is a triangle. In practice there exists a triangulation procedure known as the greedy triangulation algorithm that solves the above problem in a straightforward manner. In the following, the essence of this algorithm is summarized.

Let S be a set of n points in the plane. First, the $\binom{n}{2}$ edges between all points of S are generated and ordered by increasing lengths in a list of edges and the triangulation is initialized as empty. Second, the shortest edge is picked and removed from the list. If this edge does not intersect with any of the current triangulation edges, it is added to the triangulation or discarded otherwise. The process correctly terminates either when the triangulation is complete or when the list of edges is empty.

In the present case, triangulation is applied to adjacent sets of slices with collinear control points. This ordered arrangement of the processed MRI slice contours represents a unique situation in which the different adjacent control points derived from the Freeman chain-encoding will be triangulated using polygon approximation. The use of triangles in the surface approximation has the advantage of defined plane and plane-normal situations. Because the successive adjacent slices may have different numbers of collinear control points, the following heuristic triangulation algorithm has been developed.

Let P(k,i) and P(k+1,j) denote respectively the start control point of the slice k and the slice k+1. The following condition states when and how a triangle should be drawn (Figure 13.3):

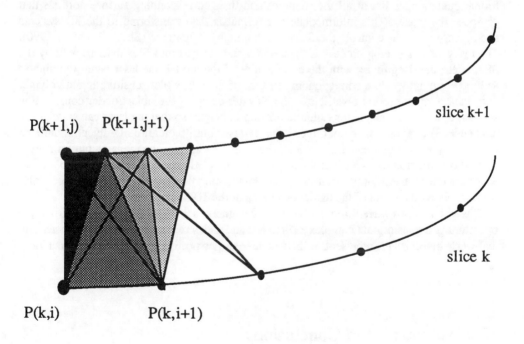

Figure 13.3. Triangulation of adjacent MRI slice contours

IF |P(k,i), P(k+1,j+1)| ≤ |P(k,i+1), P(k+1,j)|

THEN   Draw the triangle {P(k,i), P(k+1,j+1), P(k+1,j)}
            P(k+1,j+1) is the actual point in the slice k+1;

ELSE   Draw the triangle {P(k,i), P(k,i+1), P(k+1,j)}
            P(k,i+1) is the actual point in the slice k .

Figure 13.4 (see Color Section) shows the resulting triangulation of 64 MRI slice contours as used for further processing towards a corresponding physical 3D-copy.

13.5. Stereolithography

The technique of stereolithography represents a new milestone in the evolution of computer output device technology. Its operation is as follows: after the completion of a 3D-surface representation of the model under consideration, the latter is converted to a intermediate file-format containing a list of all the triangles and their corresponding surface normals that compose the model. This intermediate file-format is then transferred to the 3D systems slicing software that controls the Stereo-Lithography Apparatus (SLA) (Wohlers 1990). The result of this slicing process is then stored and merged into files that are read by the SLA controller. Beginning with the bottom slice of the model, the laser beam illuminates and therefore hardens the corresponding surface of the ultraviolet-sensitive liquid polymer contained in an appropriate vat. Next, the elevator carrying the object under construction submerges a short distance, for example 0.2 mm in height, so that the laser can solidify the next slice. The process then continues layer by layer until the entire 3D-object is built. In order to unmount the created 3D-object, the latter is fixed on the elevator platform by a support construction that separates the model from the platform. This is necessary to prevent distortion during the 3D-object building and unmounting processes. Figure 13.5 (see Color Section) shows the result of the hardcopy replica of the 3D human head.

The technique of stereolithography gives designers, scientists and engineers a unique opportunity to transmigrate complex 3D-models and data structures out of the computer into real-world objects. This represents a challenging new perspective in scientific visualization.

13.6. Summary and Conclusions

The processes used for the surface reconstruction of 3D-objects from the MRI-slices described in this chapter can be summarized as pseudo-code representation:

MRI-slice processing step:

```
FOR (Tomogram 1 TO Tomogram 64) DO
BEGIN
        Input:    Tomogram
                    Step 1)     Contour detection
                                    •  MTC-contour detection
                    Step 2)     Thinning
                                    •  Zhang and Suen algorithm
                    Step 3)     Contour segmentation
                                    •  Freeman chain-encoding technique
        Output:   Polygon approximation of a thinned contour-slice
END
```

Synthetic 3D-Surface Processing step:

```
        Input:    Polygon representation of the 64 contour-slices
                    Step 4)        Adjacent slice-contour triangulation
                    Step 5)        Wireframe model
                    Step 6)        Flat shading or Gouraud shading
        Output:   Real-time animation
```

The individual programs are written in the C programming language. Their execution runs on a Silicon Graphics super-workstation under the IRIX operating system. The execution time of the different slice processing algorithms depends on the complexity of the slices to be processed. Average performance values achieved with an MIPS Inc. R3000 processor platform and for MRI-slices with 512×512 pixel and 256 gray level are as follows: Step 1: 2s; step 2: 10s; step 3: 0.5s. Steps 4, 5, and 6 can be executed as real- time animation.

13.7. Conclusion

A fully automated surface-reconstruction procedure to create 3D-objects from MRI-slices has been developed for execution on a state-of-the-art general-purpose graphics super-workstation. The proposed method, applied to a human head, uses a new Multiple Thres-holding and Convolution (MTC) approach that provides, in conjunction with conventional skeletonization techniques, error-free and consistent contours. The results obtained are then used for subsequent vectorization and triangulation for wire-frame representation. Finally, various shading techniques are used to provide a photorealistic visualization of the processed 3D-object. Potential applications of the technique described can be found in the area of Computer-Aided Instruction (CAI) at large including stereovision and stereolitho-graphy.

Acknowledgments

The authors wish to thank A. Ungerböck and T.S. Huang, Visiting Professor at the Multimedia Laboratory of the University of Zurich, for the many useful discussions and suggestions. This research is partially supported by the Swiss Commission for the Promotion of Scientific Research and Orell-Füssli Graphic Arts Inc., Zurich.

References

Chin RT, Wan HK, Stover DL, Iverson RD (1987) A one pass thinning algorithm and its parallel implementation, *Computer Vision, Graphics, and Image Processing* 40.

Dyer ChR, Rosenfeld, A (1979) Thinning algorithms for gray-scale pictures, *IEEE Transactions on Pattern Analysis and Machine Intelligence*, Vol. PAMI-1, No. 1, pp.88-89.

Freeman H (1977) *Analysis of line drawings, in digital image processing and analysis*, (J. C. Simon and A. Rosenfeld, Eds.), Noordhoff, Leyden.

Fuchs H, Levoy M, Pizer StM, (1989) Interactive visualization of 3D medical data, *Computer*, Vol.22, No.8, pp.46-51.

Ghezal A, Stucki P (1991) 3D-Copies of Surface-Reconstructed 3D-Models, *Mustererkennung 1991*, B. Radig, Ed., 13. DAGM-Symposium, Munich.

Gonzales RC, Wintz P (1987) *Digital image processing*, Addison-Wesley, Reading, MA.

Höhne KH, Bomans M, Pommert A , Riemer M, Tiede U (1988) 3D-Segmentation and display of tomography imagery, *Proc. 9th International Conference on Pattern Recognition*, Computer Society Press.

Huang TS (1990) Modeling, analysis, and visualization of nonrigid object motion, *Proc. 10th International Conference on Pattern Recognition*, 16-21 June 1990, Atlantic City, New Jersey, USA, volume I, IEEE Computer Society Press.

Naccache NJ, Shinghal R (1984) An Investigation into the Skeletonization Approach of Hilditch, *Pattern Recognition*, Vol.17, No.3, pp.274-284.

Pavlidis T (1982) *Algorithms for graphics and image processing*, Computer Science Press.

Pratt WK (1978) *Digital image processing*, John Wiley & Sons, New York, N.Y.

Preparata F, Shamos MI (1985) *Computational Geometry: An Introduction*, Springer.

Salari E, Siy P (1984) The Rige-seeking method for obtaining the skeleton of digital images, *IEEE Transactions on Systems, Man, and Cybernics*, Vol. SMC-14, No.3, pp.524-528.

Wang PSP, Zhang TY (1989) A fast and flexible thinning algorithm", *IEEE Transactions on Computer*, Vol. 38, No. 5, pp.741-745.

Wohlers TT (1990) Practical prototypes: Thanks to recent innovations, laser-based 3D output is no longer just an expensive, experimental technology, *Computer Graphics World*.

Zhang TY, Suen CY (1984) A fast parallel algorithm for thinning digital patterns, *Communications of the ACM*, Vol. 27, No. 1, pp.236-239.

14

Interactive and Controlled Synthesis of 3D Irregular Shapes

Laurent Moccozet, Prem Kalra
MIRALab, Centre Universitaire d'Informatique
University of Geneva, Switzerland

14.1. Introduction

There have been many surface representations for modeling 3D objects for different purposes. Each representation has some advantages and disadvantages. Among existing means of surface representation, polygonal meshes are widely used. The popularity of this representation comes mainly from the fact that they can be directly handled at the hardware level by current graphics workstations, allowing rapid polygon drawing. Allan et al. (1989) provide an exhaustive list of advantages of this representation, particularly with regard to irregular shapes. Any object can be modeled using polygons, and any other representation can be converted to a polygonal mesh. Efficient rendering algorithms can render solids as wire-frame for previewing or ray-traced for final rendering. However, there exist some inherent disadvantages of the above choice, due to its polygon-base (Allan et al. 1989). Still, in the context of constructing irregular shapes such as synthetic actors, we have found polygonal surface representations to be appropriate.

3D construction/design of objects fundamentally involves natural and intuitive interaction. One of the earlier approaches for object creation uses multiple windows for the different orthographic views. This approach, though popular for CAD type applications, does not provide a natural method of object design. The objects dealing with synthetic actors need different treatment for realizing traditional concepts like sculpting and molding. We provide a sculpting tool using Ball and Mouse interaction methodology (LeBlanc et al. 1991). This tool uses the sculpting metaphor in a very natural way. Many means have been proposed to deform and manipulate polygonal meshes at either a global or local level:

Virtual Worlds and Multimedia Edited by Nadia Magnenat Thalmann and Daniel Thalmann
© 1993 John Wiley and Sons Ltd

Sederberg and Parry (1986) introduced free-form deformations, later extended by Coquillart (1990), (Coquillart and Jancene 1991) and Hsu et al. (1992), which allow deformation of a solid geometric model in a free-form manner by moving vertices of a control lattice. Allan et al. (1989) defined a methodology for local deformations based on a move-vertex operation; and Barr (1984) developed different types of local and global deformations such as bending, twisting or tapering. These deformation techniques give powerful tools for interactive modeling of three-dimensional shapes. Many of these techniques have been included in our design methodology for creating a variety of 3D shapes.

The sculpting process is dedicated to a designer who gives importance to the aesthetic aspects or the final look of the result. He/she may not be fully aware of the requirements of the processes or the specific contexts in which his/her creation may be further involved. This establishes the need for an intermediate process which may act like an adapter (Figure 14.1) to match the creation with the end use requirements. For example, a surface designed using the sculpting tool or obtained by other means may need additional treatment to be used for animation or final rendering. One of the primary requirements for polygonal structured surfaces for use in a particular situation is the ability to control the polygon resolution (number of polygons). This becomes a fundamental necessity when polygonal data is captured using devices like a laser scanner. DeHaemer et al. (1991) have developed methods to get three-dimensional objects from 3D digitizers from Cyberware, to include them in simulation, e.g. driving a jeep across a terrain. Works related to mesh decimation or reduction of data points have been developed in different areas. Fowler and Little (1979) used triangular irregular networks (TIN) in the area of terrain modeling. Schroeder et al. (1992) and Turk (1992) provided more general algorithms for removing and adding points based on curvature information, and the resulting points are then retriangulated to obtain the desired shapes. Their methods have been successfully used in the fields of data-visualization, medical imaging, and terrain and volume modeling. The requirements for the possible uses of resulting 3D shapes differ on the environments in which they are used. Two different types of environments are considered: static and dynamic. Static environments are concerned especially with rendering and texture mapping. Dynamic situations are related to animation, realistic and/or real time involving virtual reality. It is obvious that rendering thousands of polygons which are not visible for an object in the final rendered picture is inefficient. Similarly, an object built from digitized data of more than a hundred thousand polygons is not possible to include in a three-dimensional scene that has to evolve in real time. The resolution control of a surface may mean reducing or even augmenting the number of polygons of a region of interest or the entire surface, depending on the context of its end use. Such a surface resolution controller is included in our design system and permits the increase/decrease of polygons in the surface while preserving its general shape. We have adopted both interactive and noninteractive modes of operations. In interactive mode, a user can define the geometric attributes of shapes to be preserved, in noninteractive mode uniform decimation is conducted, keeping the global shape of the object.

The surface design for synthetic actors has to cater to the dynamic environment of the actors where they may move or interact with each other or with the external environment. We include facial animation as an example to demonstrate the behavior of the surfaces designed (a face) in a dynamic situation where the complete face or a portion thereof may move to mimic speech and emotions of a person. Situations with realistic and real-time animation are included.

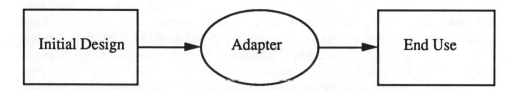

Figure 14.1. Surface design and its adaptation to the end use

The chapter is divided into sections. In Section 14.2, we give an overview of the sculpting tool. The following section presents the resolution controller for reducing or adding polygons to a surface. Section 14.4 provides a brief description of animating faces which is constructed using the included design methodology. Finally, some concluding remarks are included.

14.2. Sculpting Tool

Geometric modeling and surface manipulation have been a significant research area in computer graphics. We employ a sculpting metaphor where the process of object creation is natural and corresponds to intuitive thinking of conventional construction of objects. The surface design consists of the ability to create an object from scratch or to start from a rather simple primitive and then perform various operations locally or globally on the surface to obtain the desired shape. The variety of deformations available adequately provides methods of changing the existing models to create irregular classes of objects such as a character's face or other parts of the body. Global transformations allow the user to treat a solid as if it were constructed from a special type of topological putty or clay which may be bent, twisted, tapered, compressed, and otherwise transformed into a final desired shape. In addition, local deformations of the surface provide fine-tuning where a point or a group of points can be transformed to obtain the effects of pinching, lifting and moving a piece of stretchable material.

We employ a user interaction methodology based on a six degree of freedom interactive input device called the Spaceball. Use of this device helps a person's spatial intuitions to move and steer objects in 3D space. The mobility of the object exploits the phenomenon of motion parallax and aids 3D manipulation of the object in a single projection window. The Spaceball is used in one hand to move and examine the object being sculpted while the mouse is used in the other hand to work on the object and to activate the function from widgets.

The following sections briefly describe the main features and functions of the sculpting software.

14.2.1. Creation and Primitive Selection

Object creation may start either from scratch or by loading simple object primitives like planes, spheres, cylinders etc. created outside the software. Generally, a designer starts from an existing primitive; e.g. to construct the head of a person one may start from a sphere and to create limbs start from a cylinder. He/she will then add or delete points/polygons and move them locally or globally using appropriate deformations to attain the desired shape. Starting from scratch means creating a point and then polygonizing the set of created points. This is relatively tedious and time consuming. Combination of the two, however, provides generality when creating a variety of shapes including disjointed objects or objects with holes in the surface. In our implementation, we consider polygons to be only triangles for simplicity and homogeneity.

The software permits easy selection of the primitives; the selected item can then become a candidate for the desired operation. Group selection of the same entity (primitive) or together with other entities is also possible. This is accomplished by using the mouse in conjunction with the Spaceball: the mouse is used for marking the wanted primitives and the Spaceball for orienting the object. Change in the color of selected primitives provides real-time visual feedback. We also provide collective picking with constraints, e.g. selecting triangles of the same color, or entities within a snapped portion of the window screen. Once the desired primitive is selected, various operations can be performed on it. For example, a selected triangle may be deleted or split, its material may be changed, its normal may be flipped, etc. Similarly functions like merge, deform and delete can be performed for selected vertices, while edges can be split, deleted or rotated.

A region is defined as a set of polygons which may be related or associated in some context. Inclusion of the layer of regions provides a hierarchical manipulation of a surface. In the following section we present the system's deformation capabilities which progressively change the shape of an existing surface.

14.2.2. Deformations

We include two classes of deformations: local and global. As the name suggests, local deformations pertain to deforming locally a point or a set of points of a surface, whereas global deformations perform changes in the shape at a global level, dealing with a region or the entire surface. Combination of the two provides adequate flexibility and control adhering to the sculpting metaphor.

14.2.2.1. Local Deformation

This type of deformation produces local elevation or depression on the surface to attain the desired irregular shape. The selected vertices are moved in a controlled manner according to a decay function that is radially symmetric about a vertex called the apex vertex. When the apex vertex is moved by the mouse in space, other vertices follow it in the same direction and with amplitudes as a function of their initial distance from the apex vertex. Several functions can be used depending on the desired final shape; some of these functions are bell, cusp, single, box, sine, etc. This methodology is similar to the metaphor of pinching, lifting and pressing flexible material. For example, pushing the apex vertex inward results in the effect of pressing a lump of clay. This type of deformation helps change the basic shape characteristics of a local region of the surface: e.g., adding irregularities or peaks. It also provides a means to perform fine-tuning for surface shape features.

14.2.2.2. Global Deformation

There also exist tools to deform globally the entire object or a region of the object consisting of a group of polygons. These deformations include regular deformations (Barr 1984) and free form deformations (FFD) (Sederberg and Parry 1986). Regular deformations refer to scaling, tapering, shifting, twisting, bending, etc. These deformations are regular and well-defined and the results are quite predictable and transparent to the user. A globally specified deformation of a 3D solid is a mathematical function F which explicitly modifies the global coordinates of points in space. Mathematically, it can be represented by $X = F(x)$ where x is a point of the undeformed solid and X is the point of the deformed solid. The transformation function F is different for each type of deformation. The free-form deformations are very general and can give the desired shape by merely moving the control points of the control lattice. An FFD is initiated by defining a 3D grid of control points about the region to be deformed. The region of interest (or the entire surface to be deformed) is embedded in the grid of control points that can be interactively moved. The region/surface is considered to be made of flexible material so that when the grid of the control lattice is deformed, the object(s) inside it is also deformed. The combination of the two types of deformations, regular and FFD, gives an enhanced versatility for the sculpting process.

14.2.3. Material Editing

Each polygon has a material attached to it. The system allows manipulation of the materials associated with a surface. A user can add a material, delete a material, or change its attributes and properties. Materials information can be maintained in a separate database. The properties related to a material are color characteristics including diffuse, specular, ambient colors, reflectivity, and transparency. Each material has an assigned name. Manipulation of materials of a surface refines display clues.

14.2.4. Interaction

The effectiveness of a geometric modeling system depends on the facilities provided for fast and intuitive specification and modification of the model. A primary requirement for an efficient modeling system is the interactivity. Incremental modifications during the modeling process should be executed and visualized instantly. However, the use of direct manipulation for 3D modeling is complex as the 3D transformation parameters have to be specified on a projected 2D screen. Use of the additional device the Spaceball easily resolves this problem by providing object mobility at any time. Simultaneous use of the Spaceball and mouse (referred to as Ball and Mouse methodology) has been found an attractive communication interface between the designer and the modeler. The methodology resembles the visual interface that a real life designer would encounter. One hand is used to hold the object in place or to move around with the help of the Spaceball and the other hand is used to operate various tools to work on the object using the mouse.

Another aspect which has been considered in the design provides a graphical user interface environment. The interface has been designed using the in-house developed toolkit (Turner et al. 1990) which uses object oriented methodology. Widgets like buttons, toggles and sliders are encapsulated as 2D objects and are associated appropriately with the performable operations. Physical input devices such as mouse, keyboard and Spaceball are encapsulated in special classes of the toolkit. These input device objects communicate their data through a uniform event message protocol.

14.2.5. Examples

The sculpting tool presented offers a very flexible and natural environment for designing various types of irregular objects. It enables the design of objects from simple primitives with progressive modifications, e.g., building a head from a sphere. Figure 14.2 (see Color section) demonstrates the process for making a highly irregular object (face) from a very regular object (sphere). In addition it provides the ability to derive another irregular surface from a given existing irregular surface. Figure 14.3 (see Color Section) illustrates an example of deriving a devil's head from a normal head.

14.3. Resolution Controller

A surface created by the sculpting tool or even imported from outside may not directly fit to the requirements dictated by its intended use. A surface with extra information may have to be simplified to make the intended end task easier and simpler. This is particularly important when the effectiveness of the end use depends on the complexity of the surface designed. We, therefore, introduce a resolution controller which permits reduction or addition of polygons if needed to meet the end use requirements. In the context of animation, however, where speed has immense importance, only data reduction has been found useful for situations where extra polygons help augment surface shape features, the controller provides facilities for adding polygons. In this chapter we have focused only on diminishing the number of polygons to satisfy our requirements for animation. According to our experience, it seems that two kinds of tools for resolution control may be needed: the first category is based on interactive selection of regions of the shape as decided by the user, the other category is noninteractive and the decimation algorithm is applied uniformly over the entire shape.

The decimation algorithm developed for the interactive mode gives all the freedom to the user for his creation, and applies some corrections locally. This gives complete control to the user of the visual aspects of the shape. The design methodology corresponds to the sculpting software for consistency in the working environment.

14.3.1. Interactive Decimation

The process employed for interactive decimation (Moccozet and Magnenat-Thalmann 1992) is summarized in Figures 14.4.a-b-c-d. It starts with the selection of a region by picking triangles, projecting them on a plane and extracting the important features of the region and its border. The features are either vertices or edges and are decided by using approximation of curvature. The triangles of the three-dimensional region are deleted simultaneously, when projected triangles in the plane are removed. The projected region containing the border and the inside vertices and edges is subsequently retriangulated using constrained Delaunay triangulation (De Floriani and Puppo 1992). The new two-dimensional triangulation is finally projected back onto the three-dimensional shape. As the border is kept intact, the insertion of the region in the shape is straightforward, fitting the hole exactly .

14.3.1.1 Extracting Shape

Decimation or simplification is the process of removing extra elements of a surface without losing too much of its shape. The primary question then arises: what defines the shape of a surface? For a terrain type of a surface, shape can be defined as a set of shape-specific points and a set of segments (Fowler and Little 1979). The shape-specific points are divided into three categories: peaks defined as relative maxima, pits as relative minima and passes defined as points of intersection between ridges and channels. Similarly, the shape-specific edges may be ridges (connecting two adjacent peaks) or channels (connecting two adjacent pits). These elements are defined in terms of the heights of points relative to a plane, and are not so relevant for a three-dimensional shape. We, therefore, need other definitions to characterize shape-specific features. Koenderink (1988) defines the shape of a surface in terms of its curvature. Elements with a small curvature contribute negligibly to the overall shape and thus can be considered for removal in the simplification process. Brown (1991) has developed different methods to triangulate a set of two-dimensional points and data values at the points with minimal average absolute error. In these methods, a cost function is defined to determine the best triangulation that will minimize the cost function for a triangulation. The cost functions can imply a good way of approximating curvature. From Brown's definition, we deduce the following cost function defining the curvature of a given point. Given a point P of the initial three-dimensional mesh, let m be the number of triangles incident to P, and for $i = 1$ to m, n_i is the unit normal vector to each triangle, the normal at P is given as follows:

$$n = \frac{\sum_{i=0}^{m} n_i}{m} \tag{14.1}$$

The associated cost function at P is

$$C(P) = \frac{\sum_{i=0}^{m} (n_i \cdot n)^2}{m} \tag{14.2}$$

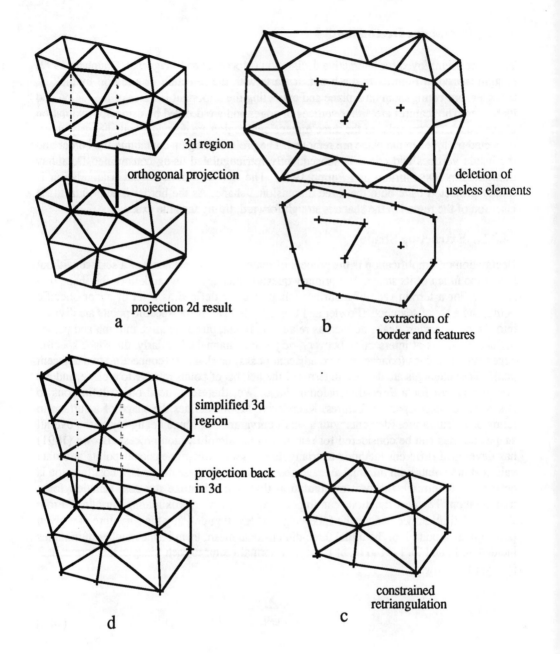

Figure 14.4. Procedure for interactive decimation.

As each dot product gives a cosine value (all the vectors are normalized), the cost function is always less than 1. A value of 1 means that normals of surrounding triangles are collinear with the average normal, so that the neighborhood of the point is flat. Given an epsilon value ε, we can now extract the shape information conducting the following test: each point P for which the curvature function is more than $1-\varepsilon$ is not a shape-specific point. When epsilon is close to 0, the value of the cost function is close to one.

Experiments show that the aforementioned procedure can sometimes lead to modification of the shape of an object. This is due to the fact that the projection on a plane causes some loss of geometric information. Consequently, in the case of a ridge, for example, keeping its two endpoints does not guarantee that the edge between these two points will be retained in the new triangulation. To overcome that drawback, edge elements are also extracted and inserted in the set of elements to be kept and to be triangulated. As we have defined a curvature function for points, we define a curvature function for edges that is applied only to the interior edges of the selected region. The border edges are selected by default. A simplified form of curvature function as proposed by Brown (1991) for edges is defined. Given an edge e, T_1 and T_2 the two triangles sharing e, the cost function is defined as the cosine of the angle between the normals n_1 and n_2 of T_1 and T_2. If we assume that n_1 and n_2 are normalized, the cost function is given as follows:

$$C(e) = n_1 \cdot n_2 \qquad\qquad (14.3)$$

The criterion for retaining edges of specific shapes is similar as presented for the points. The process can be further optimized as it is not necessary to compute the curvature function for each inside point and inside edge. Because the curvature function is more easily computed for edges than vertices and because edge selection implies endpoint selection as well, we first need to compute the curvature function for all the inside edges. The appropriate edges are then selected and kept with their endpoints and subsequently the curvature functions for all the inside points (not of endpoints of selected edges) are computed and the points of interest are retained.

The vertex curvature function can itself be optimized. We notice that as the average normal used is derived from the sum of normals of all surrounding triangles, we can say that, m being the number of triangles incident to the vertex, given an epsilon value ε, if there exists an i between 1 and m so that $n \cdot n_i$ is less than ε, then the point has to be kept. On the other hand if given an epsilon value ε, there exists an i between 1 and m so that $n \cdot n_i$ is more than $1-\varepsilon$ then the point has to be eliminated.

Once the shape-specific elements are retained, the region or the surface containing them has to be rebuilt. The following section describes the process of rebuilding the region.

14.3.2. Rebuilding the Region

A two-dimensional triangulation is built from the elements kept on the projected plane. Delaunay triangulation is chosen to build a new triangulation of the projected region. The elements retained are either inside points or edges and points belonging to the border of the region. The Delaunay triangulation gives a triangulation of the convex hull of a set of points. The choice of Delaunay triangulation is made because of its properties; the main properties of the triangulation (Preparata and Shamos 1985, Edelsbrunner 1987) are:

a) Empty circle property: the circle through the three points of one triangle does not contain any of the other points of the set of points to triangulate.
b) Max-min angle property: if the edge adjacent to two triangles giving a quadrilateral is swapped to the other diagonal of the quadrilateral, the minimum of the six internal angles does not increase. These properties ensure a well-shaped triangulation and thus make it suitable for our purposes.

As presented earlier in Section 14.3.1, keeping only shape-specific points does not guarantee that the shape-specific edges will be retained in the resulting triangulation. We therefore employ constrained Delaunay triangulation, which gives a triangulation of the convex hull of a set of points and segments/edges. The general triangulation of a set of points and segments uses a visibility test: given a set of points and segments, a "visibility graph" can be built that joins every pair of points visible from each other and includes the constraint segments. Here, "visible" means that the segments created do not intersect with any constraint segment. A triangulation is a planar subgraph with triangular faces of the visibility graph where two edges do not intersect except at the endpoints. The constrained Delaunay triangulation satisfies the extended empty circle property. The extension of the empty circle property with respect to constrained Delaunay triangulation is that for each triangle the circle going through its three vertices will not include any visible points from these three vertices. A triangulation that verifies the empty circle property is a Delaunay triangulation. A similar extension exists for the min-max angle property.

The algorithm implemented is a static version of the one presented in (De Floriani and Puppo 1992). In the first step, the Delaunay triangulation is defined as a map for a set of points and the endpoints of the constraint segments. Then each constraint segment is inserted in the previous triangulation: all edges crossing the constraint edge are removed, creating two simple polygons sharing the constraint edge. These two polygons are called "influence polygons" of the edge. According to the results shown and proved by De Floriani and Puppo (1992), there is a recursive way of triangulating these two polygons to get a constrained Delaunay triangulation for the original set of points and segments with the new constraint edge inserted.

The algorithm assumes that a user will make a clever enough choice so that the projection will not affect the topological result. Experience has shown that users choose satisfying regions by simple intuition. Problems may arise if some of the projected triangles overlap on the plane. In this case, performing the Delaunay triangulation leads to some topological aberration. The solution would be to re-create the topological three-dimensional situation on the projection. This may be done through a similar process as described by Turk (1991, 1992); it allows positioning of vertices on a three-dimensional surface by point repulsion in the context of texture generation or in retiling polygonal surfaces. According to the context, some repulsive or attractive properties may be given to the projected vertices, so that after a repetitive process of relaxation, the projected points that overlap on some already projected triangles may be moved and restored in their neighborhood. Some other ways may be experimented with, based on the projection method developed by Kent et al.

(1992). This method consists of projecting an object of genus 0 onto a unit sphere in order to merge the topology of two objects and interpolate them. The idea is analogous to inflating a balloon. In our context, a similar projection on a half-sphere of the selected region would overcome the overlapping problem. The process may be extended to the regularization of the mesh. The half-sphere can be easily and regularly meshed at any resolution. The resolution should be closely linked to the size of the smallest triangle of the three-dimensional region.

An interactive tool to control the resolution of a three-dimensional object is necessary mainly because it gives the user a way to control the aesthetic result of the decimation of points in the mesh. This is an important issue of mesh decimation. There is no precise formula to estimate the aesthetics of a three-dimensional shape. As a consequence, the best judge remains the human eye which suggests that an interactive tool is the best way. An alternative may be running a noninteractive algorithm, checking the visual aspect of the result, and rerunning the decimation with some new parameters until the visual aspects satisfy some rendering judgments.

14.3.3. Noninteractive Decimation

For a specific case, where efficiency takes precedence over aesthetics, interactivity can become an overhead. Moreover, this alternative may not give complete satisfaction in the sense that the decimation is performed uniformly on the complete shape, which diminishes the flexibility. In a systematic approach, automatic decimation governed by some formulae run on the whole shape will give much better results. Performing such a decimation on a complete object through an interactive process would be very tedious. In that context the region-based approach is not satisfactory. Experience has shown that a 'blind' selection of a region fitting the requirements of the decimation algorithm is very difficult. The decimation here is performed locally on a vertex and its incident triangles, or on an edge and its close neighbors. Some uses, especially in a dynamic context, for example virtual reality, show that after a certain level of decimation, algorithms based on removing vertices lead to shapes that no longer have the same visual aspects as the original ones. A solution to this is to use some local deformations to keep an acceptable global shape. This method consists of operations like replacing an edge by one point, assimilating the process as pinching (pressing) of its endpoints and converting an edge to a single point. The object is given some superficial elastic properties and the displacement resulting from the pinching is propagated locally to the neighboring vertices according to a range of influence.

The whole process is divided into many passes over the shape, each pass concerned with different elements (triangles, edges, vertices). At most two types of parameters are considered for each element: size and curvature for the edges, area and curvature for the triangles, and curvature for vertices. The algorithm is based on some threshold values for these different parameters. All elements for which one of the values is more than the threshold is either removed or transformed to another type of element. To facilitate the task of a user, values concerning the curvature are normalized between 0 and 1. For quantitative values like size or area, as it is difficult to know exactly the size and area of elements in the initial shape, a preprocess is performed to determine the average size of all edges, and the average area of all triangles; so the threshold values are expressed as a ratio of these average values. Another technique, more effective but computationally expensive, would be to use the median value for the size and the area instead of the average value.

All elements of the object are scanned and eventually determined as candidates for simplification (elimination) if they fit one of the criteria of uselessness. The region defined by the incident triangles of these candidates are then removed and the hole created is re-triangulated. The curvatures for vertices and edges are evaluated in the same manner as explained earlier in the interactive case. For triangles, a way of describing the curvature must be found: for one triangle, we use the given triangle and three incident triangles to it along the edges. For these three triangles, we define a circle going through their respective center. The endpoints of the diameter and the center of the target triangle are used for defining a triangle, and the angle at the center of the target triangle defines the curvature. To normalize the values of the curvature between -1 and 1 we use the cosine value of the angle. A cosine near -1 indicates a locally "flat" triangle and thus a candidate for simplification. Some other evaluations of the curvature may also be used.

An edge- or a triangle-candidate for simplification is changed to a vertex. An edge is changed to its middle point and a triangle is changed to its centroid. Extra vertices are simply removed. A local region of simplification is defined on which a retriangulation is performed. For a vertex the region is defined as the set of incident triangles to the point; for an edge, the region is defined as the set of triangles adjacent to the edge or incident to either of both endpoints of the edge; for a triangle, the region is defined as the set of adjacent triangles to the triangle, and incident triangles to the three points of the triangle. Once the region is defined, triangles of the region are removed, a point is created if needed, and the resulting hole is retriangulated. In the case of an edge or a triangle, each vertex of the border of the hole is linked to the replacing vertex by an edge. For the vertex case, vertices of the border must be retriangulated. As the polygon defined by the border is nonplanar and can be concave, care must be taken in the retriangulation. One way is to define a plane going through the removed point, and with the normal, the normal of the removed point. Vertices of the border are then projected on the plane and any algorithm of triangulation of a planar polygon can then be performed. After retriangulation, adjustments are performed locally (Allan et al. 1989). The shape is considered superficially elastic and vertices in a range of influence are moved according to a decay function. Figures 14.5.a-b-c illustrate the principle for an edge. Replacing the edge P1P2 with its middle I is considered as pinching both endpoints of the edge in opposite directions along the edge to the middle point of the edge. The decay function is a function of the distance between a point in the range of influence and I and of the cosine of the angle between the edge P1P2 and the vector defined by I, and the point to move. Given a point M on the border of the region, and M' its new position to compute, vectors IP1 and IM' are computed and normalized and their dot product is then calculated, giving the cosine of the angle. If the angle is negative, the absolute value is used. The cosine value and a stiffness coefficient K are used in conjunction to define the amount of the vector IM that M will be moved in the direction of I. The final position M' of the point M will be given by the following formula:

$$\overrightarrow{M_1M_1'}=K|\cos(\theta)|\ \overrightarrow{M_1I} \qquad \text{with } 0{<}{=}K{<}1. \qquad (14.4)$$

In the case of a triangle the decay function is more simple and just depends on the distance between the point to move and the new point. For a vertex the function depends on the distance between the point to move and the point to be removed.

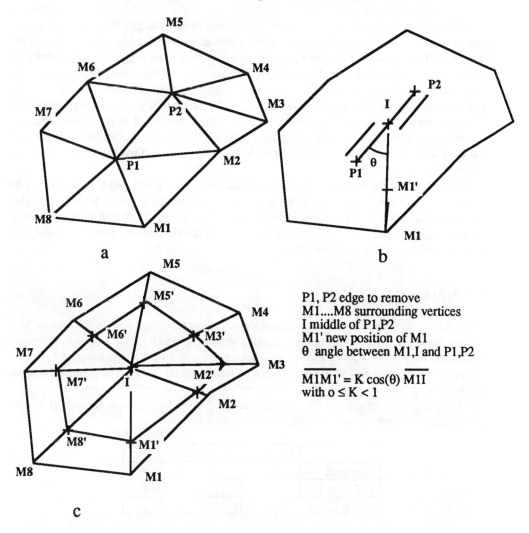

P1, P2 edge to remove
M1....M8 surrounding vertices
I middle of P1,P2
M1' new position of M1
θ angle between M1,I and P1,P2

$$\overline{M1M1'} = K \cos(\theta) \, \overline{M1I}$$
with $o \le K < 1$

Figure 14.5. Reshaping for noninteractive decimation.

Before applying the decay function to the vertices in the range of influence, the set of points is checked to determine whether some of them should be anchored. Points to anchor are those on the borders of holes. Applying the decay function on these points would modify the object by enlarging existing holes, which is not the expected effect. These points are first detected and the decay function is not applied to them. For the same kind of problem, a vertex, an edge or a triangle loses its candidature for simplification if any of the vertices composing one of these three elements is on the border of a hole. Instead of changing types of elements, like transforming a triangle to a vertex, some more direct techniques could be used, like re-triangulating the hole created by the removal of the triangles of the region of simplification without adding a vertex in replacement of the triangle. But this method may lead to some loss of information in the case of a thin triangle with a high value of curvature. Instead, different passes over the different elements may have a specific order that may increase the computation time, but will give good control on the result. Triangles are first checked for their area, then for their curvature; edges are then checked for their size and area, and vertices are checked for their curvature. In the case of a small triangle with high curvature, the triangle would be first changed to a vertex because of its small area, and then the point would be kept, because of the high curvature. In the case of a small triangle with low curvature, the triangle would be first changed to a vertex, then the vertex would be removed.

This method will be extended in order to regularize the mesh defining the shape from the initial irregular mesh. As stated earlier, some extensions would be made to find ways that can perform and control the decimation according to some specific requirements. Maintaining different levels of detail of shape would enable use of a surface for different purposes and with different requirements.

14.3.4. Results

Some results of both interactive and noninteractive methods are shown in Figures 14.6 through 14.8. Figure 14.6 (see Color Section) shows the result of the interactive method applied to a synthetic face created from a sphere. Figure 14.6A is the original head and Figure 14.6B is simplified. One may notice that contrary to a surface obtained from digitization, the number of polygons of the original surface is relatively small. The region-based approach is employed for simplification. Table 14.1 shows the result of the simplification in terms of number of polygons on each region.

	Original	Simplified	Epsilon
Forehead	28	16	0.6
Left Cheek	37	15	0.4
Right Cheek	45	19	0.3

Table 14.1. Results of interactive simplification

Figure 14.7 shows the result of different levels of noninteractive simplification applied to a sphere. Figure 14.7A is the original sphere containing 1680 triangles, 2520 edges and 842 vertices. Figure 14.7B gives the result of a first level of simplification with 1260 triangles, 1890 edges and 632 vertices. Figure 14.7C is the result of simplification with 1140 triangles, 1710 edges and 572 vertices and Figure 14.7D is the result of simplification with 906 triangles, 1359 edges and 455 vertices.

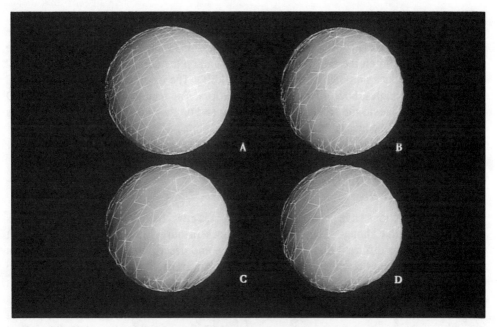

Figure 14.7. Noninteractive decimation on a sphere

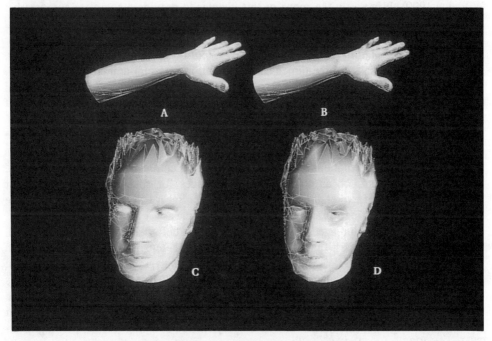

Figure 14.8. Noninteractive decimation on an arm and a face

Figure 14.8 shows another application of the noninteractive method: two objects, an arm, (Figure 14.8A and 14.8B) and a head with eyeballs and teeth (Figure 14.8C and 14.8D). The original arm in Figure 14.8A contains 2314 triangles, 3533 edges and 1359 vertices. The result with threshold on the area and length of 1/5 and on the curvature of 0.0001 has 1592 triangles, 2450 edges and 859 vertices (Figure 14.8B). The original head in Figure 14.8C contains 5227 triangles, 8026 edges, and 2807 vertices. The resulting head in Figure 14.8D with threshold value on the area and length of 1/5 and on the curvature of 0.0001 contains 3095 triangles, 4832 edges and 1743 vertices.

14.4. Facial Animation

The preceding sections have primarily addressed issues concerned with design and synthesis control of irregular shapes. These irregular shapes in our virtual world may represent synthetic actors or different body parts. The shape and description of the surface play an important role in animation. Here, we have included an example of facial animation to demonstrate how a surface (face) designed using the above methodology behaves in a dynamic situation. The problem of facial animation as such is rather difficult, particularly as we tend to relate the results to reality. However, there has been extensive research on facial animation and several models have been proposed (Bergeron and Lachapelle 1985, deGraf 1989, Hill et al. 1988, Lewis and Parke 1987, Magnenat-Thalmann et al. 1988, Parke 1982, Pearce et al. 1986, Platt and Badler 1981, Terzopoulos and Waters 1991, Waters 1987, Williams 1990). It is not in the scope of this chapter to provide a complete comparative review of the earlier or existing systems for facial animation; Parke (1991) provides a good review of the different systems.

In our system to simplify the task, we employ a multi-level approach to create, control, synchronize and visualize three-dimensional animation of facial animation (Kalra et al. 1991). The system has a hierarchical structure of controls for spatial and temporal characteristics of facial animation. From the lowest to the highest level, the degree of abstraction increases. The top level requires direct input of global actions and their duration, and at the lowest level muscle actions are integrated with their intensities to cause the desirable movement of appropriate points on the 3D face model. The system includes movements due to both emotions and speech. Higher level entities in the system correspond to intuitive concepts such as emotions and sentences for speech, which are further represented in terms of expressions and phonemes. At a lower level, Minimum Perceptible Actions (MPAs) are defined as aggregate actions of muscles.

Muscular activity is simulated using rational free form deformations (Kalra et al. 1992). We employ rational basis functions for the trivariate tensor product of Bernstein polynomials. The inclusion of weights for each control point provides an extra degree of freedom for controlling and manipulating the deformations. To simulate the muscle actions on the skin of a human face, we define regions on the facial mesh corresponding to the anatomical description of the regions of the face where a muscle action is desired. For realistic rendering of the animated face we employ texture mapping (Kalra and Magnenat-Thalmann 1993). A real photograph scanned or captured through a live video digitizer can be mapped onto the 3D facial model. Figure 14.9 (see Color Section) shows a sequence of images with facial animation.

In the multi-level approach specification and manipulation of entities are relatively easy and natural. The system allows interactive manipulation of most entities, giving almost real-time response. We offer an open system for control where the complex description of facial animation can be handled better by assigning multiple input accessories. These input accessories may be a simple script, a multi-input musical keyboard or a gesture dialogue. Integration of all means of control offers flexibility and freedom to the animator. The animation can also be driven by a real performance with real-time response. Real-time extraction of facial control parameters from live video performance is analyzed and used for the reconstruction of a dynamic facsimile of the synthetic face. Such a system provides a possibility of real-time communication between a real performance and a synthetic facial animation.

14.5. Conclusion

This chapter has presented an interactive methodology for controlled design of 3D irregular shapes. These irregular shapes are polygonally based and used for modeling synthetic actors. The methodology uses direct surface manipulation based on a sculpting metaphor which allows primitive operation where primitives like vertices, edges and triangles are accessed directly for the desired operation. A resolution controller provides the possibility to change the number of polygons of the surface while preserving its shape features. In most applications the controller simplifies the object by removing its extra elements. Examples of facial animation illustrate the application of the underlying design approach.

Acknowledgments

The authors would like to thank Hans Martin Werner for editing the manuscript. We also would like to thank Ross Racine, Arghyro Paouri and some students of MIRALab for sculpting some of the illustrated models. This research is partially supported by le Fonds National Suisse pour la Recherche Scientifique.

References

Allan JB, Wyvill B, Witten IA (1989) A Methodology for Direct Manipulation of Polygon Meshes, *Proc. Computer Graphics International'89*, Leeds, pp.461-469.
Barr AH (1984) Global and Local Deformations of Solid Primitives. *Proc. SIGGRAPH'84, Computer Graphics*, Vol.18, No.3, pp.21-30.

Bergeron P, Lachapelle P (1985) Controlling Facial Expressions and Body Movements in the Computer Generated Animated Short "Tony de Peltrie". *SIGGRAPH '85 Tutorial Notes*, Advanced Computer Animation Course.

Brown JL (1991) Vertex Based Data Dependent Triangulations, *Computer Aided Geometric Design*, Vol.8, No.3, pp. 239-251.

Coquillart S (1990) Extended Free-Form Deformation: A Sculpturing Tool for 3D Geometric Modeling, *Proc. SIGGRAPH'90, Computer Graphics*, Vol.24, No.4, pp.187-196.

Coquillart S, Jancene P (1991) Animated Free-Form Deformation: An Interactive Animation Technique, *Proc. SIGGRAPH' 91, Computer Graphics*, Vol.25, No.4, pp.23-26.

deGraf B (1989) in *State of the Art in Facial Animation*, SIGGRAPH '89 Course Notes No. 26, pp. 10-20.

De Floriani L, Puppo E (1992) An On-Line Algorithm for Constrained Delaunay Triangulation, *Graphical Models and Image Processing*, Vol.54, No.4

DeHaemer Jr MJ, Zyda MJ (1991) Simplification of Objects Rendered by Polygonal Approximations, *Computer & Graphics*, Vol.15, No.2, pp.175-184.

Edelsbrunner H (1987) *Algorithms in Combinatorial Geometry*, Springer-Verlag, Heidelberg, Germany.

Fowler RJ, Little JJ (1979) Automatic Extraction of Irregular Network Digital Terrain Models, *Computer Graphics*, Vol.13, No.2, pp.199-207.

Hill DR, Pearce A, Wyvill B (1988) Animating Speech: an Automated Approach Using Speech Synthesised by Rules, *The Visual Computer*, Vol. 3, No5, pp.277-289

Hsu W, Hughes JF, Kaufman H (1992) Direct Manipulation of Free-Form Surfaces, *Proc. SIGGRAPH'92, Computer Graphics*, Vol.26, No.4, pp.177-184.

Kalra P, Mangili A, Magnenat-Thalmann N, Thalmann D (1991) SMILE : A Multilayered Facial Animation System, *Proc IFIP WG 5.10*, Tokyo, Japan (Ed Kunii Tosiyasu L) pp. 189-198.

Kalra P, Mangili A, Magnenat-Thalmann N, Thalmann D (1992) Simulation of Muscle Actions using Rational FreeForm Deformations, *Proc. Eurographics '92, Computer Graphics Forum*, Vol. 2, No. 3, pp. 59-69.

Kalra P, Magnenat-Thalmann N (1993) Simulation of Facial Skin using Texture Mapping and Coloration, *Proc. ICCG '93*, Bombay, India, pp.247-256.

Kent JR, Carlson WE, Parent RE (1992) Shape Transformation for Polyhedral Objects, *Proc. SIGGRAPH'92, Computer Graphics*, Vol.26, No.4, pp.47-54.

Koenderink JJ (1988) *Solid Shapes*, The MIT Press.

LeBlanc A, Kalra P, Magnenat-Thalmann N, Thalmann D (1991) Sculpting with the "Ball and Mouse" Metaphor, *Proc. Graphics Interface'91*, Calgary, Canada, pp.152-159.

Lewis JP, Parke FI (1987), Automated Lipsynch and Speech Synthesis for Character Animation, *Proc. CHI '87 and Graphics Interface '87*, Toronto, pp. 143-147.

Magnenat-Thalmann N, Primeau E, Thalmann D (1988), Abstract Muscle Action Procedures for Human Face Animation, *The Visual Computer*, Vol. 3, No. 5, pp. 290-297.

Moccozet L, Magnenat-Thalmann N (1992), Controlling the Complexity of Objects Based on Polygonal Meshes, *Proc. CGI'92*, Tokyo, Japan, Springer-Verlag, (Ed T. L. Kunii), pp. 763-780.

Parke FI (1982), Parametrized Models for Facial Animation, *IEEE Computer Graphics and Applications*, Vol. 2, No. 9, pp. 61-68.

Parke FI (1991), Control Parameterization for Facial Animation, *Proc. Computer Animation '91*, Geneva, Switzerland, (Eds Magnenat-Thalmann N and Thalmann D), pp. 3-13.

Pearce A, Wyvill B, Hill DR (1986), Speech and Expression: A Computer Solution to Face Animation, *Proc. Graphics Interface '86, Vision Interface '86*, pp. 136-140.

Platt S, Badler NI (1981), Animating Facial Expressions, *Proc SIGGRAPH '81, Computer Graphics*, Vol. 15, No. 3, pp. 245-252.

Preparata FP, Shamos MI (1985) *Computational Geometry - An Introduction*, Springer-Verlag, New-York.

Schroeder WJ, Zarge JA, Lorensen WE (1992) Decimation of Triangle Meshes, *Proc. SIGGRAPH'92, Computer Graphics*, 26(2) pp. 65-70.

Sederberg TW, Parry SR (1986) Free-form Deformations of Solid Geometric Models, *Proc. SIGGRAPH'86, Computer Graphics*, 20(4) pp. 151-160.

Terzopoulos D, Waters K (1991) Techniques for Realistic Facial Modeling and Animation, *Proc. Computer Animation '91*, Geneva, Switzerland, (Eds Magnenat-Thalmann N and Thalmann D), pp. 59-74.

Turner R, Gobbetti E, Balaguer F, Mangili A, Thalmann D, Magnenat Thalmann N (1990) An Object-Oriented Methodology using Dynamic Variables for Animation and Scientific Visualization, *Proceedings of Computer Graphics International 90*, Springer-Verlag, Tokyo, pp 317-327,

Turk G (1991) Generating Textures on Arbitrary Surfaces Using Reaction Diffusion, *Proc. SIGGRAPH 91, Computer Graphics*, Vol.25, No.4, pp. 289-298.

Turk G (1992) Re-Tiling Polygonal Surfaces, *Proc. SIGGRAPH'92, Computer Graphics*, Vol.26, No.2, pp. 55-64.

Waters K (1987), A Muscle Model for Animating Three Dimensional Facial Expression, *Proc SIGGRAPH '87, Computer Graphics*, Vol. 21, No. 4, pp. 17-24.

Williams L (1990), Performance Driven Facial Animation, *Proc SIGGRAPH '90, Computer Graphics*, Vol. 24, No. 3, pp. 235-242.

15

Some Developments About Ray Tracing

Bernard Peroche
Ecole Nationale Supérieure des Mines de Saint-Etienne
Département Informatique
Saint-Etienne, France

15.1. Introduction

Since Whitted (1980), ray tracing has been a very popular technique for producing photo realistic images. More precisely, ray tracing and radiosity are the two widely used techniques for creating images when realism (or even more hyper-realism) is requested.

A great deal of work has been done these last twelve years to improve ray tracing (see for example Glassner 1989 or Bouville and Bouatouch 1988). The aim of part of this work is to increase the realism of the pictures obtained (by taking into account some phenomena like penumbra, aliasing, interference, rainbows, refraction...). The purpose of another part is to reduce the amount of time needed to produce a picture, which remains very expensive even with recent graphic workstations.

In this chapter, we will survey recent developments performed in the computer science laboratory of the Ecole des Mines de Saint-Etienne (EMSE) about ray tracing. In section 15.2, features of a new implementation of a ray tracer will be presented. We will describe a progressive ray tracing method based on a new sampling control process in section 15.3. Finally, work to include participating media in the ray tracer will be presented in section 15.4.

Virtual Worlds and Multimedia Edited by Nadia Magnenat Thalmann and Daniel Thalmann
© 1993 John Wiley and Sons Ltd

15.2. The Current Ray Tracer of EMSE

Our laboratory began to work on ray tracing in 1983. The first implementation (Coquillart 1985) was mainly devoted to producing realistic images of landscapes. A second implementation (Argence 1988) was based on a Constructive Solid Geometry (CSG) modeller and proposed a new technique to obtain antialiased pictures. A new version began to be studied three years ago (Roelens 1993).

This current ray tracer was conceived to be as generic as possible, but however well adapted to CSG modelling. It uses the following principles :

- The geometry of the model is completely separated from the associated rendering information. This allows us to simplify the modelling process and to use several rendering processes with the same geometric model.
- Scenes are described with an extended CSG modeller, where objects can be used several times. So, the model is not a tree, but a directed acyclic graph. An object may be referenced by the path joining the root of the graph to the object.
- Any vertex of the CSG graph can be provided with attributes which will be used by the rendering process. Under this general term, we can find information such as color, density, reflectance spectrum... These attributes may be volume or surface. Thus, we may distinguish a solid gold cube from a steel cube plated with gold. Among these attributes, we find textures which may be seen as volume (to define the color of an object) or surface (to perturb the normals of an object).
- Two kinds of objects, neutral and active, may be found in a scene. Neutral objects do not deviate light when they are crossed by light, and they can be superimposed in any point in space.

We focused a great deal of attention on trying to save memory. It is for this reason that we decided to use a CSG graph and not a tree for our modeller. In the same spirit, we implemented an algorithm to compact the attributes of the objects, the objects themselves or the matrices associated with affine transformations. For a detailed version of this algorithm, the reader may refer to Roelens (1993). With these rules, we have been able to visualize a Sierpinski's cube modelled by a CSG graph (see Fig.15.1, Color Section), up to level 5 (which corresponds to 20^5 cubes, i.e. 19 200 000 polygons).

The main problem arising when a ray tracer is used is the computing time. A great deal of methods have been presented to reduce this computing time. Many of these methods use various partitions, either of space (grid, octree, Binary Space Partitioning (BSP) tree,...) or of the screen. But this kind of technique is unusable with our geometric model: as objects are reused and as affine transformations can occur at any vertex of the graph, the ray has frequently to be transformed during the computation. Thus, the incremental traversal of the partition becomes very inefficient. So, in order to reduce the large computing time of ray-scene intersections, we chose to use bounding volume. Let us define a slice $(\overrightarrow{V}, \delta)$ as the set of points P of R^3 such that $\delta \leq \overrightarrow{V}.\overrightarrow{OP} \leq 0$ (it is the part of space bounded by two parallel planes). A bounding volume is the intersection of such three slices. This notion is really suited to our geometric model, because we have the following formula : if $(\vec{V}, \delta)$ is a slice containing object A, then $({}^t T^{-1}(\vec{V}), \delta)$ is a slice containing T(A), where T is any affine transformation.

Remark : In fact, we have a hierarchy of bounding volumes associated with the CSG graph.

15.3. A Progressive Ray Tracing

It is not unusual to wait a few hours, or even a few days, to obtain an image from a ray tracer. This is not acceptable when the image is not the expected one: the view point is badly located, objects are not in the right place, light effects are not those wanted... To detect this kind of mistake, we are developing a progressive ray tracing method that permits, by several successive stages, progressive generatioin of images of higher quality at little cost from a stage to another.

This method uses a new point generator associated with a sampling control process making possible a great saving in computing time.

We will review briefly the statistical technique used to solve our problem and the data structures needed for our tests and we will give some results on this method. For more details, the reader may refer to Maillot et al. (1992).

15.3.1. Sequential Analysis

Every image is composed of homogeneous and nonhomogeneous parts. If only a few points are needed to represent the homogeneous zones, it may be necessary to supersample the nonhomogeneous zones of the image. The idea for our progressive ray tracing is to refine the zones of the image that require a great level of detail and just approximate the homogeneous zones.

There are basically two kinds of approaches to detect homogeneity: one with regular sampling and fixed threshold and another one with random sampling and statistical test. Regular sampling is very prone to aliasing, so we chose the principle of a random sampling.

An ideal test method should be one that can decide by itself the number of samples needed for a desired precision on a given image. The control of the number of samples is precisely the scope of sequential analysis. It is a set of statistical methods in which the number of observations is not fixed once and for all but varies according to the results of the experiment. Sequential analysis theory has been mainly devised by Wald (Wald 1948) who developed a powerful test named the sequential probability ratio test(SPRT). This test is always faster than any other sequential test. We present here the simplest formulation of SPRT. For a complete description, please refer to Wald (1948).

On a given population, we distinguish individuals of type 0 from individuals of type 1. Let p denote the unknown proportion of individuals of type 1. We would like to know if the population is nearly of type 0. To achieve this, we choose p_0 and p_1 ($0 < p_0 < p_1 < 1$)

significant enough to say that the population is of type 0 if $p = p_0$ and of type 1 if $p = p_1$. Let H_0 (resp. H_1) be the hypothesis that $p = p_0$ (resp. $p = p_1$). If x is an individual sampled in the population, we denote $f(x, p)$ as the probability of obtaining x and $f(x, p_0)$ (resp. $f(x, p_1)$) the probability when H_0 (resp. H_1) is true. A risk is associated with each hypothesis: α for H_0 and β for H_1 ($\alpha, \beta \in]0,1[$, $\alpha+\beta<1$) such that α is the probability of reject ingH_0 when H_0 is true and β is the probability of accepting H_0 when H_1 is true. If k independent samples are drawn, the probability of obtaining the sample $(x_1, x_2, ..., x_k)$ is given by

$$p_{1k} = f(x_1, p_1) ... f(x_k, p_1) \text{ when } H_1 \text{ is true}$$

and $$p_{0k} = f(x_1, p_0) ... f(x_k, p_0) \text{ when } H_0 \text{ is true.}$$

The SPRT for testing H_0 against H_1 is defined as follows :

If $\dfrac{p_{1k}}{p_{0k}} \geq \dfrac{1-\beta}{\alpha}$ the test terminates with the acceptance of H_1.

If $\dfrac{p_{1k}}{p_{0k}} \leq \dfrac{\beta}{1-\alpha}$ the test terminates with the acceptance of H_0.

If $\dfrac{\beta}{1-\alpha} < \dfrac{p_{1k}}{p_{0k}} < \dfrac{1-\beta}{\alpha}$ the test continues by taking an additional sample x_{k+1}.

Wald has proved that the test has the desired risks and will stop with a probability of 1.

Remark: this test can be applied indifferently with a discrete or continuous distribution of x and with independent or nonindependent observations.

15.3.2. Application for Ray Tracing

To apply the results of the previous section, we should find a measure of the homogeneity of an image which is compatible with Wald's assumptions. The measures used so far are variance (Lee et al. 1985, Painter and Sloan 1989, Brown 1991) and contrast (Mitchell 1987). We chose the extent of the intensity values around their average to measure intensity variation.

Formally, if $I(y)$ represents the intensity of point y in a given image, $\overline{m}$ the mean intensity of a region R of the image with $y \in R$, and if Y is a uniform random variable on R, the measure of the intensity extent can be given by

$$P\left(I(y) \in [\overline{m}\text{-}\varepsilon, \overline{m}\text{+}\varepsilon]\right) = p, \varepsilon \in R^+ \tag{15.1}$$

To know p for a sufficiently small ε is a pertinent way to know the homogeneity of R. More precisely, we can choose p_0 and p_1 ($0 < p_0 < p_1 < 1$) such that R is declared homogeneous if $p \geq p_1$ and considered inhomogeneous if $p \leq p_0$. Consequently, H_0 is the hypothesis that $p \leq p_0$ and H_1 the hypothesis that $p \geq p_1$.

Let D_0 and D_1 be the number of points inside the interval for which its seems pertinent to say that R is inhomogeneous if H_0 is true and that R is homogeneous when H_1 is true respectively. We then put $p_0 = D_0/|R|$ and $p_1 = D_1/|R|$.

Let $X = 1_{\{I(Y) \in [\bar{m}-\epsilon, \bar{m}+\epsilon]\}}$. X is a random variable and its distribution is f(x, p) with f(0, p) = 1-p and f(1, p) = p. As the successive observations are not independent (we do not want to sample the same point twice), the joint distribution of $(x_1, x_2, ..., x_k)$ is given by

$$p_k = f\left(x_1, \frac{D}{|R|}\right) f\left(x_2, \frac{D - d_1}{|R| - 1}\right) ... f\left(x_k, \frac{D - d_{k-1}}{|R| - k + 1}\right) \qquad (15.2)$$

as long as $\qquad d_{k-1} \leq D = \sum 1_{\{I(Y) \in [\bar{m}-\epsilon, \bar{m}+\epsilon]\}}$

(where $d_k = \sum_{i=1}^{k} x_i$).

Under H_0, the distribution becomes

$$p_{0k} = f\left(x_1, \frac{D_0}{|R|}\right) f\left(x_2, \frac{D_0 - d_1}{|R| - 1}\right) ... f\left(x_k, \frac{D_0 - d_{k-1}}{|R| - k + 1}\right) \qquad (15.3)$$

and under H_1 $\qquad p_k = f\left(x_1, \frac{D_1}{|R|}\right) f\left(x_2, \frac{D_1 - d_1}{|R| - 1}\right) ... f\left(x_k, \frac{D_1 - d_{k-1}}{|R| - k + 1}\right) \qquad (15.4)$

The SPRT is then applied as follows:

R is homogeneous with the risk α if $p_{1k} \geq \frac{1-\beta}{\alpha} p_{0k}$

R is inhomogeneous with the risk β if $p_{1k} \leq \frac{\beta}{1-\alpha} p_{0k}$

otherwise the test continues with a new sample.

Remark : as $\bar{m}$ is not known, we estimate it on the first samples. This introduces a bias.

15.3.3. Data Structures

We need data structures allowing:

- to easily split an inhomogeneous region ;
- to provide a quick access to any region ;
- to perform efficiently the sampling process.

To satisfy these requirements, we chose a quadtree-like data structure which contains three substructures (see Figure 15.2) :

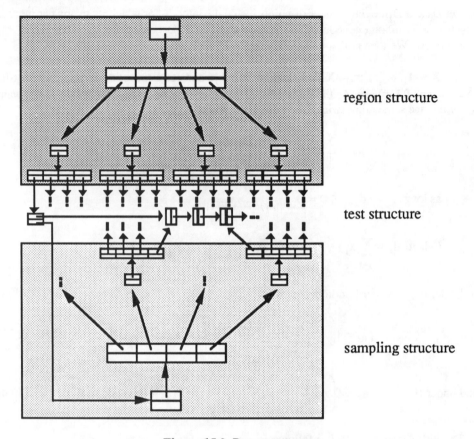

region structure

test structure

sampling structure

Figure 15.2. Data structures

- The tree of the regions: every terminal node represents a square region of the screen;

- The sampling tree with which the points have been generated. Each node of the tree represents a quarter of its father and a terminal node may contain a pointer to a point;

- A test structure is attached to each terminal node of the region structure. It contains a pointer to the list of points sampled so far on a given region and a pointer to the sampling tree.

To sample a region, the sampling tree is traversed randomly until a terminal node is reached. If the leaf has no point attached to it, then a point is sampled uniformly on its surface. If there is a point already, the leaf is split in four, the point is attached to the correct subnode and a son is randomly chosen and possibly split until no point belongs to the chosen leaf or until we run out of a resolution given by the user. In this last case, a back track is done to the last subdivision and a subnode is chosen among the ones not yet chosen.

15.3.4. Implementation and Results

The SPRT is applied separately to each RGB component. As soon as a nonhomogeneous component is detected, the region is set inhomogeneous.

A stage consists of a scan of all the inhomogeneous regions. Each of them is split and a test is performed on each subregion until a decision can be taken. Once the scan is finished, the split regions are drawn and the user decides to run a new stage or to stop the process. A set of interactive tools can be used to refine regions of particular interest for the user or to split a region covering small object parts missed by the sampler.

The interpolation scheme is the following: each cell of the sampling tree containing a point is drawn with the color of this point; if there is no point in the cell, the color used is the one obtained by averaging the colors of cells belonging to the same ancestor.

The light model used to compute the images is that of Whitted (1980).

Our method frequently leads to a saving of more than 50% in the total computing time as compared with a classical ray tracing. On average, 20% to 25% of the screen points are computed to produce the final image. The comparison of the classical ray traced image and the last stage image shows that less than 2% of the points differ significantly. The time needed by the sampling and the test represents about 10% of the total computing time.

15.3.5. Conclusion and Further Work

Based on powerful statistical results, the progressive ray tracing method provides a high speed convergence for the localization of image variations. The package is flexible as the user can interactively decide to stop the process after any stage, refine specifically any region or force the split of a missed region.

The interpolation scheme adopted so far is relatively poor and inefficient. We are trying to improve it, particularly to take into account both the surface objects and their colors.

Test and point generators form the first step of our progressive ray tracing. The next step will modify the intersection and rendering operations to include them in the progressive process.

In the Color Section, the processing of a typical scene (Figure 15.3) is shown: quadtree (Figure 15.4), difference image (Figure 15.5) and 10 progressive steps (Figure 15.6 a-j). Figure 15.7 (also in Color Section) shows an image rendered using the same technique.

15.4. Modelling and Rendering of Volume Densities

Classical ray tracing and radiosity assume that light is travelling in a vacuum between surfaces. When there are large amounts of dust or water vapor in the atmosphere, or when the distances are large enough that air molecules themselves have an effect, the initial assumption cannot be valid. Hence the need to study cases where the medium between surfaces is not a vacuum (such a medium will be called participating in the following). A lot of work has been done on the problem of the visualization of arbitrary distributed volume densities (Blinn 1982, Kajiya and Von Herzen 1986, Rushmeier and Torrance 1987, Sakas 1990...) and we developed in our laboratory two models which are linked to participating media in Fertey and Peroche (1989) and Roelens et al. (1992). These papers present methods to simulate light sources like desk lamps, automobile headlights, street lamps... Our goal was threefold: first, define directional sources that illuminate an area of the space corresponding to the type of the source; secondly, make the beam of the source both visible and transparent, as in real space; finally, render some natural phenomena such as smoke or dust in the air inside the light beam.

Light sources are neutral objects (cf section 15.2) of a CSG graph and pictures containing light sources are visualized by a ray tracing algorithm. The first model in Fertey and Peroche (1989) is completely empirical. Its purpose is to take into account the thickness of the dust crossed by the light ray. The second model in Roelens et al. (1992) is physically based. Space inside light sources is partly filled with spherical particles. The model assumes that the distribution of particles is uniform in the light source and that only single scattering occurs.

To improve these models we chose to take into account arbitrary distributed volume densities. We will now present how to model these densities and how to render them with our ray tracer.

15.4.1. Modelling Volume Densities

Three models have been implemented : the first one is a fractal model, the second one an extension of the spot noise model, and the last one a turbulence method.

15.4.1.1. The Fractal Model

Our method uses recursive subdivision of a 3D regular lattice of points which gives an approximation of the fractional Brownian motion. It is a variant of the middle point displacement method like that of Carpenter et al. (1982). We implemented the following procedure: from the sampling at frequency Δ obtained at the previous stage, we linearly interpolate new values sampled with frequency $r\Delta$, $0 < r < 1$, and a random value, with adapted variance, is added at each point. For the interpolation, the following process has been adopted: the average of the eight vertices of a cube is computed and temporarily assigned to the center of the cube. Then, the center of each face is interpolated from its six neighbors and after that the middle of each edge from its four neighbors. Then, we obtain the final value of the center of the cube from the value of the centre of each face. If vertices of the initial cube are obtained with a Gaussian random variable with variance σ^2, random displacements at the n-th stage must have variance

$$\Delta^2_n = \frac{1}{8}(1 - r^{2-2H})(r^n)^{2H}\sigma^2 \quad \text{(H is the parameter of the fBm).} \tag{15.5}$$

15.4.1.2.   The Spot Noise Model

This model is a 3D extension of that of Van Wijk (1991). The texture is defined by a function :

$$f(x) = \sum_i a_i h(x - x_i) \qquad (15.6)$$

where

> h is a spot, which is dropped in space
> $\{x_i\}$ is a set of random locations.

Several basic spots can be used: sphere, cube, cross, concentric patterns, quarter of pattern...

Spot noise $h(x)$ is synthesized through the convolution of the spot $h(x)$ with a function $w(x)$ which is a white noise ($w(x)$ is a set of random values on the 3D grid of integer points). Different types of transitions from the interior to the exterior of the spot can be used : disk, cone-shaped spot with a triangular cross-section or spot with a Gaussian cross-section.

15.4.1.3. The Turbulence Model

This model uses the turbulence function introduced in Perlin (1985):

$$\text{Turbulence (point)} = \sum_i \left| \frac{\text{Noise}(2^i * \text{po int})}{2^i} \right| \qquad (15.7)$$

where Noise ( ) is an approximation of a white noise.

15.4.2. Rendering Volume Densities

We begin with some notations about underlying physics in participating media. k_λ is a material property called the extinction coefficient. This coefficient may be expressed as the sum of the absorption coefficient α_λ and the scattering coefficient σ_λ : $k_\lambda = \alpha_\lambda + \sigma_\lambda$.

These coefficients can also be expressed as mass coefficients by dividing them by the material density ρ:

$$k'_\lambda = \frac{k_\lambda}{\rho} = \alpha'_\lambda + \sigma'_\lambda = \frac{\alpha_\lambda}{\rho} + \frac{\sigma_\lambda}{\rho} \qquad (15.8)$$

The ratio σ_λ/k_λ is also called the albedo of the participating media.

Light reaching the viewer has two origins (cf. Figure 15.8): the energy coming from the background and that coming from the light source(s) and directed toward the viewer by scattering.

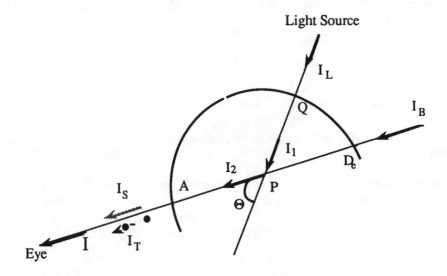

Figure 15.8. Geometry of light propagation through a participating medium.

Let I_S be the intensity coming from a light source. This light arrives at point P attenuated following Bougner's law:

$$I_1 = I_S e^{-k'_\lambda \int_Q^P \rho(t)dt}$$

(15.9)

which gives a contribution from this light source at point P toward the eye:

$$contribution = I_1 * \phi(\theta), \text{ where } \phi(\theta) \text{ is the phase function.}$$

(15.10)

This energy is attenuated along the path PA :

$$transparency = e^{-\int_P^A k'_\lambda \rho(u)du}$$

(15.11)

and a part of this energy is scattered:

$$scattering = \sigma'_\lambda \rho(v)dv$$

(15.12)

So dI_S = contribution * transparency * scattering. (15.13)

The contribution of the light source to the intensity rearching the eye is

$$I_S = \int_{D_0}^{A} dI_S I_L e^{-k'_\lambda \int_Q^P \rho(t)dt} \beta(\theta) e^{-\int_P^A k'_\lambda \rho(u)du} \sigma'_\lambda \rho(v)dv \qquad (15.14)$$

The contribution of the background is

$$I_T = I_B e^{-k'_\lambda \int_{D_e}^{A} \rho(s)ds} \qquad (15.15)$$

The total intensity I reaching the viewer is calculated as:

$$I = I_S + I_T \qquad (15.16)$$

This integral formula cannot be solved analytically for arbitrary density distributions $\rho(x)$. In Inakage (1989), an evaluation of this equation at each voxel is performed with a ray tracing method, but it is extremely time-consuming. As for us, we chose to use a sampling method, as in Sakas (1990) or Haas and Sakas (1992).

Path $[D_E, A]$ corresponding to the traversal of the density field by a ray will be subdivided into subpaths. The number of these last ones may be constant, given by the user or randomly computed.

We assume that the intensity coming from the light source and the phase angle are constant for each subpath (the values are those obtained at the midpoint M of the path). We must also compute a value of the density for each subpath. We can take the value of the nearest vertex of M, the average of the values of the height neighbors of M or compute a mean value of those encountered between the beginning and the end of the subpath by a 3D Brensenham-like algorithm.

Finally, we compute shadows like in Kajiya and Von Herzen (1984) by using a precomputed table containing negative exponentials giving the attenuation from the light source. It is less expensive than casting shadow rays toward the light source.

15.4.3. Conclusion and Further Work

This work on arbitrary density distributions (Mathieu 1992) is only a first approach in our study of participating media. It proved that our current ray tracing is well adapted to extensions like this one.

Several problems have to be examined more deeply. For example, we are not currently able to treat the case of two intersecting primitives with arbitrary distributed volume densities. Also, we would like to introduce multiple scattering in our model.

In the modelling domain, we would want to generate density fields from physical models of smokes, of clouds...

15.5. Conclusion

The ray tracer is now completely implemented for its geometric part (the CSG modeller and algorithms for intersections between a ray and the scene). To improve it, we have to develop new rendering algorithms for reflection and transmission (Cook-Torrance is currently our more sophisticated reflection model). In particular, we have to modify the current rendering algorithms to include them in the progressive process. We mentioned at the end of the previous section the developments we have in mind about participating media.

When this work is finished, we think we will have a tool allowing us to treat problems dealing with physical optics or with sophisticated geometrical optics (dispersive refraction, rainbows, interference, ...), which will be our next aim.

References

Argence J (1988) Antialiasing for Ray Tracing using CSG Modeling, *Proc. CG International' 88*, N. Magnenat-Thalmann and D. Thalmann eds., Springer-Verlag, pp. 199-208.

Blinn JF (1982) Light Reflection Functions for Simulation of Clouds and Dusty Surfaces, *Computer Graphics*, Vol. 16, No. 3, pp. 21-29.

Bouville C, Bouatouch K (1988) *Introduction to New Ray-Tracing Techniques*, Eurographics' 88 Tutorial No. 7.

Brown WT (1991) *Filtering and Adaptative Supersampling for Ray Traced Rendering*, University of Illinois Urbana-Champaign Technical Report GWRG -91-16.

Carpenter L, Fournier A, Fussel D (1982) Computer Rendering of Stochastic Models, *Communications of the ACM*, Vol. 25, No. 6, pp. 371-384.

Coquillart S (1985) An Improvement of the Ray Tracing Algorithm, *Eurographics' 85*, pp. 77-88.

Fertey G, Peroche B (1989) Sources directionnelles en tracé de rayons, *Actes de PIXIM' 89*, Hermès, Paris, pp. 219-232.

Glassner A (1989) *An Introduction to Ray Tracing*, Academic Press, London.

Haas S, Sakas G (1992) Methods for Efficient Sampling of Arbitrary Distributed Volume Densities, in *Photorealism in Computer Graphics*, Eurographic Seminars, Springer-Verlag, pp. 211-230.

Inakage M (1989) An Illumination Model for Atmospheric Environments in *New Advances In Computer Graphics*, Springer-Verlag, pp. 533-547.

Kajiya JT, Von Herzen BP (1984) Ray Tracing Volume Densities, *Computer Graphics*, Vol. 18, No. 3, pp. 165-173.

Lee ME, Redner RA, Uselton SP (1985) Statiscally Optimized Sampling for Distributed Ray Tracing, *Communication of the ACM*, Vol. 19, No. 3, pp. 61-65.

Maillot JL, Carraro L, Peroche B (1992) Progessive Ray Tracing, in *3rd Eurographics Worskhop on Rendering*, Bristol.

Mathieu G (1992) *Modélisation et rendu de densités volumiques*, Technical Report No. 92.11, Ecole des Mines de Saint-Etienne.

Mitchell DP (1987) Generating Antialiased Images at low Sampling Densities, *Computer Graphics*, Vol. 21, No. 4, pp. 65-72.

Painter J, Sloan K (1989) Antialiased Ray Tracing by Adaptative Progessive Rafinement, *Communication of the ACM*, Vol. 23, No. 3, pp. 281-288.

Perlin K (1985) An Image Synthesizer, *Computer Graphics*, Vol. 19, No. 3, pp. 287-296.

Roelens M (1993) *Algorithmes pour le tracé de rayons et la modélisation CSG*, Ph. D. Thesis, Ecole des Mines de Saint-Etienne.

Roelens M, Fertey G, Peroche B (1992) Light Sources in a Ray Tracing Environment, in *Photorealism in Computer Graphics*, Eurographics Seminars, Springer-Verlag, pp. 195-210.

Rushmeier H, Torrance K. (1987) The Zonal Method for Calculating Light Intensities in the Presence of a Participating Medium, *Computer Graphics*, Vol. 21, No. 4, pp. 293-302.

Sakas G (1990) Fast Rendering of Arbitrary Distributed Densisities, *Eurographics'90*, pp. 519-529.

Van Wijk J (1991) Spot Noise: Texture Synthesis for Data Visualization, *Computer Graphics*, Vol. 25, No. 4, pp. 309-318.

Wald A (1948) *Sequential Analysis*, Wiley & Sons, New York.

Whitted T (1980) An Improved Illumination Model for Shaded Display, *Communications of the ACM*, Vol. 23, No. 6, pp. 343-349.

Index